Sea Wolves

Sea Wolves

Savage Submarine Commanders of WW2

Tony Matthews

Pen & Sword
MARITIME

First published in Australia in 2021 by Big Sky Publishing
www.bigskypublishing.com.au
First published in Great Britain in 2023 by
Pen & Sword Maritime
An imprint of
Pen & Sword Books Ltd
Yorkshire – Philadelphia

ISBN 978 1 39906 461 3

A CIP catalogue record for this book is
available from the British Library.

Typeset by Mac Style
Printed in the UK by CPI Group (UK) Ltd, Croydon, CR0 4YY.

MIX
Paper | Supporting
responsible forestry
FSC
www.fsc.org   FSC® C013604

Pen & Sword Books Limited incorporates the imprints of Atlas,
Archaeology, Aviation, Discovery, Family History, Fiction, History,
Maritime, Military, Military Classics, Politics, Select, Transport, True
Crime, Air World, Frontline Publishing, Leo Cooper, Remember
When, Seaforth Publishing, The Praetorian Press, Wharncliffe Local
History, Wharncliffe Transport, Wharncliffe True Crime, White Owl
and After the Battle.

For a complete list of Pen & Sword titles please contact

PEN & SWORD BOOKS LIMITED
47 Church Street, Barnsley, South Yorkshire, S70 2AS, England
E-mail: enquiries@pen-and-sword.co.uk
Website: www.pen-and-sword.co.uk

Or

PEN AND SWORD BOOKS
1950 Lawrence Rd, Havertown, PA 19083, USA
E-mail: Uspen-and-sword@casematepublishers.com
Website: www.penandswordbooks.com

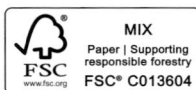

Dedication

This book is dedicated with love and admiration to my wife, Lensie.

Contents

Acknowledgements

Special mention must be made of my wife, Lensie, to whom this book is dedicated. She has worked tirelessly in assisting with the many facets of the production of this book including the photographic restoration, typesetting and indexing. For her devotion and encouragement I shall ever be grateful.

The author would also like to thank and acknowledge the following people and organisation who have assisted and have been instrumental in the research and development of this book.

Australian War Memorial

Bundesarchiv, Germany.

John Oxley Library, Brisbane.

Holly Reed, U.S. National Archives & Records Administration, Still Picture Reference Team.

Pamela Overmann, Curator, Navy Art Collection, U.S. Naval History and Heritage Command.

Jonathan M. Roscoe, Archivist, U.S. Naval History and Heritage Command.

U.S. Office of War Information Collection, U.S. Library of Congress.

Edward Petruskevich, Curator, *Wilhlem Gustloff* Museum.

Keith Clegg

Introduction

This is the story of four of the most dangerous submarine commanders of the Second World War. Two of them were Japanese, one was German and the last was a member of the Soviet Navy. These men between them killed an almost uncountable number of innocent civilians during their war operations and only one was actually punished in any significant way for his crimes.

The book begins with Hajime Nakagawa, commander of the Japanese submarine I-177 in May 1943. Nakagawa was responsible for sinking the Australian hospital ship, *Centaur* at a cost of 268 lives, all of whom were either civilian crew members or members of the ship's medical staff or an ambulance unit of the Australian Army. All were non-combatants protected by the Geneva Convention as was the ship itself which had clearly been marked as a hospital vessel and was travelling with the full protection of international law.

Why Nakagawa sank a protected hospital ship is a moot point which is discussed in detail in this book but he was never punished for this war crime. Later in the war, as commander of another Japanese submarine, the I-8, he was responsible for sinking freighters in the Indian Ocean and deliberately machine-gunning survivors in the water. This book details how these events occurred, why they occurred and what we know of Nakagawa's fate after the war.

In the second chapter of this book the author looks at the unique case of German submarine commander Heinz Eck – a handsome, well educated young man with a good family background and everything to live for. Yet despite his obvious attributes and intelligence, Eck was to become the only Nazi U-boat commander to be convicted of war crimes after the war.

Heinz Eck had been in command of the new and particularly powerful submarine U-852, when it was sent to the South Atlantic to prey upon Allied shipping in the region. This was Eck's first command of a submarine. He had been warned beforehand of the immense dangers which faced him and, at this time in the war, 1944, these dangers were immense. All the submarines that had recently been sent into this region had been destroyed by the intense Allied air presence in the zone and Eck fully realised that he was facing almost impossible odds. In fact the odds were *really* against him. Every German submarine that had already been destroyed in this area had been commanded by an experienced, battle-hardened captain. Almost all of them had come through the highly dangerous years of the war in the North Atlantic where countless numbers of ships and submarines had been sunk. All these commanders had been decorated for their successful service. Yet even these seasoned professionals had failed when sent to operate in the South Atlantic with its incredible Allied air power coupled with a strong presence of warships, particularly aircraft carriers.

What hope could Captain Eck have in such a perilous place when this was his first war patrol and his first command?

Eck's successes, if they could be called that, were modest. He sank only two ships including the SS *Peleus*, after which he callously killed almost all the survivors in the water with machine-guns or through the use of hand-grenades. Why he did so formed part of one of the more tragic stories of the war and led to one of the first war crimes trials to take place following the cessation of hostilities in 1945.

In chapter three the author investigates the astonishing story of Japanese submarine commander Tatsunosuke Ariizumi and the particularly brutal events that followed the sinking of two ships, the SS *Tjisalak* on 26 March, 1944, and the SS *Jean Nicolet* on 2 July that same year. What makes this story unique is the sheer, single-minded brutality of events following the sinking. The survivors were not simply machine-gunned in the water, in fact they thought for a while that they were being rescued by the submarine that had sunk their ships, but as soon as they had been brought on board the enemy vessel, Ariizumi had launched a bestial wave of torture and murder on the survivors including at least one woman, which would echo in tragedy and horror for decades to come.

The one Allied submarine commander to take his place within the pages of this book is the Russian naval officer Captain Alexander Marinesko, whose story as the commander of the Soviet submarine S-13 is told in all its appalling detail in chapter four. Marinesko's toll of death far exceeds any other submarine commander in history. He was responsible for sinking two former liners, the massive *Wilhelm Gustloff* and the *Steuben*, both of which he torpedoed in the Baltic Sea early in 1945, only months before the war ended. No one today really knows how many people were killed in these two tragic events. The *Wilhelm Gustloff*, upon leaving Gdynia, Poland, on 30 January,

1945, had so many people crammed on board that it had been impossible to count them all. These people were comprised mainly of refugees fleeing the coming Russian onslaught and also a large number of wounded German soldiers and nursing staff. On board the ship that day were also around five thousand children. When Marinesko slammed his torpedoes into the ship later that night he was fully aware that the vessel was crowded to capacity with civilians and wounded, yet he was perfectly willing to send the ship to the bottom of the Baltic at the cost, in some estimates, of around nine thousand lives, a large number of them being children who were either killed in the blast, drowned or frozen to death in the bitterly cold sea that night. Some of the bodies were later discovered frozen solid into ice-floes.

Not long afterwards Marinesko attacked the *Steuben*, also sending that ship to the bottom. Once again the death toll was huge. The cost in lives from that second ship has been calculated at around five thousand innocent souls. Between these two ships, Marinesko is believed to have killed around 14,000 men, women and children within just a few days.

These are true and tragic stories of the Second World War told in all their shocking detail. This book provides astonishing accounts of compelling and profoundly disastrous events that should never be lost to history.

'No man is justified in doing evil
on the ground of expediency.'

Theodore Roosevelt

Chapter One

Hajime Nakagawa

The Hospital Ship, *Centaur*

Hajime Nakagawa's steps were slow and deliberate that day as he walked towards the grim prison that would become his home for the next six years. Sugamo Prison in the district of Ikebukuro, Tokyo, was only fifty years old – relatively modern by many prison standards – but it had attained a dark reputation as a place of harsh punishment including the recent executions of numerous war criminals. Nakagawa was deeply concerned that he might become one of those former members of the Japanese Imperial Navy who would soon be swinging lifeless from the prison's gallows. He knew full well, from personal experience, that there were many very clever people working diligently behind the scenes to put him there – to stand him right on the gallows platform with an American noose around his neck.

The thought made him feel decidedly queasy.

The streets were busy that day, when were they not? he reflected moodily, and he wondered if he might never again have the pleasure of sitting at one of the outdoor stalls to enjoy a bowl of steamed rice with boiled carp and miso. No longer permitted to wear his uniform as an officer of Japan's now defunct submarine fleet, Nakagawa was dressed plainly in an off-white shirt and trousers and would not have stood out in a crowd. Slightly more than five-feet four-inches in height and weighing 139 lbs, he seemed to melt into the people around him as if he were almost invisible.

As he came closer to the main prison gates he could see there were two American guards standing on either side. Behind them were the double gates over which was an enormous sign which read, in English: 'Drive Carefully'.

Under different circumstances Nakagawa would have found the sign amusing but today there was no breath of humour left within him. In fact he rarely smiled and liked to keep to himself. He was known to be dour and at times irascible. He walked to the closest guard and opened the folded order he had received obliging him to report to the prison as he was now being officially regarded as a war criminal and that he was to stand trial for certain offences he was alleged to have perpetrated while the commander of two Japanese submarines during the war. The while-helmeted American M.P. nodded, made an entry on his clipboard, folded the paper and passed it back to Nakagawa before turning and opening one of the white-painted gates behind him. He told Nakagawa to report his arrival at the induction centre. Nakagawa, who could understand English reasonably well but found difficulty speaking the language, nodded and did as he was bid. The date was 11 June, 1948, the war in the Pacific had been over for close to three years but it had taken a team of war crimes investigators, working diligently through that entire period to be able to obtain just sufficient evidence to charge Nakagawa with a set of war crimes which they hoped would see him either end his life on the gallows or at least bring about a sentence of a lengthy term of imprisonment.

Nakagawa remained stoic as he was hustled through the prison's induction process. For a man who had commanded a submarine's crew and demanded

Hajime Nakagawa. The commander of the Japanese submarines I-177 and I-8. Nakagawa was responsible for sinking the *Centaur* and also machine-gunning the survivors of ships he later sank in the Indian Ocean. (*U.S. National Archives POW File 201*)

respect, the stringent requirements for being inducted into the prison were humiliating and irksome. He was stripped, weighed, given a thorough medical check, fingerprinted, photographed, deloused and issued not only with a drab prison uniform but also a prison number. Henceforth he was to be prisoner 2594.

Having completed his induction Nakagawa was escorted to his cell along the well-lit corridors of the prison to the cell block. As the steel door clanged closed behind him he could hear the sounds of the M.P.s' boots retreating on concrete. He looked at the sparse cell with dull eyes. His future was uncertain. After years of being dragged in for questioning and being reluctantly released he had always hoped that it would never come to this. He turned slowly, sat on the narrow bunk and leaned back against the wall of the cell. His mind began to drift back in time and he could clearly see those events which had brought him here. The bodies floating in the water, bloodied, shredded by machine-gun fire; the ships going down in flames; the cries of the dying; the look of murderous determination on the faces of some of his crew as they had obeyed his orders to kill every seaman struggling in the water after their ships had been torpedoed from under them.

Secret memories. Not memories Nakagawa would ever share with anyone. If he refused to talk, kept quite forever, if no one talked, then perhaps there was hope that he might escape the noose.

*   *   *

As the Australian hospital ship *Centaur* glided slowly out of Darling Harbour, Sydney, on that pleasant autumn morning in May 1943 she looked like something that was inherently good and courageous in life. It was almost as if the *Centaur* were the epitome of everything that was caring and just in the world.

Dressed in the colours and insignia of mercy, the *Centaur* presented a beautiful sight. Many who saw her leaving harbour that day would never forget the moment. The *Centaur* had been converted from a rather dowdy merchant ship that had once transported passengers, general cargo and even live cattle, on occasion, from Australia to Singapore. Now, however, the *Centaur* was painted a brilliant white from bows to stern and the sides of the vessel and also its funnel were emblazoned with huge red crosses, clearly defining the *Centaur* as a hospital ship and therefore fully protected from enemy attack under the Geneva Convention.

The A.H.S. *Centaur*. When the ship was torpedoed by a Japanese submarine in May 1943, in contravention to the Geneva Convention and international law, 268 people, doctors, nurses, orderlies, ambulance personnel and ship's crew, were killed. (*Australian War Memorial, Accession Number 302798*)

The *Centaur* was at the very beginning of what should have been its fourth successful voyage as a hospital ship. On board was a total complement of 332 people all of whom were non-combatants. These were comprised of crew members, permanent medical staff including doctors, nurses and orderlies, and men of the 2/12th Field Ambulance including an attached A.A.S.C. (Australian Army Service Corps) unit of ambulance drivers.

The *Centaur* was under the command of a highly experienced officer, Captain George Murray, then fifty-three years of age. Murray knew the *Centaur* like the back of his hand having been captain of the vessel for the previous seven years when the ship had been in regular mercantile service.

The date was 12 May, 1943. As Captain Murray and his second officer, Gordon Rippon, stood on the bridge that morning they had little reason to believe that they and the vessel they loved were heading into a tragedy, the reverberations of which would echo with astonishing sadness down through generations and change the lives of thousands of people forever.

The day was warm and sunny as Murray looked up at the impressive bridge while the *Centaur* slid centrally beneath its massive arch. Gulls were

Left: Captain George Murray who would go down with the *Centaur*. (*Author's collection*)
Right: Chief Officer Gordon Rippon who was the most senior officer to survive the sinking of the *Centaur*. (*Gordon Rippon collection*)

wheeling behind a lone trawler as it chugged ponderously into port. Murray, a rather introspective Scot, had been at sea for a major part of his life and the *Centaur* was his fourth command. He had been appointed its captain in 1936. Like many ship's captains of his time he maintained a certain distance from his officers and crew but was greatly admired for his experience and capabilities as a seaman. Yet when the opportunity arose Murray was also not adverse to letting his hair down a little if the occasion demanded.

The ship that day was crowded with soldiers. Many of them had never before been to sea and this voyage promised to be a hugely enjoyable and unique adventure. They sat around the decks, clustered on the tops of gratings and lockers, climbed masts and generally made their presence felt on board in a way that at first seemed innocent enough but there were quiet concerns about their very visible presence aboard the ship.

For members of the ship's crew particularly – men who had been seamen or engineers in time of peace and now also during a war, the dangers of the sea were well known and although the *Centaur* was protected by international law the fact that Japanese submarines were attacking shipping all along the east coast of Australia was disquieting enough. The sheer number of soldiers on board gave pause for thought. The ship was leaving port in broad daylight. It was a bright sunny day and there were hundreds of people around the harbour, on ferries or pleasure-boats watching it leave. Any one of these people could have been a Japanese spy and it would not be unreasonable to assume that if that were the case then it was possible that the *Centaur* might be regarded as having broken international law by allowing troops to be carried on board. If the Japanese believed that a hospital ship was carrying combatant troops then its protected status ended and the *Centaur* would become a legitimate target for attack.

This was not, of course the case. The *Centaur* was carrying only non-combatant personnel. The soldiers on board were all members of the 2/12th Ambulance or its associated A.A.S.C. drivers. The drivers were allowed to carry a weapon for the protection of themselves and their charges but that was acceptable under international law and those rifles and a small amount of ammunition for them were also on board the *Centaur*. Carrying these weapons did not disqualify the *Centaur* from its protected status and nor did the presence of so many solders in uniform. But what worried many of its crew and some of its officers was that those non-combatant service personnel might be reported to the Japanese as fighting troops en route to the hotly disputed battle areas of New Guinea and that concept was particularly disturbing, especially when the ship would be lit up like a Christmas tree advertising its presence to every enemy submarine along the entire east coast of Australia.

Standing on deck that day was Maurice Cairnie, the dapper and handsome fourth engineer of the *Centaur*. Maurice, or 'Maurie' as he was known to family and friends, was a quiet, reflective and diligent man sporting a rather swashbuckling Errol Flynn-style moustache. Cutting a dashing figure in his officer's uniform, the young ladies on shore probably adored him. Maurice was no newcomer to the sea. A Western Australian, he had been born and bred at Fremantle so ships and seafaring were like blood in his veins. He had been educated at the Fremantle Boys' Senior High School and gone immediately into marine engineering. Working as an engineer for the Blue Funnel Line, Maurie had been employed on a rotating basis on several of the company's ships: the *Centaur*, when it had been a simple merchantman, and its sister ships *Charon* and *Gorgon*. Maurie loved these ships and was well versed in their capabilities. However, even before the *Centaur* had left the wharf that day in May 1943 he not only had grave concerns about the safety of the ship but he also had a strong premonition that the vessel was going to be torpedoed.

Standing on the top boat-deck that morning Maurice Cairnie had been chatting to a friend, a sub-lieutenant in the Royal Australian Navy. The naval officer had been sure that the *Centaur's* coming voyage would be successful. He grinned broadly.

'Oh well, Maurie, at least you're on a safe ship for a change.'

Maurie shook his head, his eyes dark. 'I'm not so sure.' He paused moodily. There was an uneasy feeling crawling into the pit of his stomach. He had been at sea all through the war and this was a feeling he knew well because the other ships he had served on had not been protected by international law. 'I've got a premonition we're going to get it this time,' Maurie continued.

'Come on Maurie, really? What makes you think that old mate?'

Maurice Cairnie looked up at the *Centaur's* rigging. 'Well, just have a look up there. Soldiers all over the rigging, look at them, playing accordions, having a great time. And the only distinguishing mark is a

The *Centaur's* fourth engineer, Maurice 'Maurie' Cairnie. (*Maurice Cairnie collection*)

small patch on the shoulder.' Maurie shook his head. 'No one's going to take any notice of that mate. The *Centaur* might look like a hospital ship but it also looks like it's carrying troops and you know what that means.'

The sub-lieutenant could hardly disagree. He saw Maurie's point. It could have been a problem but there was nothing anyone could do about it now. It was too late. There were troops and spectators everywhere. Grimly, he shook Maurice Cairnie's hand and wished him good luck.

Still under the control of the harbour pilot, the *Centaur* now passed quickly through the anti-submarine boom and on to the Heads. Here Captain Murray once more took command of his ship and the pilot was transferred to shore.

As the *Centaur* sailed steadily away that day, turning onto a northerly heading that would take it along the coast of New South Wales and beyond, Murray could never have believed that his ship was doomed and that he and another 267 people on board that ship had just two more days to live.

*   *   *

Captain Hajime Nakagawa sat quietly in the tiny partitioned living space euphemistically described as the captain's quarters aboard the Imperial Japanese Navy's submarine I-177. He had been on watch for more hours than he cared to think about but that was normal for a war patrol. He was used to the long and exhausting hours but now he also needed to rest for a while, a few hours at least, before he could again take over the watch. He rolled into his narrow bunk and thought carefully about the message he had received three weeks earlier (20 March, 1943) from Rear Admiral Hisashi Mito, the commander of the 1st Submarine Squadron based at Truk Island. The contents of that dramatic message had not worried Nakagawa then, but now that he was actually on patrol, his first since having received that crucial message, a faint glimmer of concern was momentarily ignited somewhere deep within his consciousness. What if it all went wrong and somewhere down the line and sometime in the completely unforeseeable future he was called upon to give an explanation for such actions?

He held the decoded flimsy in his hands, reading those last few words again:

> Do not stop at the sinking of enemy ships and cargoes. At the same time carry out the complete destruction of the crews of the enemy's ships; if possible seize part of the crew and endeavour to secure information about the enemy.

Nakagawa folded the flimsy and placed it between a manual he was attempting to read. He shrugged. There was no need to worry; even thinking about it was a complete waste of time. Japan would win this war. He was sure of it. The very fact that the country's dedicated servicemen were willing to take difficult actions such as this was proof enough that the people of Japan would be victorious. The strong always win over the weak. He rolled over and tried to sleep.

At that moment the submarine's gunnery officer, Lieutenant Hajime Obori, pushed his head through the curtain of the captain's cubicle, his eyes shining with barely suppressed excitement. Nakagawa rolled over, opening his eyes.

'It's a convoy, Captain, heading north.'

Nakagawa climbed from his bunk, reaching for his cap. 'How many?'

'Five or six, Captain. A minor convoy. Possibly two escort vessels but they appear to be small. Corvettes perhaps.'

'Bearing?'

'182 Captain. Speed approximately seven knots.'

Nakagawa nodded, 'Dive the boat. Come to battle-stations.'

'Aye Aye Sir.'

Crew members were quietly hurrying to their posts as Nakagawa squeezed past in the narrow central communications passage. The red action lights were winking monotonously. Nakagawa raised the periscope and it hissed softly into position. He could see nothing. The night was as black as pitch and the convoy, blacked out, was virtually invisible. Now, however, it was possible to hear the faint thumping of approaching propellers; they sounded like banks of waves breaking against rocks in a discordant storm.

'It will be difficult to get close enough to select individual targets, Captain,' Obori whispered needlessly. 'But perhaps… .'

Obori's voice trailed away. Nakagawa had already come to the same conclusion. Attempting to manoeuvre into position to attack a single vessel would almost certainly be a complete waste of time, and dangerous, especially with escort corvettes or destroyers wasping about above, their asdic operators straining to hear any sign of enemy activity. The more sensible measure would be to fire a fan of torpedoes into the heart of the convoy and hope that at least a couple of them would strike a target.

Then they heard a ping on the hull, followed almost immediately by another and they knew the escorts had already found them. The sonar operator leaned urgently over his consul. 'I hear a klaxon, Captain. They are sounding battle-stations.'

Obori was beginning to perspire freely now. He hated being depth-charged. 'All six tubes are loaded Captain.' He was holding a hand-piece, ready to pass orders to the torpedo room.

Nakagawa did not respond. He was busy issuing quiet orders swinging the bows of the submarine around to starboard, finding the best position so that his fan of underwater missiles would strike at the very heart of the convoy.

'They are already scattering, Captain.' The sonar operator was holding his headphones tightly to his ears, listening with every fibre of his body.

Nakagawa remained silent, counting time, eyes glued to the periscope. Yet his view was limited; he was deliberately keeping the periscope as low in the water as possible so that the wash would not be spotted from above. The escort ships evidently knew that I-177 was about, somewhere, but there was no need to wave a flag to show them exactly where. Nakagawa flipped up the periscope handles and the instrument slid softly back into its housing.

'Fire one. Fire two. Fire three. Fire four.'

Obori immediately passed the order to the torpedo room. He was trying not to shout into the hand-piece but in the intensity of the moment he almost screamed the instruction. Moments later the entire boat shuddered as the four torpedoes left their tubes. It was as if the submarine itself had suddenly run into a wall of steel netting.

'Four in the water and running sir,' Obori looked up from his hand-piece.

'Take us down,' Nakagawa called urgently and the submarine dipped alarmingly as the planesman pushed the boat down hard and the electric motors hummed, pumping tons of water to flood the ballast tanks.

They could hear the buzzing of approaching propellers now – at least two of them – hounds on the scent. Every single crew member on the boat knew what was coming.

'Level at 340,' Nakagawa ordered. The plates of the submarine were glistening with condensation as the boat slowed, levelling evenly.

'Depth-charges are in the water, Captain.' The sonar operator looked a little frightened. This was his first time under attack.

Nakagawa said nothing. He was looking intently at his watch, counting the seconds. For a long agonising twenty seconds, while they waited for the depth-charges to reach them, they heard nothing, then there was the sound of a distant explosion. Just one. Nakagawa could hardly breath as he waited for more. There was nothing. Then it didn't matter too much any more because the first of the depth-charges began to explode all around and for the next ninety minutes everyone on board the submarine believed that they were about to die.

*　*　*

The ship that Hajime Nakagawa destroyed that night was the 8724 tons refrigerated cargo vessel *Limerick* which had been constructed at Glasgow in 1925. It was owned by the Union Steamship Company and although a tough little vessel which had seen and endured countless sea passages and, at times, indescribably severe weather, it suffered from some mechanical issues which on this occasion had forced the freighter to trail behind the other ships in the convoy.

The *Limerick* was actually part of Convoy GP 48 which was steaming north towards Brisbane under the protection of two corvettes, HMAS *Colac* and HMAS *Ballarat*. All but two of the *Limerick's* crew would survive the sinking, being rescued by the *Colac*, and while I-177 was depth-charged after the attack on the *Limerick* it would escape unharmed.

The number of torpedoes fired at Convoy GP 48 would later become an essential piece of evidence in the war crimes investigation of the operations of I-177 during this particular patrol. The submarine was equipped with six forward tubes and when under investigation long after the war had ended Nakagawa was to claim that he had fired six torpedoes at Convoy GP 48 that night. However, after years of intensive work investigators came to the conclusion that Nakagawa actually fired four torpedoes at the convoy, stating that he had claimed to have fired six in order to hide the fact that he had later used two of his torpedoes on the hospital ship *Centaur*. When his patrol had been completed and he had returned to his base at Truk Island, Nakagawa had been missing exactly six torpedoes from his standard store of armaments.

*   *   *

After leaving Sydney the *Centaur* moved steadily north following a convoluted route to avoid minefields and other potential hazards or normal navigational problems. Captain Murray had been instructed to zigzag in order to prevent being targeted for a torpedo attack but Murray believed that zigzagging was a precaution that should not be utilised by hospital ships which were travelling under international protection as such a manoeuvre might raise enemy suspicions that the entire non-combatant persona of the ship could be nothing more than a ruse – and an illegal one at that. In any case, with so many military personnel on board the question was rather academic. Anyone seeing all those uniforms swarming over the ship would certainly form their own opinion over the *Centaur's* non-combatant role.

For those on board the *Centaur* the passage meant different things to different people. For the captain and his crew this was just one more voyage in a lifetime of sea-journeying – plunging from one wave to the next in a never-ending journey through life – moving from one port to another and back again. Only the ports were different but after a while even these began to fuse into a kind of universal oneness.

Ordinarily it would have been all so routine but now there was also the war to contend with and while that normally brought additional hazards to a seaman's life, the protected status of a hospital ship meant that the crew and all those who sailed within the *Centaur* could relax and enjoy the voyage – the type of journey that many had never before experienced.

One man was particularly uneasy about the voyage: this was Lance Corporal Ron Jones, known as 'Spud' to his mates. Ron was an Englishman who had emigrated to Australia in 1927 and worked as a provisions manager at McIlraiths store in Burwood, New South Wales. When war came he had been eager to do his bit and joined the 2/12th early in 1940, just a few months after the outbreak of the conflict. He had already experienced action having been at Darwin during the Japanese bombings on the city in February 1942. A total of 236 people had been killed at that time.

Aboard the *Centaur* Jones was now very uneasy because, like Maurice Cairnie, he had a powerful premonition that the voyage was heading for disaster. He was so convinced of this that even as the ship had been heading out of Sydney harbour Spud was below decks checking how it might be possible to unscrew one of the ship's portholes. Would the porthole be large enough for him to wiggle through if he needed to get off the ship in a hurry? Spud Jones was only a small man, and slim, built a bit like a jockey, but, as he later told a national Australian magazine, he realised quickly that he was never going to be able to squeeze through that porthole. Spud's concerns were exacerbated by the fact that he was unable to swim. As a member of the 2/12th Field Ambulance he had never really expected to be in a situation that could have required him to swim for his life. He sat back on his bunk, thinking deeply about his dilemma. Having ruled out the possibility of the porthole as a possible means of escape he had at least saved himself from wasting valuable time in the event of a disaster. There was nothing more he could do at that stage but to wait until the lifeboat-drills commenced and then to pay particular attention to everything he was being told. Meanwhile, he hung his life-jacket close at hand – just in case.

Private Allan Pettiford of the 2/12th Field Ambulance was enjoying himself thoroughly. He later said, 'We were looking forward to a very leisurely trip; we weren't dreaming that we'd be hit by a torpedo. ... We thought we were really safe and most of the time we spent on deck. At times we could see the coast of New South Wales and it was really enjoyable.'

Perhaps the only events that cast any kind of shadow on what otherwise would have been a pleasant cruise towards the tropical climate of the north were the many boat-drills, the reality and urgency of which quickly dispelled the growing sense of invulnerability which was spreading over the ship's passengers and medical personnel. 'Spud' Jones, of course, was delighted to attend them.

It was well known that Japanese submarines were particularly active in the waters off the east coast of Australia at this time and reports of the scattergun instances of ships suddenly being torpedoed and sunk were frequently being published within the pages of the press. The burning question was, of course, would the Japanese disregard international law and attack a hospital ship as other armed forces had done during both world conflicts (including Allied forces) or would they allow the *Centaur* to pass unmolested? There was no way of knowing. Those travelling aboard the *Centaur* on that fateful voyage had to place their trust in fate and hope for the best. All they could accurately state was that the odds were on their side.

The really good aspect of this, appreciated by all on board, was that the frequent lifeboat-drills at least helped to placate any fears that the *Centaur* might be caught unawares, and at the same time confirmed that even though there were more than three hundred and thirty people on board, should the unthinkable actually happen there would be quite sufficient lifeboats and life-rafts for everyone. Additionally, every person on the ship was issued with a lifejacket which came complete with a small red light and whistle.

On 13 May, the *Centaur's* penultimate day of existence, two medical officers standing on the upper deck spotted what they thought might have been the conning tower of a submarine. The object was frequently being washed by waves but it was about four or five miles away from the *Centaur* and heading south, in the opposite direction. The ship's second officer, Gordon Rippon, then standing on the bridge, also saw the strange object which soon disappeared from sight. All three men were convinced that the sighting had been that of a submarine but it was impossible to state of which nationality. Had it been Japanese then perhaps the *Centaur's* clear markings of a hospital ship had already protected the vessel and all its passengers and crew, but it was equally possible that the conning tower – if indeed that was what it had been – was that of an American submarine. Speculation was rife. A distinct 'edge' had been jolted back into people's consciousness but there was nothing anyone could do so those on board settled into a rather festive but still somewhat uneasy night.

As darkness descended the powerful image of the well-lit *Centaur* was an impressive sight. When almost every other vessel was painted in the drab grey of wartime anonymity and travelled most frequently in convoy, the *Centaur* majestically sailed alone, lit up like a brilliant white star. The ship's hull was emblazoned with three large red crosses painted on both sides complete with a wide green band which went right around the entire hull of the vessel. The funnel of the ship also carried large red crosses on both sides and similar crosses had been painted on the deck of the ship so that they could clearly be seen from the air. All the decks and especially the red crosses were brilliantly lit so that at night they were not just prominent but visually dominant. If the ship were to be attacked there could be no excuse.

No one could possibly mistake the *Centaur* for anything other than a non-combatant hospital ship.

Once the fright, or at least the reasonable concern of the sighting of the 'conning tower' had dimmed that night, many of those on board moved into a kind of party mode. All over the ship people were enjoying themselves almost as if the voyage were some kind of peacetime cruise. A birthday party was being celebrated for the matron of the nursing staff, Miss Sarah Ann Jewell. Musicians struck up their instruments and the beer ration flowed happily. One crew member, the senior radio officer (and purser) Eric Summers, heard the news that he had just become a father for the first time, although sadly he and both of the other radio officers on board, Tom Morris and Bob Laird, would not survive the coming attack.

One of the ship's crew, Ron Moate, later recorded that the day before the sinking of the *Centaur* everything appeared to be very busy, principally because it was Matron Jewell's birthday. 'She happened to be a very popular person aboard the ship and all hands were out to [help] with birthday cakes and the dinner and all the rest that was served for her,' Ron recalled.

Staff Sergeant Dick Medcalf was enjoying the voyage as much as anyone on board, in fact he had been trying to get a posting to such a job for a long time. 'I had been held in Australia doing medical work', he subsequently recorded, 'and trying to get overseas all that time. Every young chap did, and

Dick Medcalf seen here during the interview he gave in 1993 for the production of *Centaur – Death of a Hospital Ship*, a television documentary on the sinking of the *Centaur*. (*Tony & Lensie Matthews collection*)
Inset: Staff Sergeant Dick Medcalf. (*Dick Medcalf collection*)

finally when I was offered this job on the hospital ship I jumped at it and was very pleased to get on board. I was very pleased to do the work I was doing because it was helpful.'

Dick Medcalf was very impressed with the *Centaur*. The vessel had been thoroughly converted to a hospital ship and although somewhat cramped for that role it had everything Dick needed to carry out his X-Ray work and medical technology.

On the *Centaur's* last night Dick Medcalf enjoyed the party ambience that had developed almost spontaneously. He later recorded: 'We had a very nice night. We had a concert on the fore-deck and various people put in bits of skits and acts. There were chaps from the 2/12th Field Ambulance and they had a pretty good comedian and one of our nurses had a lovely voice and sang two or three songs. I don't think it went on very long, probably a couple of hours.'

When the concert had finished Dick Medcalf and his good friend, Tommy Morris, the ship's second radio officer, walked around the decks chatting about nothing in particular. However, their eyes were drawn to some flashes of what appeared to have been large naval guns on the horizon, far out to sea on the ship's starboard side, but although they discussed what these flashes might have meant they did not know for certain, only believing that some kind of naval action was taking place far away. They walked back towards the stern of the *Centaur* and looked to port, towards the shore, where they could see the glow of what appeared to be a lighthouse reflecting on the clouds. Tommy Morris was then due to go on watch so he left Dick Medcalf alone on deck. Dick decided to turn in and went for'ard to the accommodation space that had been reserved for N.C.O.s of the ship's medical staff. This was situated on the second deck down, just aft of the chain locker.

Meanwhile, standing on deck that evening Private Allan Pettiford sauntered over to another soldier, Private Percy Clegg, who was serving as one of the *Centaur's* permanent medical staff employed as a theatre technician. Percy was one of those happy-go-lucky country lads who were the salt of the earth of rural Australia, good

Private Allan Pettiford of the 2/12th Field Ambulance. (*Allan and Bobbie Pettiford collection*)

natured, always willing to lend a hand, with a dry sense of humour and a wry smile. Prior to embarking on the *Centaur*, Percy, who then lived with his wife, Marjorie and young son, Keith, at Warwick on the Darling Downs, had taken leave so that he could see his family before the voyage. His brother, Leslie, known as 'Les' lived at the family property, *Sunnyside*, which was situated just outside the small, former gold-mining town of Pratten. Actually there were old gold mines on the farm but they had long since petered out. Cars were scarce in those days, in fact many of them had been requisitioned for war use and fuel was being strictly rationed so Percy had ridden his bicycle all the

Private Percy Clegg. (*Tony & Lensie Matthews collection*)

way from Warwick to Pratten, a distance of about twenty miles, in order to say goodbye to his brother and ageing mother.

Allan Pettiford had been chatting to a lot of people that day, especially the ship's medical staff, making new friends and acquaintances. Being from different units Percy Clegg and Allan Pettiford had never before met although they were both Queenslanders. When Allan introduced himself, Percy nodded and smiled. He had the face of a country lad, his eyes full of good humour. Allan asked where he lived.

'Right over there,' Percy indicated with the blade of his hand, pointing out over the darkening sea towards the north-west. 'A place called Warwick.'

Allan knew Warwick well and remembered the main street with its imposing Catholic cathedral. 'Married?' Allan questioned. In answer Percy dug into the pocket of his tunic and pulled out his pay-book. In the centre of the book was a photograph of Percy with a particularly beautiful young woman.

'The wife,' Percy smiled proudly, 'Marjorie. We have a boy now, Keith.'

Allan gave an appreciative whistle. 'She's a corker all right.'

Percy smiled quietly and tucked the photograph back into his paybook. Then he began talking about his family and Allan realised to his complete surprise that he and Percy shared a lot of friends and acquaintances. The

Percy Clegg seen here with his wife, Marjorie. Percy was a member of the *Centaur's* permanent medical staff, serving as a theatre technician. He did not survive. (*Keith Clegg collection*)

two men hunkered down for a long chat about the all the people they knew at both Warwick and Roma. Allan was a Roma lad and knew the area and people well including the Clegg family. He had grown up in Roma and had been educated there. Allan also knew the Matthews family in Warwick and Percy had married into the family so the two men had much to talk about as their families and friends shared a love of sport and other country pastimes. From another pocket Percy took out a small booklet. It was a publication about the Taronga Park Zoo at Sydney which Percy had visited just before boarding the *Centaur*. 'I got this for my boy, Keith,' Percy said, flipping through the pages which were filled with photographs of the zoo's animals. 'He's only seven but he loves animals so I thought he'd like it. I'm going to post it from Cairns.'

Allan later said goodnight to Percy and wandered away to look for his mate, Jack Lynagh, leaving Percy alone at the ship's rail. Percy looked again towards the scattered lights on the shore, the northern extremity of New South Wales. He was thinking about his family then, his wife and young son, and wondering when he would see them again. It might be months, a year, who could know? He thought of his brother too, Les Clegg, working the beautiful farm at Pratten. The brothers were close and so much alike they could have been twins.

Allan Pettiford. Photographed in 1993 at the time of the *Centaur's* 50th anniversary memorial service. (*Tony & Lensie Matthews collection*)

As the hours passed, one by one the party-goers and also those who had decided to have a quiet night alone made their way back to their bunks and cabins. Percy Clegg made his way aft to the ship's medical staff accommodation with his mate Vince McCosker, who had been actively enjoying the sing-song that night. The mess was situated right above number four hold.

Percy had enjoyed chatting with Allan Pettiford; it had been great to talk about the people they both knew. Sadly it was impossible for Percy to know that he would never see his family again. (The Taronga Park booklet never arrived, of course, although Percy had earlier posted a letter to his son to state that it would soon be on its way).

Meanwhile, Allan Pettiford and his best mate, Jack Lynagh, went for'ard to the ward where most of the 2/12th were being accommodated for the journey north. The ward was stuffy and crowded with so many servicemen in it. Allan took one of the bottom bunks while his mate, Jack Lynagh, took the top bunk. It was to be a fatal decision.

Finally the ruckus of revelry died down and the *Centaur* continued to move quietly north on a gentle sea, its watch-keepers and lookouts alone now in the vast stillness of the night.

As the long hours passed, the *Centaur* ploughed steadily on course. To a casual observer, from a distance, the ship would have looked like a star floating on the surface of the sea. Occasionally pods of dolphins or porpoises could be seen surfacing close to the ship. Creatures of great curiosity, they had been attracted to the *Centaur's* unusually brilliant light display.

At 4 a.m. the watch was changed. The *Centaur's* first officer, Henry 'Harry' Lamble, took over the bridge relieving Gordon Rippon, the second officer. Rippon went to the chartroom to write up the log and then down to the radio officer's cabin where he gave the position chit to the chief radio officer, Eric Summers. The position he gave to Summers that night would be disputed for decades to come, but Gordon Rippon would be vindicated in 1996 when the wreck of the *Centaur* would be discovered just a few kilometres from its calculated position, a minor variation perfectly acceptable in nautical terms.

Tired and ready to turn in, Gordon Rippon now headed for his cabin never thinking for a moment that there would be little chance for him to sleep that night.

Corporal Albert Taylor was a dental technician attached to the 2/12th Field Ambulance. Basically Taylor was a passenger on board the ship. He did not need to be up and about at that hour of the day but he had just visited the 'heads' (ship's toilets) and decided that it would be nice to go up on deck to get some fresh air. He walked aft and now stood near the ship's stern-rail gazing casually out at the darkened sea. It was such a pleasant night he did not wish to return to his narrow bunk. The lights of the ship, especially those shining downwards along the hull illuminating the Red Cross markings, were casting a flickering, almost hypnotic glow over the water. Taylor stood there for a few moments, enjoying the scene, watching a school of porpoises at play, when a flash of white on the surface of the sea momentarily caught his eye. He did not have a pair of binoculars, of course, and it was difficult to see in the darkness, especially as his eyes had become accustomed to the bright lights illuminating the ship. Yet as Taylor watched, leaning now slightly over the ship's rail, he wondered if the white objects he could see – two of them – were not porpoises, but actually trails in the water, just visible in the moonlight.

And they appeared to be heading directly towards the *Centaur*!

*   *   *

Today, no one really knows exactly what was happening aboard the Japanese submarine I-177 on that fateful morning. The reasons why there is such a dearth of knowledge about this one submarine at this specific time are varied and complex but at least they are clear.

The first and most significant of these reasons is that for the remainder of his life Hajime Nakagawa, the commander of I-177, refused to admit that he had been responsible for attacking the *Centaur*. His gunnery officer, Lieutenant Hajime Obori, subsequently backed Nakagawa's claims that the I-177 never attacked any hospital ships at any time. The I-177 was later attacked by two American warships and sunk with all hands so no other members of the crew were available to make statements either confirming the attack or denying it. (Details of the sinking of I-177 will be found later in this chapter). However, by the time I-177 was destroyed, both Nakagawa and Obori had been assigned to other duties. Additionally, when the I-177 was sunk any documentation which might have placed the submarine in the position of the attack on the *Centaur* was also destroyed. The submarine's daily logs, radio flimsies or copies of diaries or official orders would probably have been sufficient evidence of guilt. We shall see, however, that both men were lying when they claimed not to be responsible for the sinking of the *Centaur*.

After years of research by war crimes investigators after the war we can now be certain that I-177 was the only Japanese submarine in that area at that particular time. As to the precise sequence of events that led to the attack it is only possible to offer an educated scenario of probabilities.

At 4 a.m. on the morning of 14 May, 1943, the *Centaur* was precisely inside the designated war patrol zone allocated to the I-177 by the officer in charge of the 22nd Submarine Flotilla, Commander Nishino, at their base at Truk Island. The exact movements of all three of the other Japanese submarines operating as part of this flotilla when on patrol at this time were later accounted for and verified by various documented means. Only the I-177's movements were cloaked in a fog of disinformation, outright lies and secrecy.

It now appears that sometime before 4 a.m. that morning the submarine was almost certainly on the surface recharging its batteries. That would have been normal practice for submarines of that era, principally because the batteries usually needed recharging at least once every twenty-four hours depending upon how much time had been spent submerged. The safest time to do so was at night. If indeed this was the case then the radar operator at around this time would have been aware of a blip on his screen telling him that a ship was approaching. Indeed it hardly needed a radar to spot the arrival of the *Centaur* on the horizon as the ship was lit up more brightly than a fireworks display.

Standing in the conning tower just beneath the periscope housing Lieutenant Commander Nakagawa would have been both astonished and pleased to see the white lights of the *Centaur* coming into focus within the lenses of his binoculars. It would have been an unusual sight. Ships normally steamed in convoy, protected by escorts, and at night they were completely blacked out. Yet here was a target simply asking to be torpedoed. Its lights were a bright beacon calling for destruction. Nakagawa was only too willing to comply.

From that distance Nakagawa could not have known with certainty that he was dealing with a hospital ship, although he may have suspected that as being the case. He needed to get a lot closer. He turned to his helmsman, ordered full speed ahead and changed course to intercept.

As a precaution, more than anything else, Nakagawa would subsequently have reduced speed and submerged the submarine, ramming home the hatch clips in the conning tower as the vessel slipped silently beneath the waves. At periscope depth the I-177 would have crept even closer to its prey, Nakagawa watching the approaching ship with intense scrutiny. Finally the unidentified vessel would have come sharply into focus. What went through Nakagawa's mind when he suddenly realised that his suspicions were now confirmed and that the mystery vessel was indeed a hospital ship protected by international law? We shall now never know.

The gunnery officer, Hajime Obori, later told war crimes investigators that Nakagawa never attacked the *Centaur* or any other hospital ships at any time. He stated that Nakagawa had expressed his belief that no such vessels were ever to be attacked. However, we can only take that sentiment as another exercise in an endeavour the men later made to save themselves from prosecution and the likelihood of ending their lives on the gallows of Sugamo Prison.

Nakagawa was not having a particularly successful war patrol. He had now been at sea for weeks but had managed to sink just one ship, the *Limerick* (almost by accident), one of the vessels that had formed the small Convoy GP 48. The I-177 would soon be required to return to the submarine's base at Truk. Suddenly, attacking and sinking another ship to add to Nakagawa's lacklustre tally of kills seemed a reasonable thing to do.

Over the next half hour or so Nakagawa manoeuvred the I-177 into attack position. It is entirely possible that he alone knew that the vessel they were about to attack was a protected hospital ship while the crew remained in ignorance, believing that the ship was just a tanker or general cargo carrier. It is likely that only Nakagawa actually saw the ship through his periscope.

In any case, the exact details leading to the attack are now somewhat academic. At 4.10 a.m. the attack plan was complete, timings had been estimated and the submarine was holding position. When Nakagawa's words came, they sealed the fate of hundreds of people.

'Fire tubes one and two,' he ordered.

*   *   *

At that precise moment Lieutenant Russell Ward, the orderly officer of 'O' Heavy Battery, also known as Rous Battery, situated on the eastern shore of Moreton Island, was in the process of carrying out his rounds of the battery's position which was located approximately twenty kilometres south of the Cape Moreton Lighthouse. At that time 'O' Heavy Battery was still in its fledgling period. The unit was being housed in temporary accommodation – basically little more than a campsite with the actual battery position and accommodation for the men under construction. In fact the men were still awaiting the arrival of the battery's 155mm coastal guns with their accompanying searchlights. The concrete foundations for the large weapons were then being laid.

That night Russell Ward was sharing the duty rounds with his orderly sergeant and friend, Dermott Reilly. The two men although of different ranks got along well together and even though it was just after four in the

'O' Heavy Battery. Major Ken Fullford, (second row, 6th from right) Lieutenant Russell Ward (second row, 5th from right) and Sergeant Dermott Reilly (directly behind Ward). (*Ken Fullford collection*)

morning the weather was pleasant enough with the air fresh and invigorating. After checking that the sentries were all in place and alert, the two men stopped for a moment to have a few words with another soldier, Rudi Glass. As they stood in the sand chatting to each other the attention of all three men was suddenly drawn to a strong orange glow which temporarily lightened the sky just over the horizon. What happened next was really important to the history of the sinking of the *Centaur* because if events had transpired differently it could have meant that the ship's survivors may have been rescued earlier and it is even possible that lives might have been saved. Having said that, it should also be pointed out that

Major Ken Fullford, commanding officer of 'O' Heavy Battery. (*Ken Fullford collection*)

the three men at the battery who played a role in these events did everything in their power to ensure that what they had seen was reported promptly and properly and their actions were in no way to blame for what followed.

All three men were at first slightly confused by what they had seen. A round orange glow had lit the horizon and at first it was thought that the glow might have been the moon rising but the glow died down very quickly. Almost immediately came another orange glow which remained for only a second or two before it too died down leaving the horizon as black as before.

'That was no moon-rise,' Dermott Reilly said, slightly incredulously, his voice sounded worried.

'You're right there, Sergeant,' Russell Ward responded. 'Looked to me like a ship going up. Torpedo maybe.'

Reilly nodded agreement. There had been too many reports of ships being torpedoed by Japanese submarines. 'We'd better report it.'

'Let's go and wake the major,' Ward said grimly.

Lieutenant Ward and Sergeant Reilly hurried back to the camp which was situated about four or five hundred metres away. Once there they went straight to the sleeping quarters of Major Ken Fullford, the commanding officer of the battery. Fullford at that time was asleep in his narrow bunk but he came awake quickly when Lieutenant Ward arrived.

'There's been a strange sighting at sea, Sir,' Ward began. 'Sergeant Reilly and I saw it while checking the piquets.'

'What sort of sighting, Lieutenant?' Fullford responded sleepily.

'An orange glow, Sir. Two glows in fact, one after the other.'

Major Fullford yawned and climbed from the bunk, pulling on his trousers. 'You don't think it was just the moon rising?'

'That's what we thought at first, Major, but there were two glows and both subsided pretty quickly. It didn't look like a moon-rise to us. I think we should report it to Combined Defence Headquarters. It may have been a submarine attack.'

Sergeant Dermott Reilly. (*Tony & Lensie Matthews collection*)

Fullford nodded slowly. 'Are you sure, Lieutenant?'

'As sure as I can be, sir. And, you know, with all the attacks that have been happening lately, right up and down the coast … .'

'Well, if you're so insistent, Lieutenant, you'd better get a message off right away and we'll see what they say.'

In an interview he recorded in 1993 for a television documentary being made on the sinking of the *Centaur*, Russell Ward subsequently stated: 'As soon as possible thereafter, using the means of communication we had, which were fairly primitive because we were only in a very temporary situation on this battery site which hadn't actually been fully installed, we got a message through to C.D.H. which we logged, and that's on record in the archives, and that's our account of the happening. We were very concerned that something should be done about it.'

What happened next was a classic error of miscommunication. Admittedly the system of communications between the fledgling gun battery and Combined Defence Headquarters in Brisbane was ad hoc, to say the least, with a temporary telephone line running from the battery to the main line

Lieutenant Russell Ward (left) and Sergeant Dermott Reilly. Both Ward and Reilly witnessed the flash on the horizon which indicated that a large explosion had occurred out at sea. This was later confirmed as having been the torpedoing of the *Centaur*. These photographs were taken fifty years later in 1993 when both men were being interviewed for a television documentary. (*Tony & Lensie Matthews collection*)

which went up to the lighthouse. It frequently did not work but Ward was both surprised and pleased when he was able to get through.

It was now sometime between four o'clock and four-thirty in the morning so people were not entirely at their most alert. However, the telephone operator in Brisbane, when writing down what he was being told over the scratchy telephone line, used the word 'flare' rather than 'glare' to describe what the men at the battery had seen. This was a terrible mistake.

On that particular night an anti-submarine naval exercise was taking place about a hundred miles out to sea approximately east of the *Centaur's* position. As we have seen in this chapter, two men aboard the *Centaur* that night, Dick Medcalf, one of the ship's medical staff, and second radio officer, Tommy Morris, had seen lights flashing out to sea but had not known exactly what had been happening over the horizon. They thought it might have been gunfire.

However, the officers at C.D.H. were, of course, fully aware that the anti-submarine exercise was taking place and also aware that as a part of that exercise aircraft were dropping flares at locations where 'enemy' submarines had been spotted. It was believed, therefore, that the 'flare' that had been spotted by Ward and Russell had simply been a part of the anti-submarine exercise taking place far out at sea and no action was taken to check the sighting. Had the correct description, 'glare' been properly transcribed by the radio operators then it is possible that the officers at C.D.H. might have ordered a patrol boat or other naval vessel to be put to sea to investigate, especially when it was known that the sighting had been visible from shore, whereas the naval exercise was taking place well out to sea, about a hundred miles or more, and that a flare being dropped at that distance would probably not have been visible at sea level on Moreton Island. Had a vessel been sent to investigate, the *Centaur* survivors might have been picked up within an hour or two, rather than being left to fend for themselves in shark-infested waters for more than thirty hours.

And then there was another event which might have prevented the submarine from attacking at all. In fact this single event, if acted upon, might have brought about the destruction of I-177 and saved the lives not only of everyone on board the *Centaur* but also the many dozens of men who would later fall victim to Hajime Nakagawa's murderous actions. It's a moot point, and academic, but one worth pursuing, nonetheless.

Over the years there has been considerable confusion regarding the possible radar sighting of a suspect submarine at that time. During the war years a great many radar stations were installed, principally in coastal regions, around Australia, the main task of which was to track aircraft movements and to be early warning systems for any unidentified aircraft that might have been hostile. These radar stations were operated by the R.A.A.F. but also by the U.S. Army Air Corps. There were two stations along the coast in the Brisbane region at this time that could have tracked the movements of the *Centaur* – although, of course, as the *Centaur's* position was not known due to the requirements of radio silence, the radar operator would have recognised the 'contact' as just another ship heading north.

The first radar station was at Point Lookout on North Stradbroke Island. This had been under the control of the R.A.A.F. utilising the fairly basic M.A.W.D. system (Modified Air Warning Device). These early models of radar had their limitations and were principally designed for finding and tracking aerial contacts but they were certainly capable of picking up vessels on the surface of the sea (although not beneath the sea which was the job of ASDIC – an acronym for Anti Submarine Detection Investigation Committee).

The Australian unit on Stradbroke Island was subsequently transferred north at which time, on 29 July, 1942, ten months before the attack on the *Centaur*, an American unit took control, (apparently under the command of a rather gung-ho John Wayne style sergeant who came complete with a cigar-chomped stogie and Colt .45 automatic strapped to his belt).

This unit utilised more advanced radar equipment, a SCR 268, which had been modified so that it could detect aircraft at one hundred miles and shipping at thirty which would have brought the *Centaur* track within range.

The second radar unit was situated at Fort Lytton in the mouth of the Brisbane River and this unit appears to have been the most significant in the events regarding the sinking of the *Centaur*, although some of the information which follows came from memories or conversations of events that had occurred fifty years previously and therefore precise details have been lost due to the passage of time.

In their superb book on the history of the *Centaur* (*Centaur – the Myth of Immunity*), co-authors Professor Chris Milligan and Captain John Foley provide details of a sighting made by operators of the radar station at Fort Lytton at about 1.30 on the morning of 14 May, 1943 – the morning of the attack on the *Centaur*. The sighting was first made by radar operator Mabel Hess. This sighting caused considerable confusion because the operators were principally involved in tracking aircraft which would ordinarily appear at the edge of the screen and move across it as they were tracked. This particular sighting, however, just suddenly appeared, apparently out of nowhere, and moved only very slowly – far too slowly for it to have been an aircraft. The sighting was reported to Number 8 Fighter Sector in Brisbane (their headquarters were in a tobacco warehouse) whose job it would have been to intercept and investigate the contact but their response was less than helpful. They stated that as the contact appeared to be moving very slowly it must have been a ship or some kind of surface vessel and therefore the squadron was not interested in doing anything about it.

Then suddenly the contact disappeared just as quickly and mysteriously as it had appeared. Mabel Hess immediately guessed that the contact might have been the conning tower of a submarine. She considered again reporting what had happened but because she had already been given a rather rude and condescending brush-off from the staff at Number 8 Fighter Sector she decided against it.

The second report we now have comes from Robert Martin who had worked as a radar operator with the R.A.A.F. during the war. It's here that we see a possible lapse of memory but Martin's account of what happened when the submarine was sighted makes for interesting reading, particularly when one considers the implications that according to Martin's account, the I-177, if indeed that was what radar operators saw that night, was seen tracking a ship and apparently preparing for an attack.

Robert Martin's memory was that the sighting had come from the radar station on Stradbroke Island but according to the radar history publication *Radar Yarns*, edited by Ed Simmonds and Norm Smith, the Stradbroke Island radar unit was already under the control of the Americans by that time. Additionally, Milligan and Foley, in their book, *Centaur – the Myth of Immunity*, record that for the crucial period when the *Centaur* came under attack the Stradbroke Island unit was briefly out of operation having blown a valve, and by the time the unit had been repaired the *Centaur* had already been sunk. The radar unit on Stradbroke Island had missed the entire tragic event.

As stated above, between the time the *Centaur* had been sunk on 14 May, 1943, and the time Robert Martin gave his account of events, fifty years had passed and he had obtained his information from fellow radar operators he had known and worked with during the war. It appears that he misremembered the actual unit that saw and tracked the submarine, stating that it had been the Stradbroke Island unit rather than the unit at Lytton. Despite this lapse in memory he claimed to have important information about the sequence of events that night.

In the early part of the evening [Thursday 13 May] in 1943 [the radar station] picked up a ship heading north. … After tracking it for about and hour, approximately, another echo appeared behind it which was thought to be that of a submarine and it was subsequently vividly identified as a submarine. Not one of ours … but a hostile one, an enemy submarine, a Japanese submarine heading on the same course, behind and overtaking the *Centaur*. The radar station kept tracking it, kept plotting it; all the plots were recorded in a log book as they were required to be of all ships and all aeroplanes. … Now the submarine, over a period of approximately six hours, crept up on it and subsequently overtook HMAS *Centaur* while at this time the *Centaur* was … standing fairly well out to sea at a distance, I think, from very rough memory, of about twenty-eight nautical miles. And the submarine disappeared, as it turned out, east of HMAS *Centaur* and it was lost to the radar screen, blotted out by the *Centaur*. Shortly after that there was an enormous explosion which was the end of the *Centaur*.

It was horrid, absolutely horrible for our operators. … They were good, sensible young men who knew exactly what they were doing and they were asked frequently to check their equipment for accuracy, which they did. There was a well known procedure for doing that and they did it, and it was a real life horror drama that unfolded in front of them, even to this day, I reckon, remorseful and upset about the whole thing when I first talked to these people, at a distance in time of about six months, and then again at a year, it was still a nasty horrible dream to them to think that all those nice people went down.

The A.H.S. *Centaur*. The Japanese torpedo would strike the ship approximately where the small launch can be seen tied to the Jacob's ladder on the port side for'ard. (*Australian War Memorial, Accession Number 302794*)

Due to strict radio silence in force at that time no one, of course, could have known that an attack was being made on a hospital ship. Nonetheless, if the above information is accurate then one has to ask why a ship, or better still an anti-submarine aircraft, was not sent immediately to investigate.

*   *   *

However, to rewind now, back in time by around half an hour. Hajime Nakagawa had just illegally fired his twin torpedoes at a brightly lit hospital ship in clear contravention of international law and common decency. One of the torpedoes missed the *Centaur* completely but the other was devastatingly successful. It struck the ship on its port side for'ard of the bridge superstructure blowing a massive hole into the hull, penetrating the engine room and fuel tanks which were filled with diesel. The position of the strike could not have been worse. The fuel ignited instantly and from that nanosecond the stricken ship and more than 260 people had just three minutes to live.

As we have seen, standing on deck at that moment was Corporal Albert Taylor who had visited the heads that morning before going on deck to catch some fresh air and to watch a school of porpoises at play. When the torpedo struck he was stunned by the shock of the explosion. He saw the bridge being engulfed in flames and almost immediately a rain of oil began falling over the ship. The deck lights went out leaving only the eerie glow of the fires to illuminate the shocking scene. It had taken only a second but everything in Albert's life, in fact the lives of everyone on board, changed from that exact moment. Taylor ran aft on the port side as other men began to scramble on deck, desperately trying to get to a raft or lifeboat.

In the engine room William 'Bill' Cuthill with his wipers and oilers had just settled into their watch. They were probably enjoying their first cup of coffee for the morning when the torpedo struck. Even before the fuel tanks exploded moments later, Cuthill and most of his staff would almost certainly have been killed in the torpedo's blast or by the savage storm of heavy machinery that erupted violently in the compartment as the engine and its associated pieces of machinery were torn from their mountings to fill the air with white-hot shrapnel. Death for these men would, at least, have been mercifully fast.

The for'ard portion of the ship was almost immediately a mass of flames. Most of the men of the 2/12th Ambulance and their associated A.A.S.C. personnel were being accommodated for the journey in two hospital decks above the for'ard hold. These, and the hold itself, were turned instantly into raging infernos. All this happened so quickly that most of the men would have been killed as they slept. Those who were not, however, now faced another equally menacing danger – flooding.

Nakagawa's torpedo had blown a massive hole beneath the waterline in the side of the *Centaur* and water was now rushing into the ship with tremendous force. Both the hold and Ward F were soon completely flooded.

Over the following few desperate minutes an uncountable number of individual human tragedies and also innumerable spontaneously heroic deeds occurred as the *Centaur*, now well ablaze and sinking by the bow, began its plunge to the sea-bed.

Between decks on the stricken ship all was horror and confusion as those who had survived the initial blast and subsequent ignition of the diesel fuel struggled to climb up successive decks in a desperate attempt to live. Yet this was no easy task. The stairwells and passageways were choked with men and also the nurses. The ship was filled with smoke and burning oil; water was flooding up from below with terrifying rapidity. In panic, clusters

Ward F aboard the A.H.S. *Centaur*. This ward was almost immediately flooded following the explosion of the torpedo. (*Australian War Memorial, Accession Number 029717*)

of people wedged themselves into bottlenecks at hatches and stairwells, shouting anxiously to those in front to hurry, to get up the steps and allow those pressing from behind also to escape. Fear was an all-pervasive element which seemed to cloak and hinder all those who were trying so hard to get to the upper deck. Some assisted others while a few simply helped themselves.

George McGrath was a driver attached to the 2/12th Field Ambulance. He and his brother, Allan McGrath, had been at Darwin during the bombing of the city in February the previous year. Allan was subsequently posted to Tobruk and George to the *Centaur*. George had recently become engaged to Marie Mullins, a bombardier who was then in charge of a searchlight battery at Port Kembla. Coincidentally, the *Centaur* attack coincided with Marie's birthday

George McGrath's story of survival was a little different from most because shortly before the blast he had visited the 'heads'. He was later to attribute the quantity of beer he had drunk during Matron Jewell's birthday party to saving his life because he had needed to use the toilet at just the right moment. George's accommodation space was on the first deck in the main hospital area where about nine men had been allocated sleeping quarters. Upon returning to his bed he had been unable to sleep. He was actually sitting on the edge of the bed looking at his watch when the torpedo struck. He described it as, '… an almighty explosion followed by a fireball'. Because he was quartered midships, and on the port side, the same side the torpedo had struck, George was right at the centre of the area where the explosion and fuel ignition occurred. He was blown off his bed, striking his nose on something, possibly the bed-board, making it bleed. When he managed to pull himself together he realised that something terrible had happened but there was hardly any time to think. He knew there were about seventy of 'his lads' in the next ward and things did not look good for them. He later recorded:

> When I picked myself up I could see this fireball coming at me … we were dead midships and it would have killed everyone that was in that forward part of the ship. I couldn't see them escaping because with the double-barrelled explosion, hitting the oil tanks, it was one whoosh and of course when it exploded inside it expanded and came with a rush. I could see that fire coming after me and would say it engulfed a lot of the ones that I left behind.

An instant inner voice said to George, *Mac, don't go back for your lifebelt.* George McGrath's lifejacket was stored beneath his bunk but everything was happening so rapidly now that even moving to the bunk and scrabbling beneath it for his lifejacket seemed to be inadvisable, especially with a wall of fire heading in his direction. Time seemed to be flying past at the speed of light. Having made that nanosecond decision George raced through the larger ward, passing as he did so Major Charles Thelander of the 2/12th Field Ambulance. George McGrath and Thelander were good friends, despite their difference in rank, and when Thelander saw George racing through the ward he shouted, 'Don't panic Mac.' That was the last time George saw his friend because Major Thelander would be killed during the coming minutes as the ship was abandoned.

George McGrath now raced up the narrow companionway but the ship was already tilting alarmingly, quite obviously going down by the head. There were no seconds to be wasted. George ran up the tilting deck to the stern of the ship where he found another man attempting to release one of the inflatable Carley floats. However, they were not members of the ship's crew and in the darkness it was impossible to see well enough to understand how to release the float. One of the failures of the constant drills had been the lack of instructions on how to release these Carley floats which was an

George McGrath seen here during the interview he gave in 1993 for the production of *Centaur – Death of a Hospital Ship*, a television documentary on the sinking of the *Centaur*. (*Tony & Lensie Matthews collection*)

omission that might have cost lives, particularly as Carley floats were far better than small rafts or timber flotsam.

As the ship plunged alarmingly downwards both men jumped feet-first into the sea, realising instinctively that to dive headfirst into the water with all the wreckage around would have increased the danger. George McGrath hit the water and began swimming as strongly and as quickly as he could, attempting to place as much distance as possible between himself and the sinking ship.

George was a good swimmer although it concerned him that he had been unable to get to his lifebelt in time. He was a little concerned that someone who might not be able to swim would grab onto him and drag him down but nothing like that occurred. Then in the darkness he saw the outline of a raft with several men on it. He managed to get to the raft easily enough and was pulled on board by those who had already managed to climb onto it. George later recalled that it was severely overcrowded with about twenty-two men clinging precariously together.

*   *   *

Allan Pettiford, meanwhile, had come awake from a deep sleep but for some strange reason he was no longer lying in his bunk. He was now somehow, and against all reason, standing in the aisle between the bunks and for a few moments at least he had no idea how he had come to be there. He had not heard the torpedo exploding, his sleep had been so sound, but evidently something terrible had happened because the ward was a mass of smoke and confusion and men were scrambling everywhere almost in a frenzy. One of the officers of the 2/12th, Major Charles Thelander, was shouting above the uproar, instructing his men to remain calm and to make their way to their lifeboat stations. Still somewhat confused, Allan tried to awaken his friend, Jack Lynagh, but to Allan's complete surprise and horror Jack was already dead, just lying there in his bunk as if he were asleep. The blast of the explosion had apparently killed him instantly while Allan, lying in the bunk below, had survived. Dressed only in his vest and underpants, Allan quickly tied on his lifejacket and prepared to evacuate. He later said that there was no panic on board, at least he did not see any. He stated: 'Nobody seemed frightened but there were some of the poor beggars that were up in the forward part, they were burnt to death.'

For many of those who would survive the sinking, the boat-drills that had been performed (sometimes with monotonous and irritating frequency) certainly helped in their survival. Of course, boat-drills are one thing and reality is another. When running to the boat-deck under simulated conditions everything would usually go according to plan, but in reality, when the rush to the boat-deck suddenly became a matter of life and death, almost nothing was the same. Now, those who had miraculously survived so far had to deal with panic, fear, flooding, fire and choking smoke, most of which had the potential to kill very quickly. However, despite these terrifying realities the men, and one woman, who would survive this catastrophe did so principally because of the drills. They knew the fastest and safest routes to the boat-deck and most of them were able to grasp their lifejackets quickly as they were now trained to have them on hand ready for the drills, most of which had come without any warning.

*   *   *

Robert 'Bob' Westwood was the youngest person aboard the *Centaur* that day. Many subsequent reports stated that he was sixteen years of age and according to the articles of agreement document Robert signed when he joined the ship he gave his date of birth simply as 1927 without providing either day or month. Robert later wrote that he had been fifteen at the time of the sinking.

Robert Westwood seen here during the interview he gave in 1993 for the production of *Centaur – Death of a Hospital Ship*, a television documentary on the sinking of the *Centaur*. (*Tony & Lensie Matthews collection*)
Inset: Robert 'Bob' Westwood. Bob was about fifteen or sixteen years of age when the *Centaur* was torpedoed, the youngest person on board. (*Bob Westwood collection*)

Robert Westwood was asleep in the aft mess-room when the torpedo struck. The men were mostly seasoned seamen and fully understood the dangers they faced every day, and although no one had really expected to be torpedoed aboard a hospital ship, the very real possibility had always been there.

As soon as the torpedo struck almost everyone in the mess realised what had occurred, even the youthful Robert Westwood. He grabbed his lifebelt and followed the other seamen up the steel ladder although there was a bit of a crush and someone called out not to panic, to take things calmly and easily. Yet Bob Westwood's story of sinking and survival would be somewhat different from those later told by other survivors for rather than abandoning the *Centaur* he decided, for a while at least, that staying on the ship was probably less dangerous than actually jumping into a sea full of oil, spars, tangled ropes and sharks.

When Bob reached the top upper deck he and the other men continued towards the boat deck as they had been instructed during their lifeboat drill. There the men attempted to launch one of the boats but even Bob Westwood could see that it was futile. The ship was sinking so quickly there would never be enough time to swing the boat out. Additionally, the angle of the *Centaur* already made it virtually impossible to launch a boat successfully. Realising this in the seconds they had to appraise the situation, Bob and the other men raced back down the companionway towards the stern of the ship where the men immediately began launching themselves into the sea. Every second they paused meant that the stern rose higher and higher, thus increasing the already considerable dangers they all faced. Bob Westwood, however, remained uncertain as to what would be his wisest move. He later recorded: 'I decided to hold onto the rail for as long as possible and I actually didn't let go until the water washed me off, and by that time the ship was really vertical and I went down for a considerable time with the ship and it must have been at that stage I hit my head and came to the surface with a few other people bobbing around me.'

*   *   *

Sister Ellen Savage, a member of the medical staff, would be the only woman to survive the sinking of the *Centaur*. That night she was sharing a cabin with a fellow nurse, Sister Merle Moston. Both were asleep in their bunks at the time of the explosion. As Sister Savage was violently awakened by the blast she almost immediately realised that the ship had been subjected to a torpedo attack. Instinctively she reached for her lifebelt. As Sister Moston attempted to get over the shock of the explosion she too realised what had happened. In the dim light she could see that Ellen was pulling the lifejacket over her head and beginning strap it tightly around her pyjamas. Neither Ellen nor Sister Moston spoke during those few precious moments, words were pointless, they both knew what they must do and they simply got on with it. Every second now counted.

The two women then heard a voice at the door. 'Savage – out on deck.' They recognised the voice as that of Sister Evelyn King who was

Sister Ellen Savage. (*Australian War Memorial, Accession Number 061952*)

occupying a neighbouring cabin. Within moments all three women were running for their boat-station, tightening and securing their lifejackets as they did so. There was hardly time to think. The ship was already beginning to list alarmingly to port.

As they struggled through the darkness, smoke and chaos they ran into their commanding officer, Lieutenant-Colonel Clement Polson Manson, known to his friends simply as Clem. The nurses were completely astonished that Manson was already dressed in his full uniform, complete with cap, when most of the other people scrambling all around in almost complete darkness, including the three nurses, were wearing just night attire. Colonel Manson also had his lifejacket securely tied over his tunic. It was almost as if he had experienced some kind of presentiment about the attack.

* * *

The previous night the ship's fourth engineer, Maurice 'Maurie' Cairnie, had not been able to enjoy the party atmosphere that had prevailed aboard the *Centaur*. He had been on watch in the engine room from 8 p.m. until midnight when he was relieved. He had gone straight to his modest cabin and by 12.15 was in his bunk.

At the time of the blast Maurie was still asleep in his cabin on the boat-deck which was probably a good place to have a cabin when enemy submarines with murderous commanders were roaming close at hand.

Maurie Cairnie seen here during the interview he gave in 1993 for the production of *Centaur – Death of a Hospital Ship*, a television documentary on the sinking of the *Centaur*. (*Tony & Lensie Matthews collection*)

The sudden blast of the torpedo came as a massive shock which literally blew Maurie out of his bunk. He realised immediately that this explosion was no terrible shipboard engineering disaster – the ship was under attack, his premonition had come chillingly true. Suddenly, even while Maurie was attempting to gather his thoughts and grab his lifejacket, he heard someone banging on his door. It was Maurie's immediate superior and friend, the chief engineer, Ernest 'Ernie' Smith, who was very urgently shouting to Maurie to hurry up as the ship had been torpedoed and was going down.

By now the *Centaur* was beginning to sink so rapidly it was difficult to believe that a vessel so well founded, in such good condition, could be utterly destroyed so easily. In the semi-darkness Maurie Cairnie and Ernie Smith tried to open the deck door but it was jammed, the explosion had, apparently, warped the steel. However, they managed somehow to force the door open. As the two men arrived on deck the bows of the ship were already almost under water and the accommodation on the port side was blazing furiously with flames leaping aft towards the bridge. There was no time for the two men to consult about what they should do, everything was happening so quickly that actions came almost through reflex alone. Smith turned to starboard, going apparently to his lifeboat station (although there is also a version of events which states that he had been heading to the dynamo room

Chief Engineer Ernie Smith. (*Smith family collection*)

to try to get the lights on again). However, the sea raged over the deck and Ernie Smith was washed over the side. He would, however, survive.

Meanwhile Maurice Cairnie headed in the opposite direction, turning to the port side immediately he came on deck and dutifully heading aft for his designated lifeboat station while also strapping on his lifejacket. There he found a group of men attempting to launch a boat. It was still very dark, of course, and without light every task was made more difficult, although the flames were now providing some eerily hellish illumination. Enough men were attempting to release the boat so Maurice helpfully shone his torch to assist. However, the sudden beam of light clearly illuminated how close the sea had now come. In its beam Maurice and the other men were astonished to see that the water was travelling towards them like a steam-train. 'Jump,' Maurice shouted urgently, and not bothering to wait any longer he launched himself into the sea.

*   *   *

On the deck immediately below Maurice Cairnie, Sisters Ellen Savage, Evelyn King and Merle Moston were standing at the ship's rail with their commanding officer, Lieutenant-Colonel Clem Manson. Manson was composed and seemingly completely impervious to the dangers that threatened them all. He told his three nurses that all would be well and asked them to jump for it. The nurses were not so sure that they could do it. Right then it seemed that jumping into a cold sea full of debris, oil and struggling men would be almost as perilous as remaining on board. Ellen's eyes were wide with fright. Dressed in only her flimsy night attire, she realised that the sea at this time of year, although not dangerously cold, would be cold enough to be very unpleasant. Winter was coming but it was actually still a couple of weeks away. She turned to Colonel Manson. 'Is there time for me to go back and get my coat, Colonel?' she asked. Manson could see that she was shivering but wasn't sure if it was the result of cold or of shock. He shook his head resolutely. There was no time. It was too late. They had to jump.

Evelyn King was very frightened because she was unable to swim. Ellen Savage grasped her arm. 'I'll stay right with you', she said. 'Don't worry, I'll keep you afloat.'

At that moment they all saw Maurice Cairnie plummeting past as he jumped from the deck above. The nurses eyes were wide with fright. Water was now coming at them like a wall. There was no more time to think or procrastinate. Lieutenant-Colonel Manson climbed onto the rail, probably demonstrating to the nurses that it was easy, giving them confidence, 'Come on you lot,' he called again, then jumped. Ellen Savage climbed the rail and jumped next followed by Evelyn King who needed to stay close to Ellen Savage, and then Sister Moston.

It was all a terrible disaster.

Ellen was badly injured when she jumped. As she hit the water the suction of the sinking ship pulled her down and she became entangled in a mass of ropes. The combination of ropes and suction held her firmly underwater and she was certain that this was her time to die. She also sustained internal injuries, broken ribs and a fractured nose and palate, the result of timber spars and other debris falling on her from the ship's decks. She was kicking desperately and fighting with the ropes in a last-ditch effort to break free when miraculously she popped to the surface, gasping for air, coming up directly beneath another survivor, Corporal Thomas Malcolm.

Sadly, Ellen was unable to be of any assistance to either Evelyn King or Merle Moston. Both had been killed by falling timber.

*   *   *

Corporal Thomas 'Tom' Malcolm, an orderly, was a member of the ship's medical staff and a very experienced NCO. He had previously worked on several hospital ships and knew the ropes thoroughly. The previous night he had not joined in the partying nor had he attended the concert. He had not even realised that a party was in progress as he had spent the entire evening quietly playing cards. His family was well represented by servicemen. Tom had a brother who was a prisoner-of-war in Japan with another brother fighting the Japanese at Milne Bay.

On the morning of the attack Tom was sleeping in one of the top bunks in the for'ard hospital decks. Beneath Tom was another experienced NCO and medical professional, Staff Sergeant Dick Medcalf.

Tom Malcolm was one of the survivors who later stated that they had never heard the twin explosions that night, neither the torpedo slamming home nor the ignition of the fuel tanks. Yet Tom was awakened suddenly and realised that something was terribly amiss. He attempted to switch on the bed-lamp but it was not working. Tom did not realise that the ship's power was down because he could still see in the gloom. He then realised that he was able to see because of the illumination cast by flames. He immediately jumped out of the bunk almost landing on Dick Medcalf who had just climbed out of his. Both men were slightly confused but that did not prevent

Corporal Tom Malcolm seen here during the interview he gave in 1993 for the production of *Centaur – Death of a Hospital Ship*, a television documentary on the sinking of the *Centaur*. (*Tony & Lensie Matthews collection.*)

them from exchanging a few hurried words and reaching for their lifejackets. Tom Malcolm later said that having his lifejacket close at hand was the result of long experience at sea and he had gone through countless lifeboat station drills so the entire scenario was almost second nature to him, apart from its terrible reality. He was fully aware that this was no drill. He attempted to shake another man who was lying in a bunk close by. The man did not move. Tom was never quite sure if he was already dead because despite a violent shaking and shouting the man remained immobile. Tom then raced up the stairwell towards his boat-station with water surging behind him. He reached the deck with three other men: Staff Sergeant George Carter; Private Thomas Hegarty and Private Frederick Chidgey, all members of the ship's medical staff. It was less than a minute since the ship had been hit but time astonishingly had compressed and events were moving at a furious pace. Fire was engulfing the ship and any attempt to reach the boat-deck would have been suicidal. The three men accompanying Tom Malcolm just decided to jump for it and within moments were in the sea. Tom Malcolm did not need to jump. Seconds later he was simply swept into the water. He later recorded:

Well, obviously, I went down under water and took some time, I should imagine, coming to the surface, but having done that Sister Savage just popped up right between my arms. It wasn't a case of looking for her or reaching for her, she just came straight up between my arms and it wasn't long before I was hit on the back by something which turned out to be a crews' toilet off the deck. [Other reports claim this was the old hospital roof – author's note]. We endeavoured to get on the roof and I got on and tried to help Sister Savage on but she was a pretty big woman and I had to get back into the water and literally push her on. But the only bit of humour in the incident occurred when she called out, 'Tommy I've got no trousers on' and I told her it was a bloody nice time to think of modesty and that is absolute truth.

The three men who had gone over the side at almost the same time as Tom Malcolm: Staff Sergeant George Carter, Private Thomas Hegarty and Private Frederick Chidgey, would all survive the sinking. Chidgey's case was interesting because he had been a surgical instrument representative before the war and had enlisted in the Australian Army Medical Corps with the rank of warrant officer. However, he had agreed to be demoted to a private so that he could qualify to serve aboard a hospital ship.

* * *

The ship's second officer, Gordon Rippon, who would be the most senior officer to survive the attack, after leaving the radio officer's cabin that night had gone to his own cabin to turn in. He had climbed into his bunk and later remembered looking at his watch which showed that the time was 4.15 a.m. – a slight variation to the time normally given for the attack on the *Centaur* which usually claims it as being 4.10 a.m. One can only assume that Rippon's watch was correct as he was, after all, one of the ship's senior officers and the accuracy of his watch in navigational calculations would have had to be perfect. We also know that this was not a lapse in memory on Rippon's behalf because he wrote a letter to his father outlining these details, including the exact time, while still lying in his hospital bed in Brisbane just days later. (These details may be found in an oral history interview with Gordon Rippon, recorded by Professor Christopher Milligan on 5 October, 1979, a copy of which is on deposit with the Australian War Memorial, Canberra).

Gordon Rippon had just pulled up the bunk's blankets when the ship was violently shaken by the tremendous explosion of the torpedo. Like so many others on board, Rippon was literally blown from his bunk onto the deck. He was fortunate because his cabin was close to the bridge on the boat-deck so although located in the centre of the ship, the region most affected by the explosion and subsequent fire, he was higher up and therefore his chances of survival were far better than many others trapped below, especially those in the wards.

Rippon immediately realised what had happened. He did not want to believe that the *Centaur* had been torpedoed but it seemed obvious. He looked out of the door to his cabin and saw a sight which was to haunt him forever. Even now, moments after the explosion, the ship was already well down by the head and the forepart of the vessel was one mass of flames. Rippon later stated that it was actually raining burning oil. Slightly confused, a result of the sudden blast, Gordon Rippon at first believed that he might have been trapped himself but he was able to grab his lifejacket and scrambled out onto the deck. There he saw the ship's first officer, Henry 'Harry' Lamble, who had just taken over the watch on the bridge. Lamble had his hands over his face, having been severely burned when the bridge had burst into flames. Rippon noticed in that fleeting moment that Lamble was also covered in blood and one of his arms appeared to be limp.

Amid the roaring noise, screams, cries for help and chaos Rippon raced towards the lifeboat he had been assigned to command in the event of such a tragedy. Like everyone else on board, Rippon had no opportunity to get a lifeboat away. He subsequently stated that three of the lifeboats had been smashed and there simply was not enough time to get the fourth boat away because the ship was slipping into the water at an astonishing rate. He dashed down to the rafts and attempted to get one released but there was not enough time. Then the ship began to sink so quickly it seemed as if it was actually hurrying to put a finish to its agony. Realising that there was nothing to be done, Rippon just jumped over the side and into the sea.

*   *   *

Staff Sergeant Dick Medcalf, after chatting to the ship's second radio officer, Tommy Morris, that night, had gone to the living space which he shared with the other non-commissioned officers of the ship's medical staff, including Tom Malcolm. This area was located for'ard, two decks down and consisted of a series of cubicles or semi-cabins fitted with bunks and lockers.

The blast awakened Dick as he lay in his bunk that morning. He later described it as a 'terrific crash'. Strangely, Dick Medcalf must have had some kind of premonition the previous evening, possibly triggered by seeing flashes of what appeared to have been gunfire far out to sea. In any case, he had been very uneasy. Before turning in he had packed an army haversack with his camera (strictly forbidden), a writing case and some letters and had hung the haversack close to his bunk within easy reach. He had also tied a water bottle and a packet of malted milk tablets to the haversack. He later said that he'd had no real reason for taking this precaution but was comforted by the fact that the haversack was there if he needed it quickly.

After being blasted awake by the torpedo exploding, Dick opened his eyes to see flames all around the walls of the accommodation space. He realised later that oil-pipes had burst and these were now burning furiously. He immediately grabbed the haversack and his lifejacket, raced across the deck and began to climb the first flight of steps to the ship's second deck. Yet things were now happening so quickly that even survival seemed improbable. 'I was half way up and a terrific deluge of water came down through these two lots of gratings', Dick later recorded, 'and I lost my haversack, but fortunately I had the lifejacket and I was hanging onto the hand-rail and I went straight up to the next deck which was the hospital deck.'

Reaching the hospital deck Dick looked to his right and saw that the hospital ward, which was being used to accommodate many of the 2/12th Field Ambulance personnel, was a mass of flames. Dick was attempting to climb the next set of steps to the top deck and at the same time tie on his lifejacket but when he reached the top deck he took just one step onto the deck, which was then level with the sea, and the ship began to go down taking Dick with it.

Dick Medcalf was sucked down, held there by what seemed an iron grip. He struggled and fought to get to the surface while swallowing a lot of oil – gallons of it, he thought – then to his relief he began to rise and suddenly found himself on the surface, hanging on to a section of hatch-grating.

*   *   *

How Ron Moate, a ship's pantryman, managed to get off the *Centaur* alive was nothing short of a miracle, given how quickly the vessel had foundered.

Ron had been working hard the night before assisting with the celebrations for Matron Jewell's birthday party in the ship's saloon.

When the torpedo struck that morning Ron Moate, like almost everyone on the ship at that time, was in bed. His bunk was situated in a three-berth cabin reserved for the catering staff. In the bunk beneath Ron Moate was the head waiter, Fred 'Jock' Siddons and in the third bunk was the ship's storekeeper, John Charles Buck. Neither Siddons nor Buck would survive.

An artist's impression of the sinking of the *Centaur*. This propaganda image is a dramatic but inaccurate representation of the sinking of the ship. The torpedo actually struck the *Centaur* on the port side, not the starboard, and of course, at the time of the explosion there were no survivors in the water. (*Australian War Memorial, Accession Number ARTV 09088*)

Ron Moate was blasted awake, only to discover through his shock that he had been wedged firmly into his bunk by a wardrobe that had been blasted off the side of the ship and was now pinning Ron into his bunk. Jock Siddons was tangled up in the mess too, but was able to wriggle himself free, crawling out on hands and knees, and immediately turned his attention to assisting Ron Moate. There were flames everywhere and it was obvious that their lives might now literally be measured in seconds. The other two men were able to run for their lives and Ron followed as quickly as possible. On his way out he almost stumbled over the two bodies of Siddons and Buck. Both had been killed. Reaching the open deck, Ron ran into the ship's captain, George Murray who called angrily. 'Well the bastards have done it this time, haven't they,' (meaning the Japanese actions in torpedoing the ship). Ron replied that he had known it was going to happen. Yet this was no time to talk. Murray waved him through. 'On your way, son, do what you can for yourself,' he said, and that was the last time Ron Moate saw Captain Murray.

Ron Moate seen here during the interview he gave in 1993 for the production of *Centaur – Death of a Hospital Ship*, a television documentary on the sinking of the *Centaur*. (*Tony & Lensie Matthews collection*)
Inset: Ron Moate. (*Courtesy of Ron Moate, author's collection*)

The *Maryborough Chronicle* of 19 May that year reported that as Ron Moate had come on deck he had seen Captain Murray attempting to launch a lifeboat. He was being aided by two men, Jessie 'Jack' Stutter and Charles Carey. They had been struggling desperately to release the boat. Ron Moate had later told the press: 'The four of us were washed over the engineer's deckhouse. The last thing I saw was the mast breaking away. Only Strutter [sic] and I came up. I clung to the raft with Strutter [sic] and a badly burned man.'

In these few minutes Ron Moate realised that there would be little hope for the survival of the doctors and nurses on board; he could see that the whole central part of the ship was on fire including the saloon where just hours earlier he had been helping to celebrate Matron Jewell's birthday party. 'The nurses' accommodation and where the doctors were, that was all ablaze and there was nothing anyone could do about it,' Ron later recalled. 'There wasn't enough time and there wasn't enough gear.'

*   *   *

Brothers Mark and Trevor Hoggins were two of the ship's crew who had been at sea since they had left school. Both worked as cooks on the ship although their cabins were separated at either end of the vessel. As soon as the explosion occurred, their first thoughts were for each other and they raced down the deck in a frantic search. Miraculously, amid all that death and confusion, they found each other. When they did so they jumped immediately into the sea. They somehow managed to find a raft and clambered aboard, the *Maryborough Chronicle* later (19/5/1943) reported that Mark had been a survivor of a ship torpedoed off the Australian coast the previous year. He later told the press that after jumping from the *Centaur,* 'Seven sharks nosed around our raft and one rushed it. We pushed it off with a spar.'

The third officer, Ernest 'Monty' Banks, recalled in the same press report that this was his fourth war-time sinking. A ship in which he had been serving had been bombed and sunk off St. Nazaire on the French coast and he had experienced torpedo attacks twice before: once off Gibraltar and again in the North Atlantic.

*   *   *

Lance Corporal 'Spud' Jones was another 'miracle' survivor because he had been accommodated in the hospital wards along with all his mates of the 2/12th Field Ambulance, a disproportionate number of whom would die during the attack because they were so close to the seat of the explosion and its subsequent blast of igniting fuel.

The previous evening Spud had been playing chess and after completing the game had turned in. The premonition of disaster he had earlier experienced had not gone away and he checked to ensure that his lifejacket was close at hand. He was awakened the following morning by the blast of the torpedo. Automatically he grabbed his lifejacket and shouted to his mates: 'We're going down. Get on deck.' The other men did not reply and everything was a mass of fire and confusion so Spud, holding his lifejacket close to his chest, and believing that the other men were already on deck, groped in the semi-darkness towards the set of steps that led to the next deck. He was wearing a set of pyjamas but these were already smouldering. Spud later stated that he could never actually remember feeling the steps in his hands or on his feet because the fire was literally chasing him up them. Bursting on deck he ripped off his burning pyjamas and strapped on his lifejacket. He had sufficient presence of mind to remember his lifeboat drill

instructions and was careful to leave the back flaps of the lifejacket untied so
that the back pillow of the jacket would keep his head out of the water. Spud,
however, was puzzled about two things. The first was the lack of people on
deck: surely there should have been more, and the other was particularly
troubling because he was unable to hear anything. He seemed to be in some
kind of soundless limbo.

The two other men he saw on deck almost immediately jumped into the
sea. Yet despite the apparent security of having his lifejacket strapped in
place, Spud was terrified of jumping into the water. He attempted to release
one of the rafts strapped to the deck but it would not come free. Then the ship
was almost gone and Spud floated off with it. Suction pulled him under and
when he bobbed finally to the surface he gulped for air but only succeeded
in swallowing a mouthful of hot oil. He lay on the surface, thankful for the
lifejacket but unable to see anything as his eyes were also full of oil. After a
while he was able to grab onto a hatch-cover as it drifted past.

*   *   *

Private Allan Pettiford of the 2/12th Field Ambulance managed to get
himself up to his boat-station, another successful example of the efficacy
of the boat drill training. He paused as he came on deck, confused by the
enormity of the catastrophic events that were so rapidly consuming the ship
and devouring the lives of his mates. He had seen things in the last few
minutes that he never wanted to see again and had been forced to leave his
best mate Jack Lynagh lying dead in his bunk. The boat to which Allan had
been allocated was surrounded by men as he arrived – too many, it seemed –
as they attempted to work the winch ready to lower the boat. Allan realised
that there was nothing more he could to do help them. He later said:

I could see that things were going to happen quickly so I just hopped up
into the boat which was rather silly because it was fastened with a huge
rope, and then the next sensation was the boat breaking in two and I
was in a position that I was almost vertical, looking down at the sea,
and the other half of the boat almost flat, and the next thing I knew I
was airborne from about thirty feet and hit the water and was tossed out
of the boat and goodness knows how far I went down in the process of
being sucked down … the ship sinking caused this terrific suction, and
on the way down I lost my underpants. I was able to get back up into
the old wrecked lifeboat which was floating at the time.

To state that there was now total confusion and horror on deck would be something of a misnomer. There was confusion and there was an element of panic – a rather frantic need for individual survival. Yet there was bravery too, people helping others to don lifejackets or guiding them in the darkness to the boats. Ronald Davies Bull was the ship's writer. When he managed to get on deck he immediately began to release a raft on the starboard side but had to keep dodging fires and the rigging. Just then an orderly called a warning, shouting that a spar was about to fall. At that moment a spar fell and killed the orderly.

Ronald Bull later told the *Maryborough Chronicle* (19/5/1943) that after he had jumped into the sea he was sucked down and came up minus his false teeth. His underpants had also been torn off by the suction. His left leg was entangled in a raft but he was able somehow to get it free. He then managed to get onto a hatch-cover and linked up with a group of survivors clinging to a wall of the wheelhouse. They saw a number of flares being set off and using their lifejacket lights they began flashing an SOS in Morse. They then saw what Bull described as: '... a large red light and a large submarine on the surface. We held our breath, expecting a burst of machine-gun bullets.'

Yet amid all the flames, water, smoke, cursing and struggle there was one missing element in this cluster of confusion. And that was people. By now the decks of the ship should have been inundated with literally hundreds of people – crew, medical staff, ambulance personnel and drivers, more than 330 people were known to be on board the ship but on the smoke-swept decks nowhere near this number were attempting to get to the lifeboat stations. Where were all the people? It's likely that not too many of those on deck at that time were wondering about numbers – they had their own survival to worry about, but it was becoming poignantly obvious from the relatively few people on deck that the twin blasts of torpedo and fuel tank ignition must have been responsible for an inordinate number of fatalities that night. Some, of course, would have survived the blasts only to be trapped between decks by the rapid inrush of water. As for the remainder, the flames and choking smoke would have taken a frightful toll.

Although almost impossible to believe, considering the hundreds of individual dramas that had been enacted on the ship, it was now literally just three minutes since Nakagawa's torpedo had slammed into the hull of the *Centaur* ripping a mortal gash in its side from which the vessel could never recover. Hundreds were already dead. The people struggling in the water were in a terrible state of shock and some were injured. It was clear to them that their lives might now also be measured in minutes. None of the lifeboats had been got away, apart from one that was badly damaged, and only a few rafts had been launched or had drifted off. There had been some difficulties in releasing the rafts and in the few precious minutes between the time the ship and been hit and it had sunk it had proved impossible to get most of the rafts free.

*   *   *

Frank Davidson, the ship's butcher, later said that he had seen one of the nurses on the middle deck. He had put a life-jacket on her and told her to jump, which she did. 'That was the last I saw of her,' Davidson later told the press. He added that a crowd of men had been trying to get through the flames which had enveloped the companionway. There was nothing Davidson could do for any of them so he just jumped overboard. He subsequently stated that the sharks had been the principal concern for most of those in the water. 'We filled in a bit of time arguing whether the sharks were hungry', he later stated. 'We tested it out by throwing a coloured tin into the water. A big fellow snapped the bottom right off it.'

The majority of survivors were now either clinging to rafts or simply bobbing about in the water supported by the life-jackets. The ship they had just abandoned was continuing to sink with startling rapidity. There is a general perception that ships tend to sink slowly and almost gracefully but there was nothing slow or graceful in the last few moments of the *Centaur*. Its bows were now well beneath the surface of the sea and as the survivors watched, horrified, the stern of the vessel rose grandly before their eyes, the bridge superstructure began to crumple and buckle as if made from aluminum foil and then the entire ship was nose-diving downwards until nothing was left except its whirlpool vortex amid a terrible mess of oil, flotsam and dead bodies. Some survivors later stated that as the ship was sinking, amid all the noise of the roaring flames, escaping steam, bulkheads crumbling and rushing water, they could also hear the screams and shouts of those men and nurses who were trapped within the ship's hull. Allan Pettiford subsequently provided a chilling description of the last moments of the *Centaur*: 'The ship caught fire and at the end of it, when I was looking at it going down, it was just like a red hot coal and the poor beggars that were there were screaming and going on and had no chance of escaping, but there was no panic, no panic at all, because it happened so quickly.'

When Dick Medcalf had popped to the surface grasping a piece of hatch-grating he had been in time to see the stern of the vessel sinking beneath the waves. He was immensely pleased to be alive and realised how close he had come to death. 'They say that your whole life passes before you', he later recorded, 'but I can remember very clearly saying, "You bloody beaut!" and I hung on to that hatch-grating and that was that.'

It was still dark, of course, and Dick could see the lights of life-jackets bobbing about in the water. There were people calling for help. He was just able to see a raft close by which appeared to be supporting a few people so he paddled towards it and was dragged on board.

It is today impossible to know how many people were now in the water. Estimates provided later by survivors varied considerably and given the fact that those in the water were suffering not only from shock but also severe injuries, including savage burns, it would have been almost impossible for any of them to have been in a capable physical or mental state to be able to carry out a realistic count. It was also still dark at that time so even estimating the number of survivors would have been all but impossible. In fact the rapid disappearance of the ship was now almost as great a shock as the torpedo attack itself. It was so difficult to believe that such a beautiful ship could go so quickly.

After the fourth engineer, Maurice Cairnie, had virtually been washed into the sea, he had struggled to get away from the side of the ship because he realised that when it went down the suction would take him with it. He swam as quickly as he could to get away from the vortex he could already feel pulling at his body and he was thankful that he had managed to don his lifejacket while racing to his boat station. He soon found a small hatch-cover which measured about two metres by half a metre and grasped it thankfully. Even such a frail piece of flotsam could mean the difference between life and death. Maurie later recalled that that night he, '… never saw another living person at all and through the darkness I could hear cries, but they were mainly female cries from the nurses, but it was so dark and all the water [was so] covered with oil that you could not do anything, you couldn't tell where they were coming from, only in the distance, and by the early hours of the morning it was all dead quiet, so meaning to say that I'd either drifted away from the scene or they were all gone.'

This is an interesting statement because we have no way of knowing how many nurses managed to get off the ship that night. Only Sister Ellen Savage would actually survive the sinking but Maurice Cairnie recalled hearing the cries of nurses coming from across the water so evidently more than one of the nurses managed to get off the ship. However, what became of them is unknown.

The oil in the water was pervasive. It clogged the survivors' eyes and ears and many were swallowing it as the waves washed it into their gasping mouths. People were crying out in pain – so many had been injured, some quite severely. Others were calling in the darkness, attempting to find friends or to guide people towards the rafts. There was also a lingering fear of sharks, and at night, with flotsam swirling around, it was easy to believe that any movement in the water presaged an imminent attack.

Ordinary Seaman Robert 'Bob' Westwood may have been among the first to believe that the sharks were gathering. After being sucked into the water by the sinking ship and subsequently surfacing among the debris and other survivors he bobbed about for a while, supported by his lifejacket. Close by was another survivor who seemed uninjured but when that man suddenly disappeared Bob believed that he had been taken by a shark. He paddled rapidly towards a hatch-board and clambered onto it hoping that it would keep him out of the water and away from any sharks but the hatch-board was insufficient to hold his weight effectively and floated several inches beneath the surface of the sea.

And sharks, apparently, were not the only predator out there that night. Before dawn a number of survivors saw what they thought was a surfaced submarine close by. This is interesting in light of what we now know of the orders Japanese submarine commanders had received instructing them to kill all surviving ships' crews in the water to prevent them from manning vessels in the future.

The fourth engineer, Maurice 'Maurie' Cairnie, was one of those who later stated that he had seen a submarine silently prowling close by. It had been a moonless night, and dark, but once the men had become accustomed to the darkness they had been able to see reasonably well – certainly enough to be able to make out shadowy images. The submarine had been about a hundred yards away and even in the darkness Maurie could make out not only the conning tower but also the wires which were rigged running fore and aft from the tower. Realising that he was in considerable danger, Maurice paddled his small hatch-cover away from the submarine causing as little noise or disturbance as possible. 'After about ten minutes or a quarter of an hour it was gone,' Maurice Cairnie later stated. 'The noise had gone so they must have submerged.'

Another sighting came from the dental technician, Corporal Albert Taylor, the man who had been standing on the top deck and had spotted the two torpedo trails rushing towards the ship moments before one of them had struck. Taylor had been lucky to be up at that time of night. He too had been visiting the 'heads' and this had probably saved his life. He had later jumped into the sea after failing, with several other men, including Gordon Rippon, to release one of the large rafts.

Young Bob Westwood also saw the submarine on the surface after the attack. He later stated that it had been showing a white light, probably a searchlight.

Allan Pettiford never actually saw the submarine but he heard it clearly. After falling from the broken lifeboat, being sucked down by the sinking ship and eventually making his way to the half of a lifeboat that had launched him into the sea, Allan had finally made it to one of the larger rafts. Allan and his fellow survivors were all expecting to be machine-gunned in the water. Allan later recalled that: 'At times there I heard the motor of the submarine, and some of the other survivors said they had seen it. Our colonel claims that they heard the Japs cooeing to try to give our positions away but then he realised that if it had been an Australian Navy man he'd yell out "Ship ahoy" or something like that. Anyhow fortunately they didn't use their machine-guns.'

There is little doubt that these and several other sightings were accurate. There is also little doubt that the submarine was the I-177, the same boat that had attacked the *Centaur*, as subsequent war crimes investigations clearly demonstrated that the I-177 was the only Japanese submarine in the vicinity at that time. The only real question is why Nakagawa did not murder those oil-soaked survivors he found struggling in the water that morning? As subsequent events would demonstrate, Nakagawa had absolutely no reservations about carrying out the illegal command he had been given. He would later murder dozens of survivors of his torpedo attacks with no qualms of conscience. So why did he spare the survivors of the *Centaur*? Was it because the ship had been a non-combatant and therefore the survivors did not warrant the execution of his orders? The other theory was that Nakagawa was quite happy to allow them to remain struggling in the water and on the rafts because he was waiting for a rescue vessel to arrive so that he could attack that ship too.

As dawn rose that morning, the first of two the survivors would experience following the disaster, a terrible scene was revealed. Fourth Engineer Maurice Cairnie described it in this way: 'As daylight came on the first morning I looked around and all you could see was debris and frothed up oil on the water. I went through the day all alone, never sighted another person, and just laid on the timber, three parts submerged with just the life-jacket holding the upper part of the body above water. [I] went right through that day, no food or water, and during the night I must have drifted into unconsciousness.'

It is little wonder that Maurice Cairnie had been unable to see the remainder of the survivors because by now they were spread over a fairly wide area. The largest group comprised of about forty people but others, clinging precariously to rafts, were made up of two or sometimes three men with several other men on individual rafts or larger pieces of flotsam.

The main group was certainly in the best possible position for survival. Most had managed to climb onto a large raft or Carley float which was designed to accommodate about six men in relative comfort. Nearby, around the Carley float but still part of this one group, was a smaller cluster of men clinging to what had been the wheelhouse roof. An upturned and badly damaged lifeboat, the only one to survive the sinking, was also close at hand and contained several more men including the ship's second officer, Gordon Rippon. Of these relatively frail craft supporting so many men, the wheelhouse roof was certainly the most unstable. The raft was so small that the men had to stand on it, holding onto each other for balance. As it moved, as the men moved, the roof would tilt, sometimes quite alarmingly, tipping at least some of its survivors into the sea. There were men who appeared to be almost constantly scrambling back on the roof which then caused even further instability.

George McGrath later recorded the intense drama when people realised how many sharks were in the water: 'When the dawn came … the first thing we saw was these great dorsal fins swimming around in the oil. They were in droves actually, they were in dozens.'

Tom Malcolm and Sister Ellen Savage were also reasonably close by, clinging to the small wooden roof. Ellen, as we have seen, was suffering from numerous injuries but she remained uncomplaining. She was exceedingly concerned for the safety of her friends and all the other nursing staff. There was no sign of them anywhere and Ellen was heartbroken that so many of her friends and colleagues were now almost certainly dead. She had no way of knowing at the time but in this assumption she was correct.

Some distance away from the main group of survivors were two rafts supporting two men. Ron Moate was one of these. He had been so badly burned that his skin was shredded and he was in agony. He had seen terrible things while attempting to get to the ship's upper deck – scenes that would haunt him forever including the bodies of the two men, his cabin companions, who had attempted to escape the sinking ship with him. Several other men were scattered around including Bob Westwood, all clinging to rafts or flotsam.

There was no other way to describe it. It was a bizarre, real-life and deadly diorama, a disastrous scattering of flotsom and stunned, bewildered survivors, the result of one man's inherent inhumanity.

Gordon Rippon quickly realised that he was the senior surviving officer. There was no sign of Captain Murray so it was assumed, correctly, that he had gone down with his ship. Rippon immediately organised everyone to join together, and using their hands or pieces of wood as oars those on the smaller rafts were able slowly to paddle to the main raft. Dick Medcalf later recorded:

> We paddled over to that using bits of broken timber … and gradually through that morning, a couple more small, two-man rafts, the chaps on those paddled towards us. We tied those to the bigger rafts. They were Carley floats which had been tied to the rigging of the foremast and when she went down they broke away and thank goodness because that's what we were able to climb on to. There was one badly burnt man on one of the two-man rafts but he died, and we just sat there and waited. It was overcast; we didn't have a heavy sea. Most of the chaps had very little clothing on. My mate next to me had nothing and I had a pair of pyjamas and a singlet so I gave him my pyjama coat.

Tom Malcolm and Ellen Savage were unable to paddle to the main raft as the hospital roof they were sitting on was too large. A storeman named James 'Jim' Watterson volunteered to swim to them with a rope so that the roof and its two occupants could be pulled to the main raft. Watterson's selfless offer cannot be underestimated. Almost immediately after the hospital roof had been secured a large shark's fin surfaced close by.

Allan Pettiford, by now also on the main raft saw a pair of green uniform trousers floating by. He called out to one of the men to grab the trousers as he was naked from the waist down and the pants were plucked from the sea but Allan did not profit from this piece of luck as the trousers were given instead to Ellen Savage who was in a similar situation. 'That was the first I realised there was a woman rescued out of the twelve nurses', Allan later reported, 'and she finished up getting onto the same raft that we did. She was a marvellous woman, very devout Christian. She helped a lot with the morale of the boys while they were on the raft.'

Ellen Savage was weak from exhaustion, cold and shock but the first thing she did when joining up with the main raft was to suggest a prayer of deliverance. Everyone agreed, even those hardened sailors who had trouble believing that any kind of God could be responsible for such brutality and murder. Holding her precious rosary tightly, Ellen led the survivors in prayer.

Gordon Rippon also later stated that the men balancing precariously on the wheelhouse roof were the most in danger and some of these men were transferred on a rotational basis to the more stable raft so that they could have a rest from balancing on the roof with the constant threat of being tossed into the sea where sharks were waiting for them. Even though he was injured and nominally in command, Gordon selflessly also took his rotational turn standing on the frail roof.

Lieutenant-Colonel Dr Leslie Outridge, commanding officer of the 2/12th Field Ambulance, had also survived the sinking. He was aboard the Carley float and with the aid of a medical kit he had managed to salvage as the ship had gone down he now began to administer first aid to those in need. Outridge was himself injured, having sustained severe burns. He patched himself up as well as possible using strips of his pyjamas as bandages.

It was during this operation that a badly burnt man, Sergeant William 'Bill' Cornell of the 2/12th Field Ambulance, was transferred from a small raft to the main Carley float. Bob Westwood later recalled the story because he was one of those who helped to transfer Cornell to the Carley float and in so doing lost his place on the float and found himself stranded on a smaller, more dangerous raft. Bob had himself transferred from a tiny raft to the Carley float and was receiving some medical care for a head injury he had sustained after being sucked down by the sinking *Centaur*. He was more than happy to be on the Carley float because, as he later stated, '… it was more comfortable; that large raft had canvas sides to shelter you from the squalls and a well-deck you could sit in with your feet down into the well.'

Bob Westwood was able to remain in this relatively comfortable position until it came time to transfer Bill Cornell to the Carley float. Bob subsequently recalled:

> One of the survivors who was very badly burnt was on a small raft, about six foot square, and someone pointed out how badly injured he was; he was really terribly burnt, and so he was dragged across by a line to the larger raft with the idea of getting him aboard so he could be more sheltered and cared for. He was a very large man and when he was pulled into that corner of the raft where I was, and I was helping to pull him on, the raft dipped right down in the water very severely so I jumped onto the smaller raft to compensate and so stayed on the smaller raft … all night, actually, … and that was the first time I was

afraid because it started to get rough and the raft was a slippery flat surface and I was afraid that if I fell asleep I would let go the hand-ropes.

After bringing all the rafts together and tying them loosely to the Carley float, Gordon Rippon's next task was to ascertain how much food and water the group possessed – if any. The sinking of the *Centaur* had occurred so rapidly there had been little or no time to prepare adequately for survival in an open boat. Every lifeboat on the ship had been fully provisioned with food, water and medications according to maritime regulations. However, not one of those lifeboats and been launched successfully during the three minutes it had taken for the ship to sink, despite the fact that in accordance with wartime regulations the boats had already been pushed out on their davits in readiness for rapid lowering in case the ship was attacked.

The only lifeboat to leave the vessel that night had done so accidentally with no one on it. The boat was now upturned and was being used as a kind of raft by a small group of men. However, when it was righted it still contained a modest treasure which might mean the difference between life and death for all the survivors.

Upon investigation it was discovered that the boat held two gallons of fresh water, a tin of malted milk tablets, several tins of beef extract (heavily salted) and some dried prunes and raisins. For those with a strong constitution and even stronger stomach the boat also contained a few bars of pemmican – concentrated seal blubber. There were also two thousand Ovaltine tablets, probably the most welcome and useful of the entire hoard of foodstuffs discovered in the boat. Additionally the boat yielded up some flares, a sheet of canvas and two oars. Another survivor who later joined the group, Able Seaman Owen Christiansen, added a tin of salvaged biscuits to the commissary store.

The survivors were now either grouped together or scattered on various rafts or pieces of flotsam with sharks all around. They had been fortunate that the diesel oil in the water had not been ignited by the flames on the ship as the vessel had gone down as many of those who had miraculously managed to get off the ship would also not have survived. The oil on the surface of the water was also a problem because it got into the survivors' eyes and lungs and was responsible for burning the skin much like fire. The survivors were also suffering from the cold. Almost all were only scantily dressed, many quite naked, and although not winter, this was late autumn and the sea was cold. Their discomfort was worsened by many heavy rain squalls which left everyone chilled to the bone and dejected. The survivors attempted to huddle together for warmth but those standing on the wheelhouse roof were in the worst situation, constantly being tossed into the sea and having to scramble back on the roof before the sharks could get to them. As the sharks became more confident and aggressive the survivors on the main raft were able to fend them off with an oar.

The survivors were all, of course, considering what their chances of survival might be. It was unlikely that the ship's radio officers had managed to get a distress signal away as the ship had gone down so rapidly that it would have been next to impossible, especially with the vessel in flames. It was also subsequently reported (by G. Herman Gill, naval archivist and historian in a secret report dated 21 May, 1943) that the radio had been destroyed in the blast. Not one of the three radio officers had survived so it was impossible to know if the radio had been destroyed or if a message had been sent. The only hope, it seemed, was to be spotted by a passing ship or aircraft and as the survivors were in a shipping lane this was a very real possibility.

The day was spent in discomfort and anxiety. Sister Ellen Savage attempted to keep up the men's spirits by getting them to sing some of Australia's iconic songs but although this helped somewhat everyone was feeling uncertain about their chances of survival and the presence of so many sharks around them was reason enough for concern. Dick Medcalf subsequently recorded:

> I can tell you that no one liked them because one big shark, about sixteen feet, kept going around one raft and under the rope between the two and scratching its back on it and one chap said, 'Oh I'd like to have a great big harpoon, I'd make that fellow there move.' But yes, it was a worry because if the sea became rough it may have been hard to hang onto the rafts and there was always the worry that we had lost so many that we knew the sharks would be there all the time. It was a worry all right. The sharks were there as far down as you could see and they never left us.

Ron Moate the ship's pantryman who had been pinned to his bunk after the explosion was now sharing his tiny, half submerged raft with another man and one badly burned corpse who was actually lying between Ron's legs. The raft had become the focus of attention of one shark which was swimming repeatedly in circles around it, then swimming beneath it. The shark would come so close that it would rub roughly against the raft, making it unstable.

After a while Ron and the other survivor realised that the shark was being attracted to the scent of the dead man because the water was constantly washing over the corpse. The two survivors decided to dispose of the body which was not an easy decision because obviously it was what the shark was after and it would have been much better to have given the dead man a decent sea burial. However, circumstances simply would not allow for that. They gently pushed the body into the calm sea and it floated away. Ron later recorded, '… this was early in the morning, daylight; the body, you could see it off in the sea with the sharks swimming around it. It was unbelievable. This corpse, its arms rose up and this bloody shark, he practically bit the torso in half. That was the only shark attack I saw on the raft.'

Although the survivors saw a couple of aircraft that day, and also a ship, not one of those possible rescuers spotted the flares that were immediately set off. It was a long, tiring and frustrating day. As dusk arrived it was clear that the survivors would now be forced to endure a full night at the mercy of the wind, waves and sharks. It was a significantly daunting prospect.

It seems likely from statements later made by several survivors that Hajime Nakagawa and his submarine, I-177, might well have been prowling the area that night, although this was impossible to prove as the I-177 would subsequently be sunk and its logs lost. However, several among the survivors testified that they had heard the sounds of what appeared to have been diesel engines that night and one man, the ship's cook, Frank Martin, who was then floating on a hatch-board, claimed that he had actually seen a submarine. He had turned almost immediately and paddled silently away. If this is true then it proves that Nakagawa was awaiting the arrival of a rescue ship. The survivors were drifting with the tide, they were now well away from the actual site of the sinking and Nakagawa would have had to take measures to stay close. This appears to indicate that Nakagawa was tracking the movements of the survivors in order to spring his trap. Dick Medcalf later clearly remembered those minutes when it appeared that they might be attacked by the crew of the submarine. He was then on the Carley float with Dr Outridge, Gordon Rippon, Ellen Savage and others. He subsequently recalled:

Nell Savage was looking after the cabin boy [Bob Westwood] and he was badly shocked. Anyway we just settled down for the night and it was very dark because of the overcast clouds. Sometime during the night someone could hear a motor and someone said 'That sounds like a diesel' and it came closer and closer. Then we could hear the slapping of the waves against the hull and it was a submarine. So someone said for everyone to put out the lights on their life-jackets. We thought they'd come to clean up. It got closer and we all kept very very quiet, but thank goodness it was terribly dark and gradually it disappeared and we all breathed a sigh of relief. … I was ready to go overboard, underneath the raft, well and truly I can tell you, and I think a lot of the others were too, because we didn't think they'd leave anything of a hospital ship to show any signs of being torpedoed. No, we were quite prepared for that. Whether it was just charging batteries we don't know.

The next day a badly injured Jack Walder died. He had been a driver with the 2/12th Field Ambulance. Walder was given a Christian service led by Ellen Savage and then buried at sea. The horrors of everything the survivors had experienced and the terrible uncertainty of what might lie ahead was dispiriting for all – they had no idea if any of them would survive this ordeal or if they, like Jack Walder, would be pushed gently off into the sea after a few simple words of prayer.

Meanwhile Maurice Cairnie had remained out of sight and contact with any of the ship's survivors since the *Centaur* had gone down until he came upon three men. These were the dental technician Albert Taylor; Frederick Millar, a private with the 2/12th Field Ambulance and Kenneth Murray, a lance-corporal in the same unit. Although Maurice may have seen these men on the *Centaur* during its voyage north he did not know them at all. In fact he had not known too many of the crew because most of them had been signed on board shortly before the *Centaur* had left. He knew most of the officers really well but all the crew and every one of the 2/12th and the associated drivers were strangers to him.

Maurice later recorded: 'We were all in such a bad way we didn't get to know … names, and they [too] were on a hatch. We tied the two hatch-covers together as best we could [and] made a sort of raft which did keep us above water and we carried on with that all through that day until the afternoon and an aircraft came over and it was quite evident that they didn't see us because there was no recognition at all and we thought then that we might give up hope but not at any stage did I give up hope but I prayed a lot.'

Meanwhile, at the scene where the main groups of survivors were desperately awaiting rescue there seemed to be only a dwindling hope for survival. The sun was blistering causing severe sunburn which further exacerbated the injuries of the men, some of whom had suffered terrible burns.

And then everything changed. An Avro Anson from Number 71 Squadron was returning to base at Lowood following the completion of an anti-submarine operation in convoy support. Its pilot, Flying Officer O. Crewes, with his navigator, Flying Officer J. Keith, and wireless air-gunner Sergeant Billington, suddenly saw what appeared to be a large patch of oil on the surface of the water far below. Crewes dropped down to investigate and was astonished to discover patches of flotsam in the centre of which appeared to be groups of survivors. The fliers then saw a distress flare confirming that they had made a profound and life-saving discovery.

Crewes flew over the top of the survivors and dropped a green flare to let them know that they had been seen. He then immediately flew off towards a warship he could see in the distance. This was the USS *Mugford*, then on escort duty for a merchantman, the SS *Sussex*. Over the *Mugford* Flying Officer Keith signalled that there were survivors in the water ahead. Having done so Crewes flew back over the survivors and signalled them with his Morse lamp. Gordon Rippon read the words out loud. 'Will send help.' The survivors were too exhausted to jump for joy but some waved weakly and a few let out a low cheer. They were safe now.

What Flying Officer Crewes could not have known at that time was the fact that an alert lookout aboard the *Mugford* had already spotted either a raft or a broken lifeboat in the water, along with some other pieces of debris, and the captain of the ship, Lieutenant Commander Howard Corey, had ordered a general red alert and altered course to investigate the sighting. The red alert was the standard way of warning the crew that something was happening and that they should prepare themselves in case a general alert, more commonly known as battle-stations, was sounded. As soon as it was realised that the ship would be dealing with a possible submarine attack, battle-stations was immediately sounded and the crew rushed to their allotted positions.

One seaman aboard the *Mugford* that day was radioman Bill Records who returned to Australia in 1993 at the time of the 50th Anniversary of the sinking of the *Centaur* to reveal details of these events in a comprehensive interview for a television documentary being made at the time (by this author). Bill was able to provide very detailed information about what then happened on board the *Mugford*.

Bill Records, a tall, florid-faced, well spoken man, used his words carefully, aware that he was the voice of historical events that would be recorded forever. He was also immensely proud to have been a member of the crew of the ship that had rescued the *Centaur* survivors. In addition to

USS *Mugford*. (*U.S. Naval History and Heritage Command Catalogue Number NH 63128*)

being a radioman, Bill's general quarters station was as a 'hot shellman' at the ship's No 2 gun battery.

As the ship approached the oil slick, Lieutenant Commander Corey, standing on the bridge, ordered dead slow ahead. It was a bright clear day and the *Mugford* sailors could see for miles around. In fact more and more American sailors were now appearing on deck, gathering at the ship's rails, their eyes straining forward as the vessel slowed to walking pace. Everyone was watchful and keenly alert. Corey was worried and he had every right to be. His eyes scanned the sea, port to starboard. 'Keep a sharp lookout,' he ordered his watchkeepers, although the order was somehow superfluous. The seamen on the bridge, bridge wings and other prominent positions throughout the ship were mainly veterans. They knew the risks of stopping to pick up survivors. Any report of survivors could only mean one thing, a submarine was prowling in the area and this could be a trap.

Radioman Bill Records of the U.S. Navy. He was serving on board USS *Mugford* at the time of the attack on the *Centaur*. He remained a lifelong friend of Sister Ellen Savage. (*Bill and Marion Records collection*)

The XO (executive officer) hung up his phone and looked at Corey. 'Nothing on asdic Captain and radar is clear. Just the *Sussex* where we left her, steaming at nine knots and that tanker on the horizon with its escort.'

Corey nodded. 'Get the bosun to begin rigging scrambling nets please XO. Port and starboard.'

'Aye sir.'

'And signal the *Sussex* to increase speed to eleven knots if she can manage that and to continue zigzagging.'

The XO nodded confirmation. 'Will do Captain. The Avro is keeping watch over her too.'

Then the first raft came in sight. It was covered with diesel and almost invisible in the vast pool of oil that had been drifting on the currents with the rafts since the *Centaur* had been sunk. The oil looked like some kind of vast smothering blanket, flattening the waves. Then another raft appeared and yet another. There were people on them, also covered with oil, as if they had been camouflaged by the disaster. Some were waving feebly.

'Stop both engines.'

The order rang down to the engine room on the telegraph and the throb of the engines died away. The *Mugford*, moving now under its own momentum, was coming slowly towards what appeared to be one small group of survivors.

Balancing on the precarious oil-soaked wreckage was a small group of men who watched the *Mugford* approach through a haze of exhaustion. One of the men was the dental technician, Albert Taylor. The others included Maurice Cairnie, Frederick Millar and Kenneth Murray. All were smothered with oil and totally exhausted. It was difficult for them to know exactly what was happening. They were confused by shock and tiredness but realised happily that salvation was now at hand.

'Starboard five,' Corey ordered.

The ship turned sluggishly under its own weight. It was hardly moving now. Corey took a bullhorn from its steel rack on the bridge and stepped onto the bridge wing. 'Where are you guys from and when were you sunk?' Corey's voice, amplified by the bullhorn sounded harsh and metallic. It boomed almost too loudly over the water but the survivors on the hatch-board responded immediately. A garbled reply came from each of the four survivors almost simultaneously so that Corey was unable to understand what they were shouting. He shook his head and looked around at his officers and bridge crew. 'What did they say? Did anyone get that?' No one had understood so Corey put the bullhorn to his lips once more and repeated his questions. Once again the response was garbled. Corey called a third time but on this occasion he asked if just one person could reply. This time the response came back clearly. The men were from the *Centaur* and they had been sunk the previous morning.

'You mean this morning?' Corey asked. He could not believe that the survivors had lasted so long under such precarious conditions.

'No, we were sunk yesterday morning just after four,' the response came back.

'Have you see the submarine?' Corey called.

'Not since early yesterday morning,' came the reply.

A chill of apprehension ran through Corey. He knew full well that Japanese submarines would often wait, sometimes for days, for a rescue vessel to arrive, using the survivors as live bait, and a warship like the *Mugford* would be rich pickings. Using the bullhorn Corey told the men on the hatch-board to hang on and that he would be coming back for them. He turned to his executive officer. 'Slow astern XO.'

As the ship backed away from the hatch-board the astonished survivors could not believe what they were seeing. 'Please don't leave us,' came a weakened voice from the hatch-board.

Radioman Bill Records was standing on the deck of the *Mugford* at that precise moment, looking down at the wide-eyed, oil-soaked faces of the survivors. He could see the shock and horror of their disbelief. 'It was something that has always stayed with me,' he later admitted.

The *Mugford* was not, of course, abandoning the survivors. Quite the opposite. Despite the possibility of an imminent threat of a torpedo attack, the ship would not leave the scene of the tragedy until every survivor had been brought safely aboard.

'I want marksmen posted port and starboard,' Corey ordered as the *Mugford* moved slowly astern. There were sharks in the water, a lot of them, the crew of the ship could see them clearly. Corey now wanted to get to those survivors most at risk. The potential presence of an enemy submarine was equally important in his mind but he had to juggle human compassion and the dangers involved. The crew of the *Mugford* constituted a close-knit group of well trained, battle-hardened veterans. The *Mugford* had been at Pearl Harbor at the time of the Japanese attack and its crew had fought from the ship's moorings, bringing down three Japanese bombers in just ten minutes. As soon as the *Mugford* had been able to cast off its lines it had steamed out of the harbour firing ferociously at Japanese aircraft as it had left. Off Guadalcanal in August 1942 the ship had again come under Japanese air attack but its crew had fought effectively, downing two of the enemy aircraft while sustaining significant damage itself. Eight of the ship's

USS *Mugford*. (*U.S. Naval History and Heritage Command Catalogue Number 19-N-80114*)

crew had been killed and seventeen wounded with another ten missing, believed killed. The next day the ship was again in action and managed to shoot down another Japanese aircraft. The enemy aviators survived the crash but were not abandoned. They were later rescued from the water by the *Mugford's* crew. On the 9th of that month during the Battle of Savo Island, the ship raced to the scene of the sinking of the heavy cruisers USS *Vincennes* and USS *Astoria* and was successful in pulling about four hundred survivors from the water.

These events proved that the *Mugford's* crew were no rookies. They were all keen, intelligent, well trained men highly alert to any threat that might be posed from sea or air. At the pinnacle of action readiness, the *Mugford's* crew did what was needed to save the pitifully few survivors of the hospital ship *Centaur* and at the same time protect their own ship from attack.

A secret report of the incident, written by Lieutenant Commander Corey, dated 18 May, 1943, was later submitted to the commander of the Seventh Fleet. In that report Corey wrote:

Rescue was carried out amidst [the] usual flurry of [reports of] 'periscopes', 'disturbed water', 'Torpedo wakes'. Although none proved authentic, minimum time was spent stopped. Rafts were not sunk nor broken up [pending future use as markers for further search] and it is regretted that in one flurry what was seen to be a lifeless body was abandoned and not seen again. Survivors later reported having pushed off one dead crew member.

The weather by this time had become intermittently squally but visibility, fortunately remained good. We now have a clear picture of what the scene looked like to Corey at that time because in his subsequent report he also wrote:

… Plane circled area twice, dropped smoke flare near one remote group and departed signalling, 'Leaving – report number of survivors'.

Rescue operations were carried out as rapidly as possible, survivors being in two large groups plus three smaller groups in about a two mile radius of oil slick, wreckage and debris. Regular gas [fuel] drum rafts, hatch tops, cabin tops, gratings, large shelf structures and one wrecked lifeboat [awash] had been used by the survivors, many lightly clothed, some naked, some injured and burned and about half with lifejackets. One other life boat bottom-up was seen.

Among those on smaller rafts now being rescued were Maurice Cairnie and his companions. All were clearly in need of urgent assistance. They were very low in the water and in imminent danger from sharks.

Maurice Cairnie later recorded:

> They had a scrambling net over the side but the sailors dived straight into the water and assisted us up and all this time marksmen on deck were firing to keep the sharks away. [Before that] sharks never entered my head. I never thought of them at any stage. I just prayed and hoped that we would make it [although] we were infested with bronze fins, I never thought of them, strangely.

On the *Mugford's* deck the ship's medical officer, Lieutenant Bruce McCampbell, and his assistants checked the oil-soaked survivors before they were sent below to be cleaned and given more thorough medical attention.

As the *Mugford* turned towards the main cluster of survivors Corey used the time to signal Captain Penry Thomas, the Naval Officer in Command (N.O.I.C.) based in Brisbane. Corey advised that he was in the process of picking up survivors from the hospital ship, *Centaur*, which had been sunk by a Japanese submarine on the morning of the 14th.

That message must have been received in Brisbane with both astonishment and shock. This was the first indication the world would receive that the *Centaur* had been torpedoed. The radio officers aboard the *Centaur* never had any chance to send a distress signal and because of the standard radio blackout then in force for security reasons no one had attempted to contact the *Centaur* since its departure from Sydney. The *Centaur* had, of course, also sent no messages for the same reason. The ship had been on its way to Cairns as its first port of call before going on to New Guinea and was not due to arrive at Cairns for several days so it would have been only after the *Centaur* had failed to arrive on schedule that the authorities would have become alarmed.

As the *Mugford* drew closer to the large group of survivors it quickly became clear that the warship had arrived just in time. The people on the cluster of rafts were covered with diesel and evidently completely exhausted. Some managed grim smiles of welcome and relief; a few were able to wave feebly. As the vessel drew carefully near, everyone on deck was completely startled to hear a woman's voice coming clearly to them over the oil-heavy water.

'Look out for sharks,' Ellen Savage called. As the ship edged closer Ellen's voice came again. 'I'm Sister Ellen Savage of the hospital ship *Centaur*.'

Ellen went on to identify those on board the Carley float and the transfer of survivors began quickly. Most of the sailors aboard the *Mugford* that day would never forget the seemingly frail but indomitable sight of Ellen Savage, weakened by her injuries and terrible experiences as she called out to the ship's crew. Radioman Bill Records would remain one of Ellen's friends for the rest of her life.

As the transfer continued it soon became obvious that some of the survivors were in better condition than others. Some of the survivors needed assistance to get onto the scrambling nets and the *Mugford's* sailors went down the nets to assist them. Several American sailors again dived into the sea in their endeavour to assist those who were unable to get onto the nets, completely ignoring the very real threat of sharks.

One by one the survivors came on deck although not all could make it. One man, William 'Bill' Cornell, a sergeant with the 2/12th Field Ambulance, had been so badly burned that he had to be winched aboard on a stretcher. He did, however, survive his injuries.

Sister Ellen Savage remained on the Carley float for as long as possible, helping Gordon Rippon to direct the rescue operation. When she finally came onto the *Mugford's* deck she immediately began to work with the American medical team to assist those who were badly in need of aid. Dr McCampbell shook his head in awe and told her to go below for treatment. Reluctantly Ellen did as she had been ordered.

All this was happening with an almost agonising slowness. It was impossible to get the injured and exhausted survivors on board the *Mugford* any faster but Captain Corey, moving from the bridge to bridge wings and back again, was impatiently desperate to get his ship under way. He trusted his crew and knew they would identify any threats that might be posed but being stationary in the water like a sitting duck was uncomfortable and troubling in the extreme, especially as at least one Japanese submarine was known to be in the area and there was every possibility that there were others. Silently, Corey willed the rescue operation to move more quickly.

One man who had a unique job aboard the *Centaur* at this time was a highly experienced Torres Straits and Queensland Coastal pilot who had been coaxed out of retirement for the duration of the war. This was Captain Richard Salt, born in Scotland and therefore known to his friends as Jock. At sixty-seven years of age Jock Salt was actually the oldest person on the *Centaur* at the time of the sinking and was returning to the Torres Straits. Had the *Centaur* not been torpedoed it would have been his task to assist Captain Murray to navigate through the inner route of the Great Barrier

Reef. Jock Salt managed to survive the torpedo attack but Dick Medcalf later described the harrowing discovery of the pilot, alone in these oil-drenched, shark-infested waters. 'The old Torres Straits pilot was sitting in this life-ring and there were sharks around him too,' Dick later recorded.

This was not Jock Salt's first taste of enemy action. He had been the pilot aboard the MV *Anshun* at Milne Bay in September 1942 when two Japanese warships, the cruiser *Tenryu* and destroyer *Arashi*, had entered the bay and attacked the *Anshun*, sinking it. Miraculously Jock Salt had survived this terrible event which had killed two American gunners and wounded several other men.

About an hour and twenty minutes after the rescue operation of the *Centaur* survivors had commenced, the last survivor, Gordon Rippon, was brought up from the rafts. Corey immediately ordered slow ahead on both engines and commenced a thorough search of the entire area looking or further survivors.

Corey's secret report provides details of the subsequent search. He later wrote:

> … a thorough search was made of an oval area roughly seven by fourteen miles with a long axis 045 degrees - 225 degrees, the direction of drift as determined by the position of the sinking and of rescue, as well as extent of slick and debris.

Radioman Bill Records later recalled:

> We crisscrossed for a long time trying to find any more [survivors]. We cruised in, I think, a four mile by seven mile path, both up and back but then [we] set off for Brisbane at thirty knots and that surprised all these survivors – they didn't know anything could go so fast as that thing [the *Mugford*] knifing through the water. … We made a speed run clear to Brisbane and got a pilot to take us in then. I remember going up that river – we were moving and swamping some of those small boats but we had important people on board, they needed help.

On the *Mugford* the survivors were being treated wonderfully well. In addition to receiving medical care they were fed hot soup and coffee with more solid food for those who were able to eat. They were also given cigarettes and a few tots of spirits. Bob Westwood who was still in his mid-teens later recalled that despite his age he too was offered some strong drink although he refused. 'I'm not sure if it was rum or whisky'. Bob later recalled, 'but the medical orderly compensated for that; he had the one he was offering to me. Then I was put to bed. I had the top bunk and the nurse who survived [Ellen Savage] had the bottom bunk in the same cabin while we made our way to Brisbane.'

Of the 332 people who had been on board the *Centaur* when it had been attacked just sixty-four survived. Captain Murray had gone down with his ship, washed overboard while attempting to release one of the stubborn life-rafts. The dapper Lieutenant-Colonel Clem Manson, who had so courageously stayed with Ellen Savage and her friends right up until the last moment was also never seen again after he had jumped overboard. All the nurses with the exception of Ellen and also a total of eighteen doctors were killed that morning. It was the most disastrous maritime tragedy ever to occur in Australian waters.

Dick Medcalf was another who was later to thank the training imposed by frequent lifeboat drills and also his swiftness of foot when the attack occurred. He later recorded:

I'm quite sure, from the swiftness of the explosion and the speed with which the ship sank that very few people who were right throughout the hospital deck even knew anything that had happened because the torpedo hit the oil bunkers and they exploded right up through the middle. ... The majority of the people were inside the boat almost directly above the oil tanks. It must have been almost instantaneous. Someone told us that they found one chap on the deck with a broken leg and as the ship was sinking they threw him overboard and he was never seen again. But everything happened so quickly that none had time, I'm sure, apart from a matter of seconds, to think that they were trapped. It was very very quick. ... From the terrific explosion that woke me to the moment when I stepped on deck must have been something like twenty or thirty seconds, the way I raced up the stairs. ... It was purely and simply instantaneous reaction, that and [the] ship's lifeboat drill. We'd been told what to do and where to go, ... so although we were a hospital ship and not likely to be attacked, most people knew what to do and immediately reacted. I didn't have time to be frightened. I got out fast and that was it.

The catastrophe caused a clatter of activity within official circles in Brisbane. (The news that the *Centaur* had been sunk with significant loss of life would not be released to the general public for a few more days).

According to Lieutenant Commander Corey's secret report:

On arrival at Newstead No. 3 [wharf] at 2400 [midnight], 14 May [actually this was the 16th May – author's note] survivors were taken in custody by Australian Army authorities, intelligence interrogation being made by Lieut. Comdr. McManus, R.A.N.

Upon arrival at Newstead the survivors were segregated. The merchant seamen, thirty in number, were sent to the Brisbane General Hospital because they were, technically, civilians. The fourth engineer Maurice Cairnie recalled, 'I'd swallowed a considerable amount of oil and the oil on the outside had burnt the skin off my legs and everywhere.'

The remainder of the survivors, thirty-four in number, were all service personnel. These were sent by ambulance to the 112th Australian General Hospital at nearby Greenslopes. Also going ashore at that time was a generous amount of money totalling US$239 which had been donated to the survivors by the deeply caring members of the *Mugford's* crew.

In true Australian tradition and despite the fact that the entire affair had been so tragically terrible, some of the survivors while still on the rafts had organised a sweepstake to see who could guess the time when they would be rescued. The sweepstake was organised by Matthew Morris, a greaser, and ten men contributed with payment to be made after they had been saved. Morris was actually the person who won the sweepstake, his guess being within half an hour of their actual rescue. Details of the sweepstake would make headline news in the *Maryborough Chronicle* of 19 May, 1943.

* * *

Sister Joffrette Casey of the 112th Australian General Hospital at Greenslopes, Brisbane, or 'Joff', as she was affectionately known to her many friends and nursing colleagues, had no inkling when she awoke on the morning of 17 May, 1943, that her life was about to be changed and that the events which were soon to consume her every waking minute, and much of her nightmarish dreams for many weeks or even months, were about to begin.

Joff Casey had already experienced one astonishing adventure when she had been seconded to board the ship *Zealander* in 1940 and sent to Manila to bring back a large contingent of people who had been evacuated from Hong Kong prior to the Japanese invasion of the British colony. Although

Australia was not then at war with the Japanese, the journey had been an astonishing experience for the young nurse and one she was to write about in later life.

Yet it was now May 1943. As usual Joff dressed carefully – her uniform was always starched to crisp perfection and not a hair was out of place as she walked into the hospital that morning. The time was exactly 7 o'clock. The Greenslopes Hospital was already a busy place, tragedy, injury and medical emergencies were nothing new to its staff. The hospital was then treating large numbers of men who had been wounded or otherwise injured or who had fallen ill during the New Guinea or Middle East campaigns.

Coming down the stairs leading to the wards on the upper floors that

Sister Joffrette Casey of the 112th Australian General Hospital. Sister Casey nursed the most seriously injured survivors of the *Centaur*.(*Joffrette Case collection*)

morning was the hospital's matron, her face a mask of concern and anxiety. Joff realised immediately that something was wrong. She looked around at the faces of the other nurses and staff. Everyone seemed busy – too busy. Joff began to feel decidedly uneasy.

'Ah Sister Casey.' The matron paused in her stride for a moment then marched straight towards Joff Casey. 'I'm going to send as many staff as I can to your ward.'

Joff was perplexed. She knew that everything in her ward had been functioning perfectly well when she had gone off duty the previous night. The ward had been in an orderly condition, there should be no reason for additional staff.

'Whatever is the matter, Matron?' she asked.

The matron did not pause but her face was already flooded with the tragedy she had witnessed over the past few hours. 'The *Centaur* has gone down, sister, it's gone down… .'

The news hit Joff Casey like a brick. She had friends who had boarded the *Centaur* for the New Guinea voyage: nurses and doctors she had admired and even loved. *They couldn't have been… .*

'It was torpedoed a couple of days ago,' the matron continued. 'They were in the water for almost two days, I'm sorry Joff, we all have friends on board.'

Joff Casey could hardly speak. Her legs suddenly felt weak. 'How many have survived, Matron?'

The matron shook her head. 'I'm told it's a little more than sixty. We have all the service personnel here but… .'

'The nurses, Matron, and the doctors, how many?'

The matron's face filled with anguish. 'I'm sorry, Sister, the nurses are all gone but one, Sister Savage.' She saw the colour drain from Joff's face. 'I'm sorry Joff, really. We have more than thirty of the survivors here. They arrived last night. I've put the most severely injured in your ward.'

Joff tried but suddenly found that she couldn't speak. She turned away, hurrying to her ward, almost running.

The ward when Joff Casey arrived was a beehive of activity with nursing staff and doctors everywhere but it was functioning with quiet efficiency, everyone going about their duties almost silently. The first thing that Joff noticed was how quiet the ward was. For some reason she had been expecting a scene of terrible desperation and cries of the suffering but all remained in order. The ward was just much more busy than normal. It was also in this ward that Sergeant Bill Cornell was being treated. Cornell, as we have seen, had been so badly burned that he had been winched aboard the *Mugford* on a stretcher. His care now became a focus for the nurses. Joff Casey later recalled:

They were [all] deeply shocked, suffering from immersion. We had some severely injured, badly burned, flash burns, sunburn patients as well, fractures of the limbs which had to be assessed. Naturally we had to go to the seriously wounded first to see what we could do. Sergeant Cornell, was in the Field Ambulance. He was a very large man, very heavily built and was seriously injured and badly sunburned, full of blisters from head to toe. As well he had flash burns. He was swathed in bandages, coming from the ship [*Mugford*] which did a very good job on him. I think we transfused him for a while and then we had to find a place to give him these injections to ease the pain. Well, Sister Marshall and I, she was the next senior Sister to me, went over Bill very carefully and found a place that was quite free of any scarring or burning injury and gave him his injection there. … They were all badly dehydrated. It was continuous nursing, very heavy nursing. I might add that when [some of] the dear boys who were able to get around from the medical wards, the survivors, they'd stay outside, waiting [with an] anxious look on their faces for a smile from the [more seriously injured] boys in the beds. ... it was very sad, the whole episode, of having the dear boys there.

Joff Casey lost all track of time that day. One patient became ten, then twenty, and the incredible suffering everywhere was an almost tangible element that would stay with her forever. She was heartened to learn, however, that Lieutenant- Colonel Dr Leslie Outridge, the commanding officer of the 2/12th, had survived. Outridge, then forty-two years of age, was well known and respected among the army medical fraternity. Joff Casey had known Dr Outridge since she had been in training at Maryborough. Just before she went off duty that night Joff went to see him as she had worked with Dr Outridge when he had been coming up to Maryborough for training exercises with the 5th Light Horse.

As Joff walked into the room where Dr Outridge was lying in bed. Outridge turned to Joff, his face a mask of sadness, and Joff could clearly see the tears in his eyes. 'I've lost all my men, Casey!' His words were choked.

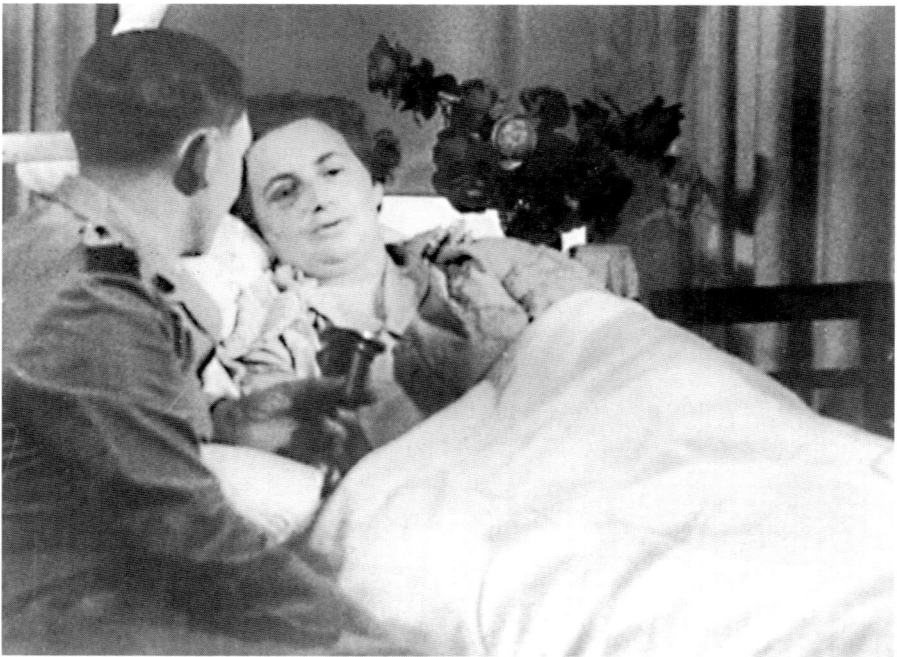

Sister Ellen Savage being interviewed at her hospital bed in Brisbane following her rescue. (*Australian War Memorial, Accession Number 044428*)

Sister Drynan nursing a *Centaur* survivor at Brisbane. (*John Oxley Library, Brisbane, 171125A*)

A.H.S. *Centaur.* (*John Oxley Library, Brisbane, 60917*)

Joff Casey later recalled: 'I just patted his hand in an understanding manner just [to show that] I understood what it would mean to Les. He was a devoted man to his troops. He said, "Will you tell my brothers that I'm okay?" I said I would.'

Meanwhile, over at the Royal Brisbane Hospital, the situation for the *Centaur's* seamen was much the same as that of the service personnel at Greenslopes.

Working at the Royal Brisbane at that time was an attractive young trainee nurse named Joan Patch who had been assigned to Ward 9. Like Joff Casey at the 112th, and largely due to the secrecy which had cloaked information regarding the sinking of the *Centaur* for a few days, Joan had known nothing about the tragedy until she had gone on duty on the morning of the 17th. Joan was an intelligent, conscientious young woman and although she was not due to begin her shift until 7 a.m. she actually arrived at the hospital early, 5.30 to be precise, when it was still largely dark, so that she would have sufficient time to complete all the many tasks normally assigned to young nurses in training.

Joan Patch, one of the young nurses who worked at the Royal Brisbane Hospital at the time of the sinking. She cared for surviving crew members. (*Joan Patch collection*)

Immediately she arrived, Joan was advised that the *Centaur* had been torpedoed and that all the surviving crew were now being cared for at the Royal Brisbane. Unlike Joff Casey, Joan did not know any of the army nursing staff who had been on board the *Centaur* but the event shocked her nonetheless. Arriving at Ward 9, Joan looked around in awe at the mass of human suffering. 'Now you keep an eye on these people; we can't let anything more happen to them,' the ward sister ordered.

Joan threw herself into her work that day with considerable vigour. The men were suffering much the same injuries as the service personnel over at the 112th although there was one very visible difference to their general wellbeing and that was being provided by members of the Mission to Seamen. Joan later recalled:

Everybody was concerned regarding the health of the patients because they had been exposed and people were worried that they may get pneumonia, but that side of it was taken care of by the nurses, naturally. What impressed me greatly was the dedication of the Mission to Seamen and the way they looked after these men. They contacted relatives, brought clothes; they were trying on shoes to make sure they got the right sizes and clothes were coming from all over the place. It impressed me greatly, the dedication of these volunteers. After that it was just nursing [care] then until they were well enough to go home and get over the shock. That's the very small part I played in this.

In fact the hospital was then caring for a number of survivors from other shipping disasters. Maurice Cairnie was extremely grateful for the care that was being given to him but realised that the staff were being stretched to the limit. He later recorded:

There were all breeds and colours in the hospital from all the other ships that had been sunk off the coast. I was put into a bed and the first thing they brought around to me was a steak and kidney pie and I'd had a stomach full of oil. Naturally I just could not look at it. I was going downhill fast … so the chief engineer, Mr Smith, came along and noticed that I was sinking in health and he rang the superintendent in Sydney who was a Mr Wong. He flew up and had me transferred to a private hospital out in Strathfield and they put me on stomach pumps and bowel wash to get rid of the oil. I was in that hospital for a fortnight.

After leaving hospital the surviving merchant seamen were fitted out with clothing and sent off on the usual six weeks of survival leave. Maurice Cairnie took a train and travelled all the way home to Western Australia to be with his wife, Alex. It was a long and boring journey but one event stood out in Maurice's mind and remained with him for decades.

Even at that early stage, shortly after the *Centaur* had been sunk, there were rumours that it had been torpedoed because it had either been carrying arms or had been used as a troopship, or both. Maurice Cairnie never believed for a second that there was any truth to these rumours. Had the ship been loaded with arms or munitions he would certainly have been aware of the issue. In fact he had earlier seen a graphic example why no contraband goods or personnel could have been on board the ship. He later recorded:

To give you an idea of how the ship was run, on the trip before [the sinking] we were in New Guinea loading hospital cases of our own and also we took on Japanese wounded prisoners-of-war. When they came on board some of the [Australian] army personnel came on board from shore with full equipment, fighting equipment. They said they would have to travel with the ship to Australia to guard these prisoners. Anyhow, our colonel was definitely against it and the ship was held up in a war zone for nearly twelve hours; he would not allow the ship to sail with armed personnel on board and they were taken off eventually and we sailed. So that's proof in itself. It's enough to show the way the ship was run, and as far as ammunition or commandos or anything else, never at any time were they on board.

During the journey across Australia taking Maurice home to his wife the train had contained a number of women and also a high ranking airforce officer. Maurice had been travelling in civilian clothes, not his officer's uniform, so remained incognito. Naturally people were discussing the war news and the story of the sinking of the *Centaur* was a particularly hot topic, especially the fact that it should never have been sunk due to its protection under international law. Suddenly the airforce officer piped up: 'Oh well, they were probably carrying troops and deserved what they got. We do the same. We go out for tonnage regardless of what it is.'

Maurice Cairnie immediately saw red. 'What would you know about it?' he said. 'I happen to be one of the survivors.' After that, according to Maurice, the women took to the R.A.A.F. officer angrily. 'We never sighted that chap from then right through the trip back to Perth.' Maurice later said. 'He went into hiding.'

*   *   *

There were countless examples of how members of victims' families were to be affected by the *Centaur* disaster. The deliberate murder of 268 people was an event that changed lives forever. Perhaps the very first example of the terrible heartache that was to flow down through the years may be expressed in the activities of Lieutenant Commander Theo Haultain, captain of an Australian destroyer, HMAS *Lithgow*. At that time the *Lithgow* was operating out of Brisbane. In fact at the time that the *Centaur* was attacked the *Lithgow* was in those very same waters carrying out exercises with an American submarine.

Lieutenant Commander Haultain had a very special connection to the *Centaur*, his sister, Helen Haultain, was one of the nursing sisters serving aboard the hospital ship at the time of the attack and when news of the sinking reached Brisbane Lieutenant Commander Haultain's ship was one of the naval vessels ordered to go immediately to sea in an endeavour to find any survivors who may still have been in the water. Other vessels with similar orders were USS *Helm* and four motor torpedo boats, all of which were tasked not only to look for survivors but also to seek and destroy the Japanese submarine.

One of the seamen on board the *Lithgow* at that time was Gordon Stenhouse, a visual signalman. He later recalled that after completing the exercise with the American submarine the *Lithgow* had returned to Brisbane, tying up at Hamilton wharf, and Lieutenant Commander Haultain had immediately gone ashore and had been whisked away in a Jeep. There was a lot of activity on the wharf so it was evident that something important was going on. When the *Lithgow's* captain returned, activity around the wharf increased dramatically; doctors and other medical staff were being brought aboard and Lieutenant Commander Haultain, evidently now in a state of grim determination, ordered that preparations should immediately be made to go to sea.

As the ship left the wharf and headed down the Brisbane River, the same river the warship had steamed up just a few hours previously, Lieutenant Commander Haultain cleared lower deck, mustering all hands not on watch and informed the ship's company that the *Centaur* had been torpedoed and that they were going out in search of survivors. Everyone on board was shocked and horrified and there was an additional sense of loss and grief among the crew because all on board realised that the captain's sister had been serving on the *Centaur*. Gordon Stenhouse even recalled a previous occasion when the *Lithgow* had steamed past the *Centaur* in Brisbane and the captain had asked Gordon to signal a personal greeting to his sister on the hospital ship. In 1993 Gordon Stenhouse told a documentary production crew that:

> I don't think that anybody that's been to sea could have anything else but fear and trepidation for the survivors. We searched that area for five days in every manner, hoping to find survivors, but we didn't see a thing. The fact that the captain's sister was on board the *Centaur* gave it double meaning and he, well I don't think he left the bridge hardly for five days. He just kept us at it and kept himself at it because if there

was any possibility of finding his sister or anybody else alive, we had to keep going at it. ... We had a strong feeling of frustration that we couldn't find any survivors and probably a very strong feeling of anger that we couldn't have a go at the submarine that sank her. ... They [the asdic operators] would have been looking I'm sure. Lieutenant Commander Haultain – the anguish that he must have been going through – he would have made sure that every effort was made to locate the submarine.

One of the many men who did not survive the sinking was, as we have seen, Private Percy Clegg, a member of the medical staff aboard the *Centaur* who had enjoyed such a long talk with Allan Pettiford on the night prior to the sinking. Percy Clegg was something of a Jack-of-all-trades and could just about turn his hand to anything. His job on the *Centaur* was vitally important in the operating theatre and it was his responsibility to maintain all the surgical instruments. His death, of course, had a profound impact on his family, not only his wife, Marjorie, and son, Keith, in Warwick but also his brother, Les, and mother, Emily Maude, both of whom still lived on the family farm at Pratten, near Warwick. However, news of Percy's death, and, naturally, the entire tragedy of the sinking of the *Centaur* also had a strong influence on one man who was then serving with the A.I.F. in New Guinea. The impact was such that Percy's friend later wrote an account of first hearing of the *Centaur* disaster and he and his fellow soldiers swore revenge on the Japanese. He later wrote:

Our boys have the Japs well on the run so we considered it safe to bring our little portable wireless into action. Picture, if you can, 20 of us camped in the jungle. ... The tips of our cigarettes seemed to glow like furnaces in contrast to the blackness; fog as thick as mud; everything damp, but we were listening to the world outside and what matter other things?

Suddenly 20 men stiffened; dead silence reigned; the jungle seemed for a moment to hold its breath, no sound only a small voice announcing: 'Outside Moreton Bay a Japanese submarine has sunk the hospital ship *Centaur*. The loss of life, it is feared, has been heavy.'

Suddenly someone blurted out, 'By God they'll pay for that.' Nineteen men humbly said, 'Amen.'

Strange as it may seem we all seemed to know somebody on that boat or somebody's cousin or aunt or some in-law knew someone at one time living next door whose grandfather knew one of the crew. Of course, I knew Percy Clegg.

I marched into Redbank. One of a squad of 40. As far as I can learn I am the only one of that 40 who is still going. But nothing hit me as hard as that. It was just murder. … In the jungle I took the hand of 19 men, vowing, 'By God we'll make them pay. We will.'

*   *   *

At the same time that the *Centaur* survivors were being transferred by ambulance to the two Brisbane hospitals, I-177 under the command of Hajime Nakagawa was either in the process of returning to its base at Truk Island or preparations were then being made by its commander and crew to head north once again for their return to base. Nakagawa was later to claim that he had arrived back at Truk on 20 May, just six days after the *Centaur* had been attacked, but if that were true then the I-177 could not have sunk the *Centaur*. Six days was not sufficient time for the submarine to travel from the position of the sinking all the way to the Carolina Islands – a distance well in excess of a thousand miles.

In fact Nakagawa was lying when he later told war crimes investigators that he had arrived at Truk on the 20th and it appears clear from the investigations subsequently carried out that he actually arrived at Truk on the 23rd of May. Nakagawa was now to lie consistently as he attempted to cover his trail of murderous war crimes. He also lied to investigators about the number of torpedoes he had fired at Convoy GP 48, when he had succeeded in sinking the *Limerick*. He had actually fired four torpedoes during that attack and the other two torpedoes missing from his arsenal when the submarine arrived at Truk had been fired at the *Centaur*, one of which had missed.

Nakagawa knew that he had committed a war crime in sinking a hospital ship but it was not something he was in the least concerned with at that stage of the war. In 1943 Nakagawa almost certainly believed that the vast military might of Japan was invincible and that no matter what crimes he committed he would never be called upon to answer for them. This hypothesis is clearly supported by Nakagawa's subsequent actions.

Lieutenant Commander Nakagawa remained captain of I-177 until he left the submarine on 29 August, 1943, slightly more than three months after he had sunk the *Centaur*. He was subsequently posted as the commanding officer of I-37 and it was while Nakagawa was serving in that capacity that he committed at least three more war crimes while the vessel was operating in the Indian Ocean.

At that time, and over the course of just one week – from 22 February, to 29 February, 1944, Nakagawa sank three more ships and on each occasion was responsible for ordering the massacre of the ships' crews when in the water.

The I-37 was a cruiser type submarine, a larger, more powerful and better equipped boat than the I-177. It had been constructed through late 1940 and 1941 at the Kure Navy Yard in Japan, being launched on 22 October, 1941, but not actually commissioned until 10 March, 1943. It had originally been designated as I-49 but subsequently given the identification of I-37. The boat was capable of speeds up to 23.5 knots when surfaced and could therefore easily outpace most of the merchant ships it would be hunting. It had a range of 14,000 nautical miles (26,000 kilometres) before it needed to be refuelled and could dive to a depth of 330 feet. In the bow were six torpedo tubes as its principal armament and it carried a total of seventeen torpedoes. It was also equipped with a 5.5" deck gun and two 25mm anti-aircraft guns. In short the I-37 was a formidable submarine but in real terms it was to have a fairly brief life.

By the time Nakagawa took command of I-37 the boat had already carried out two successful war patrols and had sunk several ships. One of these attacks had been accompanied by a specific act of war criminality. Survivors of the attack on the ship *Scotia* later reported that they had been machine-gunned while in their lifeboat and eight men had been killed.

The I-37 later docked at Singapore then, of course, firmly in Japanese hands, in order to undergo a major overhaul at the Seletar Naval Base. On 27 December, 1943, while the boat was still at Singapore, approximately seven months after he had sunk the *Centaur*, Hajime Nakagawa became the submarine's new commanding officer. It sailed on 12 January for Penang. On 10 February the submarine departed Penang for its third war patrol off Madagascar in the Indian Ocean. The submarine was also equipped with an E14Y1 seaplane which would aid the submarine in its hunt for victims. The seaplane was also capable of carrying a small bomb-load that could be used to attack shipping.

Four days later, while in a position south of Ceylon (now Sri Lanka), Nakagawa spotted a lone merchantman and immediately prepared to attack the ship. However, the vessel was evidently a modern and fast ship; it was travelling so quickly that even on the surface the I-37 was unable to catch up with its intended prey.

On 22 February, 1944, at a position south-west of Addu Atoll in the Maldives, the I-37 attacked an armed tanker named *British Chivalry*. The ship had been constructed in 1929 and was owned by the British Tanker Company. With a quadruple expansion steam engine its top speed was just ten knots (19 km per hour) and therefore the ship could easily have been outpaced by the submarine.

The time was now 10.30 in the morning. The *British Chivalry* was then en route from Melbourne to Abadan at the top of the Persian Gulf where it was scheduled to take on board a cargo of oil. At the time of the attack, however, the ship was in ballast which was, at least, a small blessing for its crew. Had the *British Chivalry* been loaded with oil, or worse, petrol or aviation spirit, the entire ship would have burst into a fiery explosion – probably incinerating everyone on board. As it turned out, the immediate future for the crew of the ship was almost as bleak.

Nakagawa launched two of his torpedoes at the tanker, however, both torpedoes were spotted in the water and evasive action was quickly undertaken but it could not save the vessel. One torpedo missed but the other slammed into the starboard side of the *British Chivalry*, striking the engine room compartment. The detonation immediately disabled the engines and killed six of the ship's crew.

Yet, unlike the *Centaur*, the hull of the *British Chivalry* was still sound enough to prevent the ship from sinking. Frustrated, Nakagawa surfaced I-37 and began pounding the tanker with shells from the submarine's powerful deck-gun. Meanwhile, the crew of the *British Chivalry*, led by Captain Walter Hill, abandoned the ship in two lifeboats. The shelling of the ship also did not sink the vessel so Nakagawa fired a third torpedo which effectively formed the vessel's *coup de grâce*.

The tanker was quickly sent to the bottom of the Indian Ocean after which Nakagawa ordered the men in the two lifeboats to draw alongside the submarine. As they were being menaced by Japanese naval ratings armed with automatic weapons, the survivors had little choice but to do as they had been ordered. The medical officer of the submarine spoke reasonable English and quickly interrogated the survivors, asking the name of the ship, its cargo, where it had come from and where it was going. Captain Walter Hill was then ordered to board the submarine, having been informed that he was to be taken prisoner. At the same time he was made to hand over a briefcase containing a quantity of about fifty diamonds and sapphires.

The submarine then moved away for some distance and, in keeping with what little we know of Nakagawa's personality, he ordered his crew to machine-gun all the survivors in the boats. Captain Hill, cursing roundly and struggling with his captors, was made to watch as many of his men were murdered. This relentless attempt to kill every one of the survivors went on for two hours as the submarine circled the boats, its crew firing at anything in the water that moved. How anyone survived the massacre was a miracle. Finally the submarine moved away, leaving the dead and dying to their fates. Fourteen men had been killed outright with a further five mortally wounded. A total of thirty-eight survivors – an astonishing number considering the relentlessness of the atrocity, managed to survive at sea, drifting for the following thirty-seven days. They were finally rescued by another British ship, the MV *Delane*. What became of the briefcase of precious stones is not known.

Captain Hill was taken to Singapore. He was held captive at Penang for the remainder of the war and released following the Japanese surrender. For whatever personal reasons he may have had he subsequently refused to give evidence to the War Crimes Commission. Privately he was willing to speak about the torture he had received at the hands of the Japanese but somehow he could never bring himself to discuss the sinking of his ship and the murder of his crew. He had been loved and highly respected by his men and had always been full of good humour.

This instance of brutal atrocity reveals that Nakagawa felt he was in no way responsible for the killing of the ship's crew. Ordinarily one would think that he had attempted to kill everyone so thoroughly, wasting another two dangerous hours on the surface, in order to keep the crime a secret, but Nakagawa believed that he was simply following orders and that his actions were therefore in no way criminal. Apparently he had never considered the moral or ethical implications of such actions or the legality of obeying orders that were internationally illegal. Evidence of this is the fact that he had taken Captain Hill prisoner when Hill had personally witnessed the massacre of his crew. Nakagawa was not in the least concerned that Hill might one day bear witness against him. Nakagawa was fully convinced that Japan was going to win the war; he was simply following orders. He believed that there had been no crime. Therefore it did not matter if there was a witness to the slaughter.

Nakagawa now continued his hunt for shipping which might easily fall prey to his torpedoes. Four days after the sinking of the *British Chivalry* he found another target, the MV *Sutlej*.

The *Sutlej* (sometimes reported as being named *Sutley*) was a steel-hulled motor vessel and general cargo carrier that had been constructed at Glasgow in 1940. Its life was to be painfully short.

The date was now 26 February, 1944. The *Sutlej* was en route from Egypt and Aden to Fremantle, Western Australia, with a cargo of rock phosphates and mail. Hajime Nakagawa attacked the ship at night when it was sailing alone in the Arabian Sea approximately 150 nautical miles to the west of Diego Garcia. Ships travelling alone were easy prey for lone wolves like I-37. Nakagawa had no trouble at all in planning an attack on the relatively slow moving ship and manoeuvring his boat into position. He then launched a torpedo which struck the *Sutlej* somewhere between number 1 and number 2 holds. Like the *Centaur*, the ship very quickly filled with water and went down in about four minutes. Aboard the *Sutlej* everything was in complete darkness and chaos as the crew attempted to save themselves. The unexpectedness of the attack and the rapidity of the sinking prevented any of the ship's boats or rafts from being launched. The men on board were left with no option – they just jumped into the sea. As with any torpedoed ship, the scene at the site of the attack was one of total devastation. The sea was a mass of oil and debris and the survivors were disoriented, frightened, injured and afraid. Some were dying. There were no life-rafts or boats in sight apart from one small and quite frail raft that had normally been used to float men alongside the ship when in harbour in order to paint the hull. It had simply been lying on deck unsecured and therefore had floated off when the ship had gone down.

It was at this point that the situation became immeasurably worse when the I-37 surfaced suddenly close by. What must have been going through the minds of the surviving seamen is not too difficult to guess. The atrocities of the Japanese were well known and news that they were slaughtering ships' crews in the water after destroying their vessels was the talk of every bar and seaman's mission from Portsmouth to Mombasa. Therefore the *Sutlej's* seamen watched the ominous surfacing of the submarine's hull with considerable trepidation. It was almost impossible to see in the dark but then the whole scene was clearly illuminated when a searchlight on the conning tower of the submarine suddenly burst into life. The piercingly bright beam began to scour the sea and wreckage, apparently in an effort to locate survivors. When the remnants of the ship's crew were sighted, treading water and holding on to the frail raft, they were asked what ship they were from and if the captain had survived. Presumably the voice belonged to the submarine's medical officer – the same person who had questioned the crew of the *British Chivalry* just before that crew had been machine-gunned. The men in the water now shouted back, giving the name of the ship and its cargo and stating that the captain had been killed. He had gone down with the ship. This seemed to be all the Japanese wanted to know for after receiving that small amount of information the submarine surged forward in an attempt to ram the raft and presumably drown the men by running over the top of them. This attempt at murder failed as the bow-wave of the submarine simply pushed the raft aside. The survivors were then subjected to a hail of machine-gun fire, the bullets tearing into them and into the sea all around.

In a pattern that closely resembled the attack on the survivors of the *British Chivalry*, the submarine continued pouring machine-gun fire into the survivors for a full hour while cruising around the area. Finally, probably believing that no one could have survived such carnage, the submarine left, its sinister hull simply disappearing into the darkness.

After such a terrifying hour of blood and destruction it would have been difficult to imagine that any of the crew could still be alive, but some were. They came out of the darkness, gathering together, eyes wide with fright and horror at what they had just endured. They managed to cast around in the night and were fortunate enough to find a raft to which they clung grimly. The raft was far too small to support all the men clinging to its sides but luckily they managed to find two of the ship's life-rafts which had also floated off. These were larger and better equipped and came with the standard issue of water, food and flares. The men now realised that they might just have a small chance of survival.

Cursing the murderous Japanese and lamenting the loss of their friends, the survivors could do nothing now but to wait for dawn to break and hope fervently that the sunrise would not also bring the submarine back to ensure that no one had been left alive.

At dawn the exhausted survivors carried out a headcount and it was revealed that all too many were missing, presumed dead. This particular group of survivors (there would be another) was now comprised of twenty-three men although one of these would die soon afterwards. The ship's crew had numbered seventy-three including a number of D.E.M.S, gunners. (Defensively Equipped Merchant Ships).

The men in this group were relieved when the rogue submarine did not return to complete its butchery but that was the only piece of good luck the survivors were to receive that day. Another night came without any sight of help or rescue. However, the following day the men came upon one of the lifeboats that had floated off when the ship had gone down. This had been discovered floating upturned by another smaller group of six survivors who had managed to climb onto the boat's keel and then right it. They had soon been joined by a D.E.M.S. gunner who had found them after spending many hours clinging desperately to a piece of flotsam. The lifeboat was damaged but relatively seaworthy and the men quickly had the boat baled out. When the survivors on the raft sighted the lifeboat they attempted to get closer so that they could join up. However, the current was too great and finally the men were forced to concede defeat.

The saga that now followed was split into three separate and equally terrifying stories of courage, despair and endurance. The two rafts containing the bulk of the survivors managed to stay together but the lifeboat eventually drifted out of sight. The rafts drifted for the next thirty days, the men becoming progressively weaker and more desperate. The most senior officer on the rafts was the ship's chief engineer and he now decided that it might be better to split up the rafts in the hope that one would be rescued and could then direct help to the other. The men agreed and that same day they separated, drifting slowly apart. It was a difficult parting because there was every likelihood that they would not see each other again and even if one raft was rescued there was no guarantee in the vastness of the Indian Ocean that the other would ever be found – even if a rescue ship had been alerted to its presence.

About twelve days later, the forty-second day after the *Sutlej* had been sunk, the men on the raft containing the chief engineer and his little group of survivors spotted a ship on the horizon. A number of distress flares were set off but there appeared to be no response from the ship. Had the raft been seen and simply ignored? It was impossible to tell but even the question was infuriating. By now morale was at an all-time low. The survivors had endured incredible hardships and there appeared to be little chance of rescue. However, several days later a Catalina flying boat appeared suddenly, circled overhead and dropped emergency rations and water to the survivors. Rescue appeared to be close at hand and the men's hopes soared.

The following day another Catalina appeared. Flares were set off to help the aircraft find the tiny raft in the vastness of the ocean and it too finally circled overhead. Smoke from a ship's funnel far on the horizon could now also be seen and it appeared clear that the Catalina was radioing the raft's position and circling so that those on the rescue vessel could more easily locate the survivors.

The vessel now racing to the survivors' aid was the British warship HMS *Flamingo*, (L 18) a Black Swan-class naval sloop which was being used extensively on convoy escort duties. (Ironically this ship would later (1959) be sold to Germany and remain operational until 1964).

The *Flamingo* was now charging towards the raft at full speed. On board that sloop were also the survivors who had been on the second raft. They had been sighted and rescued approximately twenty five miles away.

The survivors who had been in the lifeboat also had experienced an astonishing journey. The boat had been under the charge of the *Sutlej's* third officer, just twenty-five years of age. After failing to link up with the other two rafts the lifeboat had headed south and then south-west in an endeavour to get to the naval base at Diego Suarez situated at the southern tip of Madagascar. They never made it to the base but the endeavour had been valiant and the young officer had managed to navigate the boat a total of 1200 nautical miles. After forty-two days the boat had been sighted by another naval vessel, a requisitioned former trawler HMS *Solvra* which had been converted to anti-submarine duties and utilised in both the Mediterranean and Indian Ocean.

A total of forty-one crew members and nine D.E.M.S. gunners died during this disaster.

After machine-gunning the survivors of the *Sutlej*, Hajime Nakagawa continued with his murderous war patrol. Just three days after sinking the *Sutlej*, on 29 February, 1944, he found another victim. This was the 7005 tons British armed cargo steamer *Ascot* which had been constructed just two years earlier in 1942. The ship was owned by Watts, Watts and Co. of London. Its captain was James Fawcett Travis. Despite being a modern ship the *Ascot* was not known for its speed. It was capable of just eleven knots, making it another fairly easy target for submarine attack. Lookouts aboard the submarine spotted the *Ascot* eight hundred miles north-west of Diego Suarez while the vessel was en route from Calcutta either to Port Louis, Mauritius, or Diego Suarez (accounts vary), carrying 9000 tons of general cargo. Nakagawa immediately saw the vessel as easy prey.

This ship was dealt with in much the same fashion as the *Sutlej*. Easily catching up to the slower moving merchantman, the *Ascot* was attacked with a torpedo. One of the D.E.M.S. gunners on watch at the time actually saw the trail of the torpedo as it raced towards the ship. However, before he could shout a warning the torpedo struck the *Ascot* on its starboard side in the fore part of the engine room. As so often occurred during torpedo attacks, the engine room or boiler room staff were frequently among the first killed on a torpedoed ship and this was certainly the case aboard the *Ascot*. Four men died instantly.

The ship immediately began to settle in the water. Both the starboard lifeboats had been smashed during the explosion but the crew managed to get the two port lifeboats away. The attack had occurred close to midday so the survivors were not hampered by attempting to abandon ship in darkness. The crew, although dazed, injured and disoriented, also managed to launch a raft.

About ten minutes later the survivors saw a submarine surfacing on the starboard quarter about a mile away. The submarine circled the crippled *Ascot* while a gun-crew closed up on the deck-gun and began shelling the ship.

As Nakagawa brought I-37 closer, the *Ascot's* survivors examined it carefully. There were no identification marks on the conning tower, these had been removed, but the *Ascot's* crew, those few who survived, would later be able to identify the submarine type from a silhouette shown to them while they were being questioned about the event. They also told investigators that the crew of the submarine had been Japanese and that they had been dressed in khaki shirts and trousers. They had also been wearing the ubiquitous Japanese soft peaked caps. The survivors quite interestingly also claimed that there had been a white man on board who had worn a European style of officer's cap. This was probably Captain Walter Hill of the ship *British Chivalry*, although why the Japanese would allow their captive to come up to the submarine's deck at such a time is a moot point.

The submarine's medical officer now shouted across the water demanding to know if the master or any senior ship's officers were among the survivors. At first the men called back that all officers had been killed by the torpedo, including the captain. This angered Nakagawa who instructed one of his men to fire a machine-gun burst as a warning. Captain Travis then called across that he was the ship's master and both he and the chief officer were taken aboard the submarine for interrogation. Captain Travis was carrying a dispatch case, apparently containing the ship's papers. This was taken from him. He was questioned briefly, called an 'English swine' and slashed with a knife before being pushed back into the water where he was picked up by one of the lifeboats. Accounts vary but apparently the chief officer was also thrown overboard.

Nakagawa subsequently ordered that the ship's lifeboats and raft, in total containing fifty-two men, should be rammed and sunk. The survivors were also machine-gunned. One of the lifeboats was sunk after it had been rammed. The men jumped into the water in a desperate attempt to prevent being hit but there was really nowhere to go, apart from attempting to protect themselves by getting behind the boats and raft. The toll in lives was shocking. Soon the sea was tainted with blood.

Nakagawa then ordered his gun-crew to shell the *Ascot*. About thirty shells were fired at the ship until the vessel was a mass of flames. It sank soon afterwards. Only then did the submarine leave the scene.

The survivors of the attack now crawled back onto the boats but half an hour later, no doubt a timing carefully planned by Nakagawa, the submarine returned and seeing that there were still survivors Nakagawa once more ordered the boats to be raked with machine-gun fire. The men in the boats dived into the sea and sought the flimsy and wholly inadequate protection of the far sides of the boats. One man named Richardson had been wounded and was unable to get back into the sea so one of his companions, a D.E.M.S. gunner named Walker, very bravely remained with his mate to look after him. From the raft Walker was able to see the submarine clearly as it moved about seeking further victims and was able to advise his friends in the water where the submarine was and how best to hide from its murderous crew. Richardson was now hit by a bullet once more and killed while Walker was struck twice, badly wounding him. However, he told no one about his injuries as he continued to offer advice to his mates.

The submarine prowled around the area until dusk that day, periodically pouring more machine-gun fire into the boat and raft until finally stealing away into the gathering darkness. Thankfully it did not return. At that time the men who had managed to survive in the water climbed onto the raft and hoisted a small sail. Walker, meanwhile, despite his wounds, remained stoic and uncomplaining.

The following morning was 1 March. Seven crew members were now perched rather precariously on the raft. One of the lifeboats was seen in the distance but it appeared to be damaged and was soon lost to sight. The following day the lifeboat was again seen and it was clear there was at least one man on board. By noon that day the boat was able to come alongside the raft and it was seen that it was manned by a man named Hughson. Fortunately the lifeboat, although badly damaged and in no condition to remain afloat for too long, also held the standard lifeboat provisions and an adequate supply of water. These were transferred with Hughson to the raft.

Once he had been safely transferred to the raft, Hughson had a terrible story to tell to his mates. He said that when the submarine had first begun shooting at the survivors he had been in one of the lifeboats. He had seen the submarine ram the second lifeboat, sinking it and tossing its occupants into the sea. The submarine had then turned towards Hughson's boat with the apparent intention of ramming it too. All the men in the boat with the exception of Hughson had then jumped into the sea but had been killed by the machine-guns. Hughson had dropped to the bottom of the boat pretending that he had been shot and killed. Meanwhile the lifeboat had been taken in tow, presumably with the intention of preventing any survivors in the water from boarding it again. Hughson remained quite still and after about ten or fifteen minutes the boat had been cut adrift and then rammed once more by the submarine just for good measure. The ramming had failed to sink the boat but succeeded in inflicting further damage to its port side.

All that night Hughson had kept quiet, frightened that the submarine was still lurking close by, but by morning, with the enemy nowhere in sight, Hughson had hoisted a foresail and sailed all that day in freshening conditions with the boat now almost waterlogged. Then on 2 March he had sighted the raft and steered towards it to join up with his mates.

At just after 1.30 on the afternoon of 3 March, the day after Hughson had joined up with the men on the raft, the few remaining survivors were rescued by the Dutch steamer, the MV *Straat Soenda*. They were subsequently landed at Aden. Captain James Travis was not among the survivors.

*   *   *

Nakagawa was later transferred from the I-37 and under another commander the vessel went on with its deadly war patrols. However, its fate was sealed.

On 19 November, 1944, just one year and eight months after the submarine had been commissioned, USS *Winterberry* sighted a submarine at the western approaches of the 'Kossol Roads', Palau. The time was 08.58 in the morning. The *Winterberry* alerted a minesweeper, YMS-33, of the sighting and also the port director of Kossol Passage. YMS-33 immediately went in search of the submarine but failed to locate any sign of it.

At about 09.15 hours that morning Lieutenant Commander Edmund L. McGibbons, the captain of USS *Conklin*, and Lieutenant Commander Edwin K. Winn of the USS *McCoy Reynolds* were ordered to track down the enemy submarine and destroy it.

Both ships were relatively new American destroyers. The *Conklin* had been commissioned on 21 April that year and the *McCoy Reynolds* just twelve days later on 2 May.

The crews of both destroyers now launched themselves into tracking down the enemy. The hunt continued well into the afternoon and for a while it appeared that the submarine might have slipped away. However, at 15.04 hours (3.04 p.m.) both destroyers received a sonar ping from the submarine. The hunt was now on in earnest. For an hour the ships' crews worked diligently to establish exactly where the submarine was hiding and at 16.03 hours (4.03 p.m.) the *Conklin* re-established a sonar contact and quickly launched its 'Hedgehog'. The Hedgehog was a forward-throwing anti-submarine weapon originally developed by the Royal Navy. The system was used to fire up to twenty-four spigot mortars ahead of a ship while attacking a submarine. The weapon was largely used aboard destroyers and other convoy escort ships. It was a powerful and effective weapon.

Several underwater explosions were clearly heard but operators also reported that they still had sonar contact with the submarine. Lieutenant Commander Winn aboard the USS *McCoy Reynolds* now launched twelve depth-charges which were set to detonate at the known depth of the submarine. Soon afterwards came a massive explosion and also a large air bubble rose to the surface. At 1700 hours (5pm) another underwater explosion was heard which was so large it shook the destroyer quite violently. About a minute later a massive air bubble surfaced and this was followed by the sounds of several smaller explosions. Sonar operators reported that they had lost contact with the submarine. Oil and debris were soon floating to the surface. Just before the sun went down sailors aboard the USS *McCoy Reynolds* were able to recover several items believed to have come from the submarine. These included a piece of wood stencilled with Japanese letters; pieces of what appeared to have been an instrument case and also some deck planking. The American seamen also retrieved a rather gruesome chunk of human flesh with pieces of steel embedded into it. It was now assumed that the submarine had been destroyed and this assumption was later confirmed through Japanese documentation. The I-37 had gone down with all 113 hands.

Interestingly, and not unsurprisingly, the I-177, the submarine that had been responsible for the destruction of the *Centaur*, while operating in the Palau area on 3 October, 1944, suffered a similar fate. Spotted by a radar operator aboard the USS *Hoggatt*, a destroyer, the USS *Samuel S. Miles*, was immediately sent to investigate the sighting. At 04.40 the submarine was seen on the surface and the destroyer raced towards it. However, the I-177 crash-dived. The *Samuel S. Miles* fired its Hedgehog charges and after a second round of charges had been unleashed the submarine was sunk with all 101 hands.

* * *

The complex war crimes investigation later conducted into the activities of the wartime service of Hajime Nakagawa was intense and methodical. It is not intended to go into that investigation here other than to say that is has been clearly described in the highly recommended book: *Centaur, the Myth of Immunity* by Professor Christopher Milligan and Captain John Foley: (Nairana Publications 1993).

While awaiting trial in Sugamo Prison, Nakagawa was keenly aware of his likely fate. He was a man bursting with the knowledge of his murders but afraid of admitting to them and claiming that he was absolved by orders from his superiors because he knew full well that those orders were illegal under international law.

In 1930 the London Naval Treaty had come into existence. Signatories had been the United States, Great Britain, France, Italy and Japan. This agreement specifically designated the rules of engagement under international law for submarines when taking action against merchant shipping. This law stated in part that submarines and surface warships: '... may not sink or render incapable of navigation a merchant vessel without having first placed passengers, crew and ship's papers in a place of safety.' This law was laid down in such a way that it would remain in force without time limit. Japan had also signed a protocol in London on 6 November, 1936, which incorporated the same agreement.

However, such niceties of international law never really meant very much to Adolf Hitler and he believed that his allies should also disregard them. In talks he held with the Japanese ambassador to Germany, Baron Oshima, on 3 January, 1942, shortly after the United States had entered the war, Hitler pressed the Japanese government to abandon any laws protecting merchant shipping. He did this because he realised that with the United States entering the conflict a massive number of additional merchant vessels would soon be available to aid in the Allied war effort. It was important to Hitler that as many of those ships were destroyed as quickly and as effectively as possible and any international laws would therefore only hinder that undertaking. Hitler had already ordered his U-boat crews not only to sink merchant ships without any consideration of law but also to exterminate their crews. He believed that rescued crews simply went on to man other ships but if both the ships and the crews were destroyed then eventually the flow of merchant vessels on the seas would slow dramatically. Hitler explained to Oshima that the Japanese would need to follow his lead. The Americans were building ships at an incredible rate but without crews they would rust at the wharves. Merchant shipping was the lifeblood of the Allies and they had to be stopped at any cost, even if it meant disregarding international laws completely. Oshima not only agreed with these views but according to a memorandum written at the time of the meeting he, 'heartily agreed', adding that Japanese submarine crews would also now adopt these tactics.

This agreement found force in an order which was issued by the commander of the First Submarine Force at Truk Island on 20 March, 1943. The order stated quite categorically:

> All submarines will act together in order to concentrate their attacks against enemy convoys and totally destroy them. Do not stop at the sinking of enemy ships and cargoes. At the same time carry out the complete destruction of the crews of the enemy's ships; if possible seize part of the crew and endeavour to secure information about the enemy.

Of all the commanders operating out of the Japanese submarine base at Truk, Hajime Nakagawa was the one who took this order immediately to heart and was determined to carry it out to the letter.

Over the course of several years and during a number of intensive interviews with war crimes investigators, Nakagawa continued to deny that he had sunk the *Centaur* saying that he had been on his way back to the submarine's base at Truk Island at the time the *Centaur* had been sunk. However, the investigators, trawling through years of Japanese naval documents and speaking to dozens of witnesses, were able to ascertain that only the I-177 had been on the Queensland coast in that approximate position at that particular time and the evidence for that was clear. However, there were no firm witnesses to the event that could categorically state they had seen the I-177 and identify it positively as the submarine that had attacked the ship. Additionally, all the crew members of the I-177 now appeared to be dead with the exception of Nakagawa himself and his gunnery officer, Lieutenant Hajime Obori, who also told investigators that Nakagawa had not torpedoed a hospital ship, at that time or ever. The evidence against Nakagawa was damning but it was also circumstantial.

Yet investigations into the attacks and destruction of the *British Chivalry*, the *Sutlej* and the *Ascot* firmly established that the I-37 had been the submarine that had attacked those ships while Nakagawa had been in command and it was for these war crimes that Nakagawa was subsequently charged.

Nakagawa pleaded guilty at the Class B war crimes trials in Yokohama knowing there was enough evidence to convict him of the massacres of the ships' crews. That evidence included comprehensive testimony from survivors of all three ships who stated categorically that Nakagawa had ordered the ramming of their rafts and boats and the deliberate machine-gunning of the men in the water.

The evidence was irrefutable. Nakagawa pleaded guilty in the belief that by doing so he might just escape the hangman, which proved to be true. He was sentenced to eight years hard labour in Sugamo Prison, Tokyo, but released on 2 October, 1954, after serving less than six years. He was fifty-two years of age at the time of his release. For the hundreds of lives Nakagawa had so maliciously taken, this punishment could hardly be called justice. He died on 27 May, 1986 at the age of eighty-four years.

All his life Nakagawa maintained a total silence about the *Centaur* and refused to discuss the sinking of the hospital ship with anyone. He obviously had his own reasons for remaining quiet through all those years although no one could know for certain what those reasons were other than the fact that he might have feared being charged once more for war crimes. These were times when war criminals were being brought to justice decades after carrying out the crimes they had committed and Nazi war criminals in particular were sometimes being apprehended and even kidnapped, like Adolf Eichmann, to be placed before war crimes courts. Eichmann ended his life on a set of Israeli gallows in June 1962 so it was important to Nakagawa that he never be brought to trial.

Nakagawa had never been charged and tried for the sinking of the *Centaur* therefore he would be unable to fall back on the defence of double-jeopardy even had it applied in whatever legal jurisdiction he might be tried.

He probably also felt vulnerable for other reasons. Time had moved on, the traditional Japanese ways and customs were fading with each passing year as Japan regained its economic strength and a respected place on the world stage. More liberal and humane attitudes (to a certain degree) had begun to prevail and it's possible that Nakagawa now feared being despised for his criminal activities, especially the deliberate destruction of a hospital ship along with hundreds of innocent lives. If the truth had become known he might have lost the respect he had enjoyed after the war in a society that actually placed the names of war criminals on sacred memorials reserved for war heroes. That was just the Japanese way. Nakagawa had served his country in time of war and in a society where the truth remained hidden, Nakagawa was not a war criminal, he was a hero. Only the truth could alter that fact.

Nakagawa was never going to admit to his criminal activities. He had served almost six years of a sentence which he believed he should never have served. Even while in prison he had attempted to be released under parole stating that he had done nothing wrong but had simply followed his orders. The Japanese government was also not going to admit responsibility for sinking the *Centaur* but the strong circumstantial evidence remained and for those who were interested it was damning. Acknowledgement of Nakagawa's guilt came finally in a rather oblique way through a book subsequently published in Japan by a submarine warfare expert and historian, Rear Admiral Kaneyoshi Sakamoto who, in his book, *History of Submarine Warfare*, stated that there was only one submarine that could have committed the crime, the I -177. As Professor Chris Milligan wrote in the *Courier Mail* on 31 October, 1981, 'The ship can rest in peace, its good name is clear, and its killer identified.'

*   *   *

The *Centaur* had a tragic end but the ship that came to the aid of the survivors also ended its days rather tragically, especially for a warship that had experienced many actions during the Second World War. After rescuing the *Centaur* survivors the *Mugford* participated in many of the war's great naval actions in the Pacific winning significant honours. At the end of the war it was one of the vessels chosen to repatriate former prisoners-of-war back to their homeland.

By this time, however, the battle-hardened ship had served its purpose and in 1946 the *Mugford* was chosen as one of several American and captured Japanese and German warships to take part in Operation Crossroads – the nuclear weapons tests which were being conducted by the United States at Bikini Atoll that year.

The specific purpose of Operation Crossroads was to discover what damage a nuclear explosion would make on warships. The tests have since been described as, 'the world's first nuclear disaster'.

One of the captured warships used in this operation was the German cruiser *Prinz Eugen*, which, with the *Bismarck*, had been responsible for the sinking of the British battlecruiser HMS *Hood* on 24 May, 1941, with the loss of more than 1400 lives.

The decommissioned USS *Mugford* survived the nuclear blast at Bikini Atoll and was later used for training exercises in nuclear fallout decontamination. Finally, on 22 March, 1948, having been utilised in about every way possible, the ship was scuttled (along with its radiation) off

Kwajalein Atoll in the Marshall Islands. It had received seven battle stars for service in World War Two.

Over the years there was significant and almost continuous speculation as to where the remains of the *Centaur* might lie and several searches for the wreck ended in failure. In 1995 a man named Donald Dennis claimed to have discovered the shipwreck and for some time this was considered as being the actual site but the theory was later proved to be false. Then in December 2009 a search team headed by David Mearns discovered the wreck 56 kilometres east of Moreton Island which was only 1.9 kilometres from the last known position coordinates which the second officer, Gordon Rippon, had given to the ship's chief radio officer, Eric Summers, a few minutes prior to the attack. Underwater footage revealed the ship's identification number, the vessel's markings as a hospital ship and even the ship's bell on which the name had been embossed. The site was subsequently designated as a war grave protected with a navigational exclusion zone under the Historic Shipwrecks Act of 1976.

Actually there is a strange coincidence here. David Mearns had also been the person responsible for locating the wreck of the Australian cruiser HMAS *Sydney*, in 2008, which had been sunk by the disguised German auxiliary cruiser *Kormoran* on 19 November, 1941. The sea battle had taken place approximately 280 kilometres south-west of Carnarvon in Western Australia. After a particularly fierce battle both ships had limped away, mortally wounded. The *Sydney*, blasted by a massive storm of 5.9" shells and also struck by a torpedo had later gone down with all 645 hands. The *Kormoran* also sank after being scuttled but 318 men of its crew of 390 had survived the battle. It was, however, an astonishingly humiliating defeat for the Royal Australian Navy.

After being adrift for weeks in lifeboats, some of the *Kormoran* survivors had been spotted by Australian aircraft, and the *Centaur,* which had then been operating simply as a commercial freighter between Fremantle and Singapore, was ordered to investigate and pick up survivors. Many of the *Kormoran's* survivors aboard other lifeboats had already been found and others would be located alive and well shortly afterwards.

The *Centaur* at that time was under the temporary command of Captain Walter Francis Dark who had relieved George Murray so that Murray could take some well deserved leave. This was an interesting development because Dark was extremely wary of Germans and did not trust them for a moment, having been torpedoed twice while captain of the ships *Titan* and *Ixion* in the South Atlantic. His home at Liverpool had also been bombed by the

The *Centaur* prior to its conversion to a hospital ship when it would run regularly between Western Australia and Singapore with passengers, general cargo and cattle. (*John Oxley Library, Brisbane, 108359*)

Germans. The *Titan* had been destroyed by U-47 on 4 September, 1940, and the *Ixion* was torpedoed by U-94 on 7 May the following year. It's probably fair to say Captain Dark had no love of Germans.

The *Centaur's* crew had rescued their particular batch of *Kormoran* survivors, more than sixty in number, all of whom had been crammed aboard one lifeboat. One of the survivors was the *Kormoran's* captain, Theodor Detmers. The sick and injured had been taken on board the *Centaur* while the remainder were left aboard the lifeboat as Captain Dark believed that taking such a large number of enemy seamen on board an almost unarmed merchant vessel could have been a hazardous undertaking. The lifeboat with its survivors was taken in tow to Carnarvon although during the voyage the boat became swamped (there is a theory that this occurred deliberately in order to get on board the *Centaur*) and the Germans had to be transferred to two of the *Centaur's* lifeboats. At Carnarvon the Germans were placed under arrest and interrogated to discover what had happened to the *Sydney*.

One has to wonder what would have happened had Captain George Murray been in charge of the *Centaur* at that time. Murray was a kind and keenly intelligent officer but he did not have the antipathy which Captain Dark felt towards Germans. Would Murray have allowed the German survivors on board the *Centaur* and if so what would have happened? The

Bill Records seen here during the interview he gave in 1993 for the production of *Centaur – Death of a Hospital Ship*, a television documentary on the sinking of the *Centaur*. (*Tony & Lensie Matthews collection*)

Centaur was virtually unarmed. It had a couple of Lee Enfield rifles which had been issued to destroy mines if they were seen and apart from a deck-gun that had been installed on the ship's foredeck there were no other means of defence on the ship. More than sixty well trained *Kriegsmarine* crew – men who had just sunk the pride of the Australian fleet and who were being led by their battle-hardened captain – could probably not have prevented themselves from attempting to take over the *Centaur* and to sail the ship to a German port. If such an event had happened the crew of the *Centaur*, seriously outnumbered, would probably have stood little chance of putting down the uprising.

Of course this is only speculation, but worth considering. It is also worth considering that the kindness given to the *Kormoran* survivors would go unnoticed and unrewarded by the Axis powers. This was November 1941 and within a few weeks Japan would be entering the war – an event that would soon bring about the destruction of the *Centaur*.

It is purely coincidental and therefore worthy of note that David Mearns, who discovered the wreck of the *Centaur* was also the person responsible for discovering the wrecks of both the *Sydney* and the *Kormoran*.

The last words in this chapter about the dramatic and completely unwarranted sinking of the *Centaur* have been reserved not for an Australian but for an American, Bill Records, the eighteen years old radioman aboard the rescue ship, *Mugford* who later became a good friend of the *Centaur's* only female survivor, Sister Ellen Savage. Fifty years after the events, in 1993, Bill Records admitted to a television documentary crew that the events surrounding the sinking of the *Centaur* not only affected all those who had been on the ship at that time but also many people on the *Mugford*. During that television interview Bill recorded for the cameras:

[They were] just everyday people, wonderful people, missed by not only family but friends. I've thought a lot about it and I know it changed my life, it jarred me because that was the first bit of action I ever saw as a result of war. It was horrifying. I would say that those 268 people who died, killed, murdered, left several thousand people who mourned, who still mourn to this day. Children lost their fathers, one girl came up to me [at the *Centaur* 50th anniversary commemoration ceremony] who had lost her grandfather … these were just educated people, trained, and that's why nobody was screaming and ranting and raving when we picked them up. They were very calm, they were hurt, they were suffering, but they were trained to be calm in front of other people, apparently they had to deal with so many mental cases as well as wounded people, shell-shocked people. So they were wonderful, innocent people who didn't deserve to die – not that way. … I was shocked. I felt sorry for them. I still do.

*   *   *

Chapter Two

Heinz Eck

The *Peleus* Affair

Kapitänleutnant Heinz Eck ducked his head slightly beneath the frame of the doorway as he entered the office. The headquarters of BdU – the *Befehlshaber der Unterseeboote* in Berlin – was busier than he remembered, but there seemed a greater urgency now, and that urgency was slightly grimmer, more desperate, as if there was a kind of hollowness to it all. The faces of the officers Eck had seen in the anterooms and the looks on the secretaries were not defeated or even depressed, but they all had that look of intensity that seemed somehow to betray their inner concerns.

'Heinz, it's so good to see you.' *Korvettenkapitän* Adalbert Schnee's face beamed with pleasure as he stood from behind his desk and came forward to pump his friend's hand enthusiastically. 'Sit down Heinz. You look so well. God we have such a lot to talk about.'

Heinz Eck sat at the desk while Schnee went to a small cabinet beneath the room's only window. 'You'll take a small glass of schnapps, of course?'

Eck nodded, looking around the wood-panelled room with its glassed bookcases and framed photographs of famous U-boat commanders and their crews. Schnee's mahogany desk was cluttered with folders and reports, every one of them marked with a red stamp: '*Streng Geheim*' – 'Top Secret'. There was also an ashtray spilling over, and two small cups in saucers, both half -full of cold coffee. Schnee brought the glasses and a bottle and set them on the desk before pulling up another chair and sitting beside Eck. He picked up his glass. '*Prost*! To your first patrol as commander of a U-boat.'

Eck lifted his glass. 'I will drink to that.'

'And good luck to you and your crew.'

Eck looked a little wistfully at the medal ribbons on Schnee's uniform and more particularly the prominent cross at his throat which hung over the knot of his black tie.

'You've done well for yourself, old friend.'

Schnee modestly fingered the Knight's Cross with Oak Leaves. 'It was just luck, you know,' he smiled. 'Every one of my crew deserved one too, but … you know how it goes.'

Eck reached across and tapped the medal gently with his finger. 'You're being too modest. You don't get one of those just for luck. What was it, nearly 90,000 tons of merchant shipping in one year alone, and two British warships?'

'Well one was just an anti-submarine trawler,' Schnee smiled modestly. 'Armed to the teeth with bloody depth-charges though, but they could hardly be called warships.'

Eck leaned back in his chair and looked happily at his friend. He had known Schnee since they had both graduated as part of Crew 34 all those years ago. They had come through all the trials of military training together.

Schnee grinned, pouring more schnapps into Eck's glass. 'You'll have a chance to win your own soon. Congratulations, by the way, on taking command of U-852. It's a fine boat.'

Eck sipped from his glass. 'We completed sea trials out of Kiel and have been working up the crew for a few months now. We leave for the South Atlantic in a couple of weeks. You know all this of course,' Eck grinned, looking at the untidy scatter of secret files. 'You probably know more about my orders than I.'

'It's your first command since your transfer from minesweepers, Heinz. Nothing is going to be the same any more.'

Eck nodded, 'It's a big change but I prefer U-boats. Minesweeping is all right, but it's not the same as taking the fight to the heart of the enemy. That's what I'm really itching to do.'

'Yes, a big change but I've seen your training commander's reports and I know you are ready for your own boat, Heinz.' Schnee reached across his desk and fingered through some of the folders until he found one marked with Eck's name. He placed the manila file onto his knee and flipped it open, reading for a few seconds as Eck watched him silently.

'You know I'm glad you could come today,' Schnee looked up momentarily. 'As you know it's my job to give all U-boat commanders a final briefing before they depart on war patrol and usually that's a fairly standard procedure but … .'

'But this is no ordinary patrol,' Eck finished for him.

Schnee took a French cigarette from a packet on his desk and lit it with a gold lighter. He leaned back looking at Eck through drifting smoke, his eyes narrowing.

'I want to tell you what it's like down there?'

Eck looked carefully at his friend. 'You're ranked number twenty-two among Germany's most successful U-boat aces, and a good friend. Whatever advice you can give me will be greatly appreciated, believe me.'

Schnee drank from his glass. 'Do you like your new boat Heinz?'

Eck nodded. 'It's the best in the flotilla right now. Yes, of course I like her. It's new, so there are a few teething problems but we're working on those. And I hear all the problems other commanders have had taking out the older boats, despite the repairs and overhauls. So it's really exciting to be going out on a mission with a boat that's not already done tens of thousands of sea miles. I feel good about that.'

Schnee tapped his cigarette into an ashtray.

'But you are going to have to be careful Heinz. There are more dangers out there than you know.'

Eck leaned forward, his face clouding slightly now. 'That's why I'm really pleased to talk to you before I leave. I do have some concerns.'

Schnee paused for a few moments, thinking. 'It's a good boat Heinz. If everything goes well you will have the best chances of success. As you say, a new boat is usually a good and reliable boat. But you must be aware of the boat's limitations and I'm only telling you this because you are my friend.'

Eck nodded carefully. 'They say that this particular type is a bit of a sitting duck. Can that be true? You must tell me what you know. You're responsible for correlating the reports of commanders and instructing the outgoing commanders of submarines. Tell me what I need to know.'

Schnee lowered his voice and pulled his chair closer. 'Listen Heinz,' he said softly, 'I'll tell you what I know and what you must do.'

'Go ahead, please.'

'The Type IXD2 are strong, well armed, effective, but they're heavy, and can be sluggish when manoeuvring. They're easy to hit from the air because they're too big. They are the largest boats we have ever built and make big targets. In my opinion they have been designed for strength and firepower, which is all very admirable, but at the cost of stealth and speed and that's a mistake. You are going to have to be extra careful, Heinz. When surfaced you can't have enough lookouts posted. The R.A.F. have superb bomb-sights. They're deadly. But the main issue is speed. When you hit a ship there will be wreckage in the water and you will need to get away from that as quickly as possible. It's a marking sign that U-boats are in the area and the hunt for you will ramp up enormously.'

Taking a piece of paper from his desk and a gold propelling pencil, Schnee quickly began drawing. 'Look, this is the Atlantic narrows, between Freetown here, where you will find lots of ships and convoys to strike, through to here on Ascension Island. Now the British know that we are hunting though this entire area. It's where we have to be to catch the convoys coming through, but it's now equally as dangerous for us and it will be especially dangerous for you in that boat. There's incredible air-cover there for the convoys and even for independent shipping. Air patrols are also constant and their crews are well trained. Once they believe a U-boat is in any specific area the British are capable of maintaining three, maybe four or five aircraft in the air permanently, day and night until the U-boat is found and destroyed. Aircraft from Freetown and Ascension are working in coordination with carriers to saturate the area. Once they locate you, they will hound you forever. They will never let you escape. Even submerged they will find and track you on asdic. Warships will flock around you. You will be in a trap. The only way to survive all this is to remain invisible, Heinz.'

Eck took the drawing and studied it for a few moments. 'I've been thinking along the same lines. It's been worrying me.'

Schnee stubbed out his cigarette and poured another schnapps. 'You probably already know that all four type IXD2 boats like yours have been lost either in the South Atlantic or near Ascension, U-847, 848, 849 and 850. All gone, just like that, the newest and most modern of our entire submarine fleet. It's been a bloody disaster.'

Eck nodded. 'Not officially. As you know they try to keep a lid on news like that but there's talk, of course, especially up at Kiel.'

Schnee shook his head. 'It's very peculiar, Heinz. These were boats commanded by well trained and highly experienced captains. Most of them had the Iron Cross with Oak Leaves. Their experience and capabilities and also their dedication and courage were beyond question.'

Schnee paused, leaning forward slightly. 'You know that part of my work here includes a role on the planning staff, Heinz. Everything we do is aimed at destroying as many Allied convoys as possible and the South Atlantic zone is very difficult for us right now. You're going to have to be smart, careful and, dare I say it, ruthless.'

Eck stared at his friend unblinkingly. 'How so?'

Schnee shrugged. 'When you sink a ship, you will have two choices. Get out of there was quickly as possible or sink the wreckage first and then get out of there. It will be our choice.'

'Destroy the wreckage? You mean the boats? The lifeboats, the rafts?'

'Anything that floats Heinz. But it has to be your choice. If you get rid of the evidence of a sinking then you might be able to evade the pursuit that will follow automatically, but you're the commander, Heinz, and the operational decisions will be yours. You will have to make those decisions according to the conditions which prevail at the time.'

'If I sink the wreckage, the boats, what about survivors?'

Schnee shrugged. 'As I say, Heinz, it has to be your decision but you know what the official position is on survivors. It's your U-boat and your crew and they will be placing all their trust and faith in you. Make the right decisions and you will return safely to Kiel. Make the wrong decisions and you will end up at the bottom of the Atlantic like every other commander I've sent into that area over the past few months.'

Schnee looked at his watch. 'I'm sorry Heinz, I have another appointment. Look, if you need anything more just telephone. You have the number here.'

Eck nodded thoughtfully. 'Thank you for everything. Maybe I shall see you when I get back.'

'Come', Schnee stood, taking his friend's hand, 'I'll show you out.'

As the two officers walked down the stairs leading to the foyer of the building they saw a highly polished black Mercedes, driven by a young naval lieutenant pull up at the entrance. The driver opened the car's rear door and an immaculately dressed, silver-haired officer climbed out of the rear seat. 'It's the Lion,' Schnee said quickly. 'Grand Admiral Dönitz. He still keeps an office here which he uses sometimes.' Eck nodded, straightening his black uniform tie as the admiral came purposefully into the building, briefcase in hand. This was the first time that Eck had seen the man who had once been the commander of BdU and was now the *oberkommando der marine*, the commander-in-chief of the entire *Kriegsmarine*. Both Schnee and Eck stood aside and saluted, stiffly at attention as Dönitz brushed past, hardly pausing. Then Dönitz stopped suddenly and turned, an enquiring look on his slim face. 'Ah Schnee. Who have we here?'

'Allow me to introduce *Kapitänleutnant* Heinz Eck, Admiral. He has recently taken command of U-852.'

Eck saluted again – the Nazi salute which he knew had largely been introduced into Germany generally and the German military by this very man. 'It's a pleasure to meet you Admiral.'

Dönitz carefully took off a leather glove and shook Eck's hand. 'Captain Eck. I'm pleased to meet you. You know I had some reservations about giving a young officer like yourself the command of one of our most modern boats but when I read your record in minesweepers, which is first class, by the way, and what your commanding officers had said of you, any reservations I might have had disappeared completely. You are going to the South Atlantic soon, I think?'

'Yes Admiral. We leave from Kiel in a week or two. We have recently completed our workup and my crew is ready. We are arming and provisioning at this very moment.'

Dönitz nodded, half turning away, then paused to look at Eck once again. 'Captain Schnee has no doubt given you your briefing here today, and what he has told you is of the utmost importance, Eck. It pains me to know that we have lost so many good men down there recently, good men and good boats. But you must be strong, strong and vigilant. Soon we are expecting an invasion from across

Admiral Karl Dönitz (also recorded as Döenitz) who complied with Hitler's order to murder all merchant ships' crews. (*Catalogue 208-PU-52 P-1, U.S. National Archives. Naval History and Heritage Command*)

the Channel, that is a certainty now, and our U-boats will continue to play a major part in strangling the supplies to the enemy. You have your part to play in all this, Captain, so play it well and keep in mind the directive I sent to all U-boat commanders. You have read it I assume?'

'Yes sir, of course. You have directly ordered all commanders not to pick up survivors and to be steadfast and strong.'

'Have a care for your own boat, Eck. Strive for success. We must be harsh to win this war. The enemy began this war to destroy us, Eck. But by God we will finish it. Let nothing stand in your way and remain silent and invisible. You must be a ghost down there Eck, but you must also be a deadly ghost.'

'Yes Admiral. I fully understand.'

'Well good luck Eck, and happy hunting.'

'Thank you sir.'

Dönitz turned, nodding briefly to Schnee and walked carefully up the stairs to the top floor. Neither Eck nor Admiral Dönitz could have believed in that moment that within a year both would be facing war crimes trials and that Eck's coming actions in the South Atlantic would be one more piece of a monstrous jigsaw puzzle that would ultimately place his admiral into one

A U-boat in heavy seas. (*Catalogue Number NH-61821. Naval History and Heritage Command*)

of the most dangerous positions he would ever find himself during his entire life: a showdown at Nuremberg and the distinct possibility of joining a host of other top Nazi leaders on an American scaffold.

Heinz Eck left BdU headquarters that day with a dark feeling of foreboding rising in the pit of his stomach. He had expressed his concerns but when he thought about it he had also been given no real answers. Too many highly experienced U-boat commanders had gone into that death zone and never returned. They had been the cream of the U-boat fleet and in command of the latest, most powerful submarine ever constructed in Germany. How was he, a first-time U-boat commander, supposed to survive that kind of test by fire? Since the outbreak of war the British and Americans had been perfecting their U-boat hunting techniques and more sophisticated and deadly technological advances had been made. Eck walked on for a while, the ruins of bomb-shattered Berlin all around. Then the air-raid sirens began to wail once again and suddenly he was running for the nearest shelter as the muted explosions of bombs could be heard falling far away to the north of the war-torn city.

*   *   *

At times Heinz Wilhelm Eck believed that he had been born to be at sea. He loved it so much. The freedom, the openness, the opportunity for adventure and excitement. Eck had been born on 27 March, 1916 at the massive and extremely busy port of Hamburg, so ships and seafaring were second nature to him but much of his younger life had been spent in Berlin, then one of the most culturally diverse and beautiful cities in the world. The thought of life as a naval officer had always fascinated Eck and on 8 April, 1934, when he was just eighteen years of age, he had joined the *Reichmarine* as a member of Class 34. He would spend the next three years under intense training in specialty naval schools to qualify him to be commissioned as a *leutnant sur see*, graduating on 1 April, 1937. He had been promoted to *oberleutnant* exactly two years later on 1 April, 1939. The following five years were to be spent on minesweepers, taking command of one of them in 1939 and being promoted *kapitänleutnant* on 1 December, 1941.

Yet Eck had now taken command of his first submarine, U-852, and it continued to worry him, his concerns deepening after the quiet conversation with his friend Adalbert Schnee. And these concerns had in no way been alleviated when, just days later, he had met with another U-boat ace, *Korvettenkapitän* Günter Hessler who, in addition to being the son-in-law of Admiral Dönitz, was also the chief of staff to *Konteradmiral* Eberhardt Godt, the man responsible for directing the day-to-day conduct of the U-boat war. Hessler was one of the best informed men in the Third Reich at that time – at least as far as the U-boat campaign was concerned. There was little he was not aware of. Yet his words to Eck had been profound. 'Be careful Eck,' Hessler had warned. 'Absolutely avoid anything that might pinpoint your position to the enemy. If they find your boat you will not survive.' The words had exactly mirrored what Grand Admiral Dönitz and Adalbert Schnee had already said.

Eck had returned deeply worried to Kiel. Nobody had talked in quite this way before. The war was as good as won; there was every reason to be happy with progress; the Third Reich was invincible and every part of it superior to anything the enemy could throw at it. That is what everybody was saying. Why then were three highly placed naval officers so nervous? Why were they advocating extreme caution and intimating even more extreme measures in order to remain safe? Eck shrugged. There was nothing more he could do. His crew was fully trained. The boat was ready, and if everything went well they would all return to Kiel and a heroes' welcome.

*   *   *

Heinz Eck had already received his written orders. He took them now from the small safe in what passed as the captain's cabin aboard U-852, opened the stiff paper and read them through once again. He was to leave Kiel tomorrow, 18 January, 1944, and take his submarine on what was known as the 'north-about' route over the top of Scotland and into the North Atlantic then sail south to the west coast of Africa and commence attacking shipping and convoys wherever possible. He was later to join with *Gruppe Monson*, the wolf-pack group operating out of George Town at Penang in Malaya.

Standing on the bridge of U-852 on that bitterly cold morning Heinz Eck wondered if he would ever return to Germany. Kiel was not the port he had once known. Intense Allied bombing raids had wreaked enormous damage to the harbour and its facilities and there was every reason to believe that by the time he returned – if ever he did – the port would have received considerably more damage to the point where it would be almost unrecognisable. This was Eck's first war patrol as the commander of one of Germany's latest and most formidable submarines. He should have been overjoyed, happy to be taking the war into the heart of Allied operations, yet he felt nothing but sadness and a cold kind of apprehension that would not leave him.

Once clear of Kiel's defensive nets and mines, with the grey sea washing heavily over the bows of U-852, Eck ordered his lookouts below, turned to gaze one last time towards the grey outline of his homeland, now just a smear on the horizon, and stepped down into the conning tower hatch, slamming it closed behind him and spinning the lock into place. 'Take it down,' he ordered as he stepped off the steel ladder into the crowded control

Tankers were particularly prone to attack and, laden with fuel, they would often go up like bombs. This is a photograph of the ship *Empire* which was torpedoed on 24 January, 1942. (*Catalogue Number NH-54371. Naval History and Heritage Command*)

room. 'Standby main vents. Latch up main engines.' The men could hear the hiss of the vents closing as Eck moved to stand behind the hydroplane operator. In the nearby radio shack the keys of the Enigma machine could be heard clacking as the operator sent the boat's last position before diving.

'Blow negative tank.' Eck ordered quietly. 'Ease stern plane to ten degrees.'

The men could feel the bows dipping into the sea now, water washing heavily over the U-boat's hull as the battery-powered screws began to bite, thrusting the boat deeper.

'Bow up 15. Stern up 10.'

'Levelling off sir,' the hydroplane operator called.

'Shut all main vents. Come to periscope depth.'

U-852 was now a grey shadow just beneath the surface of a darkening sea.

Prior to heading out into the open sea, U-852 called into Kristiansand, Norway, where the vessel remained for two days before proceeding on its war patrol, passing between Iceland and the Faroe Islands before setting course for the South Atlantic.

For the following weeks Eck kept U-852 submerged all day, surfacing only at night to recharge the boat's batteries and to increase speed. Yet even with

Torpedoes were so powerful that at times ships simply disintegrated. This is a photograph of a vessel carrying barrage balloons. It was sunk in July 1942. (*Catalogue Number NH-71302. Naval History and Heritage Command*)

A German U-boat returning to its base in Norway in 1943. (*Catalogue Number NH-111305. Naval History and Heritage Command*)

the additional distance he was able to achieve by using his diesel propulsion system at night it still took him close to two months to reach his area of operations around the Equator. During all that time Eck attacked no ships and remained as far as possible completely invisible to enemy eyes. Obviously he was heeding the warnings he had been given prior to departure. U-852 was a good boat and it would wreak enormous damage on Allied shipping, Eck was sure of that, but both the training workup prior to departure and this long voyage south had very clearly demonstrated that the submarine had its faults, and its enormous size, causing sluggish manoeuvrability and visibility on the surface, was one of them. On two separate occasions the submarine had come close to being spotted. On both occasions Eck had been running on the surface before submerging for the day and his lookouts had spotted aircraft in the vicinity but Eck had managed to emergency-dive the boat before they had been spotted.

Then fate dealt Eck a card which was not only to change his life and the lives of many members of his crew, but would also lead directly to his own death and the deaths of many of his comrades and crew members aboard the submarine.

It was now the afternoon of 13 March, 1944. U-852 was on the surface, recharging its batteries with its lookouts scanning the horizon in search of any possible victims. The submarine was located about five hundred miles north of Ascension Island which was dangerously within range of British aircraft operating from Ascension. Those aircraft had an operational range of around six hundred miles around Ascension but shipping stuck as close as possible to that vast circle knowing that they were better protected within it. Therefore, Eck reasoned, the best pickings would also be within that circle, even if it meant additional risk to his submarine and crew. Eck really did not have a great deal of choice. He had now been on patrol for almost two months and had not sunk even one ship. The risk of placing himself within that protective circle might prove beneficial if he could attack and sink a ship and then clear the area as rapidly as possible. He was now fully aware that three other submarines had been sunk within that protective circle: U-848 on 5 November, 1943, south-west of Ascension; U-849 just twenty days later almost directly west of Ascension and almost right on the edge of the operational range of the British aircraft, and then U-177, which had been sunk on 6 February, 1944, also right on the edge of aircraft range south-east of the island. These sobering events were causing Eck to have very serious concerns about the safety of his boat but if he was to emulate the feats of some of the Germany's best U-boat aces, including his friend, Adalbert

As the Atlantic War progressed, Allied anti-submarine tactics improved enormously. Heinz Eck had every reason to be cautious but it was this fear that led directly to the *Peleus* massacre. (*Catalogue 80-G-224927* (*above*), *U.S. National Archives. Catalogue NH 109978 (below), Naval History and Heritage Command*)

Not all submarine commanders carried out Hitler's order to kill the crews of merchant ships. However, survivors of torpedo attacks such as these were constantly in danger of being murdered. These survivors are from the steamer *Carlton*, part of Convoy PQ-17. The photograph, dated 5 July, 1942, was taken from the submarine that had just sunk the ship. (*Catalogue NH 71305, Naval History and Heritage Command*)

Schnee, then he would have to take some risks. It was war. Everything was risky.

'Contact starboard.' The lookout turned his head slightly as he called, but his heavy Zeiss binoculars remained glued to his eyes.

Eck, standing in the centre of the bridge tower turned quickly, raising his own binoculars. It was 1700 hours. The sun was now lowering on the port quarter and its russet light glinted momentarily on the sides of a vessel, just on the starboard horizon.

'Looks like a freighter, *Kapitän*. Maybe five or six thousand tons, bearing two-four-zero. Speed approximately ten knots, course approximately one-eight-zero.'

Eck felt an almost vivid sense of excitement in his chest. 'Right five degrees rudder', he ordered. 'Steer two-one-zero. Come to battle-stations.'

As the submarine turned to starboard and the battle order was passed below decks, Eck turned to his three bridge lookouts. 'Watch the skies', he ordered. 'And watch like a hawk. All our lives depend upon it.'

*   *   *

The ship sighted that day was the SS *Peleus*, a Greek freighter of 6659 tons which had been built by William Grey and Company in 1928. The vessel had now been taken over by the British War Transportation Ministry and at this time was en route in ballast from Freetown, from where it had departed five days earlier, for the River Plate near Buenos Aires. On board the ship was a crew of thirty-five men, only a few of whom would survive the coming attack and the murderous events that would soon follow. The ship was commanded by a Greek officer, Captain Mavris Minas, who would also not survive.

One of the men on board the ship that day was Antonios Cosmas Liossis, the chief officer. Liossis had an interesting background. Born at Kiles in Greece on 7 November, 1906, he had first gone to sea in 1923. He was in Greece during the German occupation but managed to escape from the Germans on 16 July, 1943, travelling to Suez were he joined the crew of the *Peleus* as its chief officer. From there the ship had sailed to the U.K. and then to Canada before returning to London. After loading at Immingham docks on the Humber Estuary the vessel had sailed to Algiers and from there with its intended destination being the River Plate calling firstly at Gibraltar and then Freetown. The *Peleus* had sailed from Freetown on 8 March, 1944, just days before it was torpedoed.

Even at full speed it took U-852 almost two and a half hours to overtake the freighter, remaining well to the east on the ship's port beam so that the submarine would remain out of sight. The time was approximately 19.20 hours (7.20 p.m) before Eck had his submarine in position to be able to launch the attack. Having overtaken the ship Eck had closed with his target, turning to wait as the *Peleus* came across the bows of the submarine. During all this time U-852 had remained on the surface, Eck being fully aware that he needed to do so in order to be able to catch up to the ship. He was also keenly aware that by doing so he was inviting an air attack on his boat but there was not much he could do about that. In any case, night had now fallen, the moon was yet to rise, and the sea was in darkness. Although the *Peleus* was completely blacked out, its outline could still be seen as it steamed steadily south-south-west with a creamy bow-wave showing at its head. Basically, it was a target too good to miss.

'We will attack on the surface,' Eck said, never taking his eyes from the binoculars trained on the ship. 'Right five degrees rudder. New course two-seven-zero.'

'Steady on two-seven-zero, sir.'

'Flood tubes one and two. Master-sight to the bridge.'

'Tubes one and two flooded sir.'

'Come to two-six-zero. Stand by to attack.'

The master-sight operator kept his eyes glued to the dark image of the ship, now in profile steaming unwittingly into the trap only about a kilometre ahead.

'Range 1100 metres sir.'

'Open bow caps one and two.'

'One and two open, Captain.'

Eck paused for a few moments, mentally checking his calculations.

'Hold for bearing.'

Eck paused again, but only for ten seconds.

'Tube one, fire.'

The submarine lurched slightly as the torpedo launched from its bow tube to slide into the sea. Eck was not watching it. His eyes remained firmly on his prey. He waited for only another five seconds. 'Tube two, fire.'

The second torpedo hissed from its housing to begin its deadly journey towards destruction.

'Do you wish to submerge, Captain?' the watch officer asked.

Eck said nothing, just shaking his head slightly as he watched the twin trails of the torpedoes racing directly towards their target. It was a lone ship without an escort. There was no need to strike and hide. Not this time. The submarine was wallowing sluggishly now, almost invisible in the darkness. 'Slow ahead,' Eck ordered. 'Bear two-four-zero.'

Standing on the bridge that night was Antonios Liossis, the ship's chief officer. Even in the darkness Liossis could also see those twin white trails in the water, approaching on the port beam. He immediately ordered an alteration of course in a desperate attempt to avoid the torpedoes but even as he did so he realised that it was hopeless.

A few seconds later both explosives detonated, just a few seconds apart.

The first torpedo struck the *Peleus* in its number 2 hold. A breath later the second torpedo exploded in number 3 hold. Both explosions were massive and it was obvious that the ship was immediately doomed. Eck would later testify (at his war crimes trial) that, 'Both torpedoes had magnetic fuses. The *Peleus* burst into pieces completely. The detonation was impressive.'

It took only a few minutes for the ship to slip beneath the waves. The impact of the two magnetic explosives was catastrophic. When asked during his subsequent trial how long it had taken the ship to sink, Eck testified that it sank, '... immediately after the detonation of the explosives', adding, '... but you could not talk about a ship, it was just pieces, wreckage.'

It is not too difficult to imagine what it must have been like for those on board the *Peleus* at the time of the attack. A fourth of the crew would have been on watch, on the bridge or in the engine-room or boiler-room but all the others would either have been eating their evening meal or resting before going on watch. No one today knows how many men were killed during these twin explosions or how many managed to jump overboard, or were blown into the sea before the ship went down. Everything happened so violently and so quickly that there was hardly time to think.

The chief officer, Antonios Liossis, was knocked directly off the bridge by the blast of the explosions and fell unconscious into the sea. When he recovered consciousness he managed to clutch onto a hatch-cover. 'While I was hanging onto the hatch-cover I heard someone whistling,' Liossis later testified. 'I found that it was a sailor named Dimitrios Constantinides (also reported as Konstantinides) who said he had nothing to cling to so he joined me. We made for a raft which we could see in the distance.'

Another man, Rocco Said, was a greaser who had been off watch at the time of the attack. Standing on deck with a number of other crew members, Said realised that the ship was sinking so quickly there was literally no time to do anything other than jump into the sea. They and all the others did not have time even to find a lifejacket or launch a boat or raft. They just jumped.

No more than three minutes after Eck had fired his torpedoes it was all over. Some reports later stated that it had taken just two minutes for what was left of the ship to sink. The *Peleus* had gone and the dark night sea was littered with floating wreckage, oil and struggling men, most of whom were either clutching at hatch covers or the few loose rafts that had floated free of the ship as it had gone down.

How many survivors were now in the water was impossible to know. Quite obviously the ship had literally disintegrated after the twin detonations of the torpedoes and many of its crew would have been killed either in the blast or trapped in the broken wreckage as it had gone down. Eck was later to testify that he had brought his submarine close to the spot where the ship had disappeared and although it was dark and he had made no real effort to discover how many survivors were in the water at that time he believed that there might have been only twelve.

Two of the survivors, the chief officer Antonios Liossis, and Dimitrios Constantinides, both clinging to their hatch-cover, swam towards one of the rafts. As they did so the hull of the German submarine came slowly towards them, nosing like a shark among all the flotsam and wreckage. Both men stopped swimming, treading water as they watched the enormous hull

In these two photographs we can see a German U-boat nosing into a mass of oil and flotsam caused by the sinking of a steamer. Heinz Eck feared that such wreckage would give away his position to patrolling Allied aircraft. (*Catalogue number* (*above:*) *71307 and* (*below:*) *71306. Naval History and Heritage Command*)

of U-852 slide past and when it had done so the men grasped the raft and clambered on board.

Almost all the crew of the submarine were now below decks. Those on the bridge could hear whistles and men shouting in the water all around. They could also see faint lights coming from the rafts which were bobbing about on the sea.

At this moment another man joined those on the bridge. This was *Oberstabsarzt* (superior medical officer) Walter Weisspfenning, the submarine's doctor. Weisspfenning's only reason for coming on deck that evening was curiosity. He wanted to see what was going on. The sinking of an enemy merchantman was an unusual event and he wanted to be sure he missed none of it. As it turned out for Weisspfenning, it was to be a fatal decision.

Eck was under standard operational orders that whenever it was feasible he was to interrogate important survivors, especially the captains or chief engineers of the ships he sank to discover the names of the vessels, their tonnage, where they had come from, their destinations and any other intelligence that might be useful. However, Eck did not speak English so he sent a message below asking his chief engineer, *Kapitänleutnant (Ing)* Hans Richard Lenz to come on deck. Lenz spoke English fluently. When Lenz arrived on the bridge Eck ordered him to go to the submarine's bows to question survivors in the water. Lenz acknowledged the order, and climbed down from the bridge tower to the deck taking with him the second watch officer, *Leutnant sur See* August Hoffmann. Hoffmann was also the artillery officer and wireless officer aboard the submarine.

For all these officers this was to be a defining moment in their lives. Hoffmann, like the boat's doctor, Walter Weisspfenning, had no official reason to be on the bridge that evening. His watch had finished at 1600 hours (4 p.m.) about an hour before the *Peleus* had been sighted by the lookouts and he should have been below decks as he was not due to take over the bridge watch until midnight. Yet like everyone else on board curiosity was overtaking sound reasoning and Hoffmann could not resist coming on deck to see what was happening. He too was able to speak English although not with the proficiency of Lenz. Yet he went forward with Lenz without being ordered to do so as he believed that he might have been able to assist with the questioning.

Heinz Eck now manoeuvred U-852 into a position to come alongside a raft which carried several men. These included the freighter's third officer Agis Kephalas; a greaser named Stavros Sogias; a Russian seaman named Pierre Neuman and a Chinese fireman whose name no one could later recall.

As U-852 came alongside the raft, Lenz could see that one of the raft's occupants was an officer so he ordered Agis Kephalas to climb onto the submarine's housing. From Kephalas, Lenz learned that the ship had been travelling in ballast from Freetown to the River Plate. Kephalas also told Lenz that the *Peleus* was being followed by another ship which had been unable to keep up. Both ships, Kephalas advised, were under orders to steam to the same destination. Lenz also questioned Kephalas about convoy routines, the number of warships then at Freetown and whether or not merchant shipping was being escorted by aircraft carriers. Lenz also demanded to be given a lifebuoy carrying the name of the *Peleus*, presumably to assist with identification of their victim.

Having obtained this information Kephalas was ordered to climb back onto his raft. He was told by Hoffmann that all the survivors would be rescued by the British the following day. Hoffmann even helped Kephalas back onto the raft before both German officers began to walk back towards the bridge to give the intelligence to Eck.

As the submarine nosed away from the raft, Lenz and Hoffmann climbed back onto the bridge. Lenz told Eck what they had learned but Eck was suspicious about the alleged intelligence derived from Kephalas that another ship was following behind. 'It was too much of a good thing,' Eck later claimed.

Agis Kephalas would later die from wounds he would receive during the following massacre but before doing so he would make an informal deposition to Rocco Said, the man who was nursing him on a raft at the time, stating that the information he had given to the Germans that night had been all lies and deliberately misleading. The Greek officer had provided Lenz with a range of false intelligence, including details of another slow ship that was supposed to be coming up behind, which never actually existed. This disinformation was intended to mislead the Germans about Allied operations and was also an attempt keep the submarine in the area knowing that British aircraft and warships would soon be hunting for the submarine.

By now the bridge of the submarine was actually somewhat crowded. In addition to the two lookouts, there were five officers present. These included, of course, Captain Heinz Eck; his first officer, *Oberleutnant* Georg Colditz; the second officer, *Leutnant* August Hoffmann, the chief engineer, *Kapitänleutnant* (*Ing*) Hans Lenz; and the doctor, *Oberstabsarzt* Walter Weisspfenning. Both Hoffmann and Weisspfenning were standing apart from the other three officers and, if their later statements were to be believed, they did not take part in, nor could they clearly hear, the conversation that immediately followed.

Eck was now evidently very concerned. This was exactly what his friend, *Korvettenkapitän* Adalbert Schnee, had warned him about. He had just sunk a ship. The sea was littered with wreckage, the submarine was well within the area of operations of enemy aircraft flying from Ascension Island, and suddenly the submarine was in even greater danger than ever. Eck told both Lenz and Colditz that the wreckage all around was a beacon and that it would easily be spotted by aircraft flying either from Ascension or from Freetown and once that happened there would be a frenzied air and sea search for U-852. Eck was more than aware of all his fellow submariners who had recently lost their lives in these very waters and he had no intention, he said, of joining them. Since the sinking of the *Peleus* he had been calculating his chances. His best opportunity to escape was now to leave the scene as quickly as possible and run at full speed on the surface all through the hours of darkness. However, he realised that by the time the sun came up the following morning he would still be within range of the British aircraft. The only alternative, he believed, was to sink all the wreckage to get rid of the evidence of the destruction of the *Peleus*. Adalbert Schnee, the very same naval officer who had advised Eck that attempting to get rid of wreckage was a viable option, later told the war crimes court in Hamburg that in his opinion Eck at this precise moment, '… lost his nerves'.

'I want two M.G.15s brought up on deck,' Eck ordered grimly.

Lenz and Colditz protested vigourously. 'If you machine-gun the wreckage then you machine-gun the survivors, *Kapitän*,' Lenz stated anxiously. 'You can't do that. It would be murder.'

But Eck remained adamant. It was an operational necessity, he told them. There would be little hope of escaping out of the range of the aircraft if the evidence of the sinking were allowed to remain in place. Lenz was furious. Unable to change Eck's mind, he went below decks. Meanwhile two machine-guns were brought on deck. These were mounted on both port and starboard sides of the conning tower. Eck now ordered that all the rafts were to be sunk with gunfire. He made no mention that the people on them were to be shot, but everyone on the bridge at that moment fully realised that by shooting the rafts with a shredding volume of machine-gun fire, the rafts and the people on them would be completely destroyed. It was also realised that even if any of the men on the rafts managed to survive the gunfire, then without rafts or lifejackets it would be a miracle if any of them survived.

Eck was not actually thinking straight that night. Despite the fact that he was knowingly condemning many men to death, believing that it was justifiable (as he later attempted to explain) as a legitimate act of war, he had not taken into consideration that even if he managed to sink all the rafts and the many other items of flotsam in the water, he would never be able to disperse the pond of oil that had settled on the surface of the sea – a clear indication that a ship had been sunk. He was also under the illusion that the rafts could easily be sunk. He believed that they had been constructed on hollow floats and that once the floats had been filled with bullet holes they would quickly sink. However, the floats on these rafts had been professionally filled with a buoyant material, and even when fired upon they would still float reasonably well.

It was now around 2000 hours (8 p.m.). About forty minutes had passed since the *Peleus* had been sunk. It was a dark and, at that time, a moonless night. The rafts were all around, Eck realised that, but some of them could not be seen as the men on them had extinguished their survival lights. Those rafts closer to the submarine were, however, still visible. Eck now turned to Doctor Weisspfenning who, at that moment, was standing close to the starboard machine-gun. 'Fire on that one there,' Eck is said to have ordered, pointing to a raft bobbing about in the water about two hundred metres away.

Doctor Walter Weisspfenning was a non-combatant. Under international law, and also under the regulations of the *Kriegsmarine*'s submarine service, he was not permitted to handle weapons unless it was for the protection of himself or his patients or medical staff. However, he now had no hesitation in swinging the heavy machine-gun around, pressing its butt firmly into his shoulder, taking aim along the barrel and firing a few bursts at the raft. Within moments, however, the gun jammed. Weisspfenning's inexperienced bursts may have been a little too long for the automatic mechanism to handle. *Leutnant* Hoffmann stepped forward. He was familiar with the machine-gun being the U-boat's weapons officer and was able quickly to clear the jam. He sighted the weapon and continued firing at the raft. Weisspfenning stepped back and watched but took no further action against the survivors. Despite the intensity of the machine-gun fire that had been directed against the raft it stubbornly remained floating on the surface of the sea. Eck ordered that a searchlight be switched on. He could not understand why the raft was still afloat and wanted to see why. However, he was unable to determine why the raft had such resilience to the gunfire. He ordered Hoffmann to continue firing at whatever rafts could be found while the submarine cruised around the wreckage. It did not appear to be a problem to Eck or anyone else on the bridge at that time that many of the rafts were manned by survivors and although some of the men were able to throw themselves into the sea many were either incapable of doing so, having been injured during the sinking of the *Peleus* or wounded by the machine-gun fire.

The gunfire was now intermittent. Only Hoffmann was firing and neither Eck nor *Leutnant* Georg Colditz actually manned the guns. As the minutes and then an hour slipped past it finally became clear to those officers on the bridge that this method of destroying the evidence was never going to work. Hoffmann turned to Eck and suggested that the 37mm gun should be used on the rafts as it fired explosive rounds which would surely destroy them. Eck also considered using the massive 105mm deck gun which had enough power to destroy a ship but shelved that idea when he realised that it would be impossible to depress the weapon sufficiently to hit any of the rafts. However, he did order Hoffmann to try using one of the 20mm machine-guns but this too proved ineffective against the rafts which seemed now to have taken on a stubborn life of their own. Another suggestion was made to destroy the rafts by placing demolition charges onto them but Eck refused to do so as he did not want any crew members to leave the submarine. Yet the concept had given him another idea: he would destroy the rafts with hand-grenades.

U-852 was manoeuvred closer. Hoffmann was the officer designated to throw the grenades. It is not known how many rafts were targeted in this way or how many men were killed during this phase of the operation but not one of the rafts was destroyed. It was quite evident that whoever had designed these little flotation platforms had known exactly what they were doing. They were literally designed to survive just about anything the sea (or Germans) could throw at them.

Hours had now passed. Wasted hours. These were hours of darkness that Eck could have used to escape the area, travelling rapidly at full speed on the surface and then submerging at dawn to keep moving farther away from the area that would soon be swarming with enemy aircraft and surface ships.

Meanwhile, below decks on the submarine, the crew, ostensibly at least, remained in complete ignorance of what was going on above. Evidently something unusual and violent was happening. The order to place machine-guns on the conning tower bridge, the intermittent sounds of them firing, the order to bring hand-grenades and even small-arms to the bridge, the sounds of the grenades exploding and also the even more disturbing chatter of the heavier 20mm machine-guns was telling. It did not take a genius to work out that there was something terrible happening above.

Only one man below decks that night knew with certainty what was in the process of occurring above. This was the chief engineer, *Kapitänleutnant* Hans Lenz. He had been present on the bridge when the decision had been made to begin the mass slaughter but, after protesting, he had not remained there. Instead of staying on the bridge to witness the killings, Lenz had gone below and for several hours, while listening to the murderous havoc coming from above his head, he had been writing a detailed report of the conversation he had conducted with the ship's third officer, Agis Kephalas, concerning the possibility of another vessel coming up behind the *Peleus*. He had also gone forward and supervised the reloading of the two torpedo tubes that had been used to attack the *Peleus* and had then checked on the boat's trim. As the chief engineer it was his responsibility not only to ensure that the engines were in perfect running order but that every other mechanical part of the boat was functioning as it should including the submarine's ability to submerge at a moment's notice.

The time was now midnight. Almost five hours after the attack on the *Peleus* had taken place. It was time for the submarine's watch to be changed. Hoffmann, who had been manning the machine-gun on the conning tower and doing a particularly murderous job of his work, was relieved by another crew member, *Gefreiter* (equivalent to leading seaman) Wolfgang Schwender. As Schwender came onto the bridge Eck ordered him to man the port machine-gun and commence firing at rafts and other large pieces of wreckage. Schwender was not a well liked member of the submarine's crew, considered to have been something of a bully, he would show no mercy to those who may still have been alive in the water. Schwender swung the machine-gun towards one raft, about thirty metres away and commenced firing but after a few short bursts the gun jammed. At that moment the chief engineer *Kapitänleutnant* Hans Lenz once again appeared on the bridge. Schwender had just cleared the gun's jam when Lenz pushed him aside and took over the weapon. Lenz was later to explain his peculiar actions in this way. He disliked Schwender intensely and the raft that Schwender was then targeting carried a number of men including, Lenz believed, the freighter's third officer, Agis Kephalas, the same man whom Lenz had questioned and whom Hoffmann had assured would be rescued the following day. Lenz later told war crimes investigators that he could not stand the thought of Kephalas being, '… hit and killed by bullets which had been fired by a soldier who in my view was bad'. Lenz completely disagreed with this massacre but for him it was a point of honour that if Kephalas had to die then he should be killed honourably, not by some brutal and callous crew member. Lenz fired only at that one raft then lowered the barrel of the machine-gun and stepped away. Yet this one action was enough for him later to be charged with war crimes.

This event was witnessed by another officer of the submarine's crew, *Leutnant* Woldemar Ranft, who would testify at the subsequent war crimes trial, providing evidence that may well have saved Lenz's life. Ranft had been below decks when the massacre had first started and had only gone above after some time had lapsed. There he had seen Lenz taking over the machine-gun from Schwender. During his testimony Ranft very pointedly stated that Lenz had, '…pushed Schwender away with some force', before taking over the gun.

By now it was 0100 hrs (1 a.m.). Nothing had been achieved except mass murder. Eck finally realised that he had been a fool. He had been unable to destroy any evidence that the *Peleus* had been sunk; the dark sea remained littered with flotsam and oil and now also with dead bodies, and it was evident that from the air the scene would look like a disaster zone. Dawn was now only six hours away and Eck had wasted all those precious hours when he should have been running like a hare. He turned the U-boat away from the area and ordered full speed ahead, running south.

*   *   *

For those on board the rafts the night had been, obviously, a terrible nightmare. The sinking of their ship had been bad enough although everyone on board had known that one day such a tragedy might happen. These were dangerous times and merchant seamen and their ships were always at the heart of enemy action. Thousands had already died in this war and thousands more would also probably die before it was all over. Yet when that first torpedo had struck, and then almost simultaneously the second, it was clear that it was the end of the *Peleus*. Its time had come. Abandoning ship, for those who survived the explosions, had been almost an unconscious act of self-preservation and although no one now knows how many were in the water when U-852 had nosed in amongst them, it had, apparently, been a significant number of the crew.

They had all watched from various rafts as the submarine had edged up to the raft carrying the freighter's third officer, Agis Kephalas. They could only guess at what was being said but with luck all would be well and the men would be rescued the next day. Kephalas had returned to his raft and the submarine had edged away. The men breathed a small sigh of relief. Then suddenly the firing had commenced.

The raft holding the ship's third officer, Agis Kephalas, and two other seamen, was subjected to almost immediate attack. Both seamen were killed while Kephalas was badly wounded. However, Kephalas was able to slip from his damaged raft and swim to the raft occupied by the ship's chief officer, Antonios Liossis.

Rocco Said was a ship's greaser who would luckily survive the massacre. He had been born at Constantinople in 1905, his father being a British subject while his mother had been Greek. Between the years 1924 and 1935 he had lived in France but had then moved to England where he had taken up the trade of furrier. However, during his youth he had worked on merchant shipping and in 1941 he again volunteered to serve in the merchant marine at a time when crews were badly needed for the war effort. He served as the third engineer aboard the *Mount Taurus*. Illness forced him to leave this ship and he remained ashore for some time recovering until he was well enough to join the SS *Peleus* in January 1944.

Following the torpedoing of the ship, Said now found himself on board a small raft with a group of other men when Hoffmann turned his murderous attention on them. Said and all the other men were able to jump into the water but Hoffmann also raked the water with gunfire and, as Said later testified, all the swimmers around him 'threw their hands up' as they were machine-gunned in the water. Their bodies quickly sank from view.

The following morning Said was able to climb onto another raft on which he discovered the body of a dead Chinese man who had been a member of the crew. Said later recalled that this man had sustained injuries to his face and chest, apparently from the grenade explosions. Said was able to get on board the raft and then assisted another man to climb aboard; this was Dimitrios Argyros. Both men surveyed their dismal situation. The raft had been badly damaged by gunfire and explosions and although floating well it was not the best place to be with sharks circling. The two men remained on that raft for the entire night and the following morning managed to find another raft which was in much better condition. They transferred to that raft.

Meanwhile, the chief officer, Antonios Cosmas Liossis, later testified that after the submarine had left the third officer's raft it had made a sweep of the area. Liossis had been able to see most of the crew in the water; almost all of them had been clinging to wreckage and blowing whistles. Liossis and Constantinides, with whom he was sharing the raft, had called to their fellow crew members, letting them know that they were coming to lend what assistance they could. Liossis and Constantinides managed to lash two rafts together and as they were approaching the submarine, having been hailed to come closer, the Germans had opened fire. Both Liossis and Constantinides had ducked for cover. Liossis could hear cries of pain from Constantinides who had been struck by bullets in several places. Both of their rafts were now riddled with bullets but remained afloat. The Germans tossed grenades at the rafts, one of which wounded Liossis. At that time his head was beneath a bench but he was struck in the right shoulder and back. The Germans also threw three grenades at another raft. Someone on the bridge of the U-boat was now also using a lamp, apparently to check what damage had been done and to see if anyone was still alive. Liossis lay very quietly, his back was covered with blood and he later testified that in his opinion the Germans probably thought he was already dead and did not continue firing on the raft. The submarine then continued to nose around the floating wreckage, firing long bursts from their machine-guns. Liossis later said that after the submarine had departed the scene of the carnage he had crawled from beneath the bench and found that Constantinides was dead. Liossis was quickly joined by the third officer, Agis Kephalas, who had fallen from his raft into the sea and had been hanging onto Liossis' raft. He had been badly wounded in the right arm. Sharks were now gathering around the wreckage and as the two men did not wish to witness Constantinides being eaten, they decided to wait until nightfall before placing his body into the sea.

These two men were now in great pain but fortunately were able to find some drugs and medicine on the raft – part of the normal survival stores which were maintained aboard all the rafts on the ship. There was also a quantity of ship's biscuits and water. They were, additionally, able to make an awning to protect themselves from the sun.

Four days after the sinking the two men sighted another raft in the distance. It evidently had two men on board who would subsequently prove to be Rocco Said and Dimitrios Argyros. After a few days the two rafts came sufficiently close together to enable Said and Argyros to transfer to Liossis' raft, abandoning theirs. Twenty-five days after the sinking the third officer, Agis Kephalas, who had been cared for by Rocco Said, died of his wounds. The remaining three men had been able to fashion a sail and using an oar as a rudder were making slowly for the coast of East Africa. On the 20th of April they sighted a Portuguese steamer in the distance. The ship was the *Alexandre Silva*. Lookouts on the bridge had seen the pathetic little sail on the raft and the steamer altered course immediately to come to the men's assistance. The three survivors were helped aboard, provided with food, care and attention and seven days later the ship arrived at Lobito.

Dimitrios Argyros, the third survivor of the ship's sinking also later made a statement providing investigators with details of the event. In addition to corroborating everything that had already been attested, Argyros added that at the time of the torpedoing he had distinctly smelt gas, leading investigators to believe that the Germans might have been using not only explosives but also chemical weapons against the ship's crew. This theory was, however, later discounted.

*   *   *

After fleeing the scene of the carnage he had created, Heinz Eck took U-852 rapidly south, moving through what remained of the night at top speed. While the men below decks might have suspected what had been occurring above their heads at the scene of the attack, the confirmation of the massacre was to affect the morale the crew. Even Eck later stated that he became aware of the men's sour mood and, in fact, had been afflicted by the same malaise. 'I was under the impression that the mood on board was rather a depressing one,' he later stated. 'I myself was in the same mood.'

The crews of submarines formed a tightly-knit unit. Life on board those vessels was harsh and primitive by today's standards. Quarters were cramped, food was usually just basic rations, the boat was always stinking of oil, cooking and body odour. Anything that might affect morale was considered to be a serious impediment to the effective and efficient functioning of the vessel. Realising that his men were completely demoralised by events (some might have been worried about possible war crimes trials), Eck decided to explain his actions to them. Using the boat's loudspeaker system he told them that he had never intended killing anyone but that it was only necessary to destroy the wreckage. He added that he regretted that some of the survivors might have been killed. He said, very pointedly, that the men should steel themselves to such events and think of their families at home who were then being brutally subjected to massive Allied bombing where tens of thousands of innocent civilians were being killed.

Eck, however, failed to alter the men's mood of disaffection. He was unable to convince them that the destruction of the rafts had been an 'operational necessity', as he termed it. The crew might not have gone through an officer's training course but even to them it seemed obvious that to spend five hours machine-gunning wreckage that refused to sink, while also killing an unknown number of civilian merchant seamen, was unbelievably idiotic and dangerous. Any fool should have realised that the site was stained with a quantity of oil and that oil would remain in place until disbursed by the sea. Worse, it demonstrated that Eck was not an experienced submarine commander. He was untried, an unknown quantity. If he continued to make such poor decisions might he not eventually get them all killed? Submariners were a suspicious lot. They normally placed great trust in their captains. For experienced submarine captains, men like Eck's friend *Korvettenkapitän* Adalbert Schnee, most submariners would have moved heaven and earth to serve under them. They were considered not only lucky but also highly experienced – men who knew how to carry out an attack and get their crews away safely to fight again another day. Eck's attack on the *Peleus* had been easy, a novice could have done it. The ship had been unescorted and was a sitting duck, but what had happened after the ship had gone down had placed the entire crew in extreme peril. They would not soon forget that.

However, what those crew members could not know was the fact that they were all heading into destruction. Heinz Eck was a brash, inexperienced young man who would lead them to a series of terrible fates. Some would be killed during action, two men would suffer lengthy periods of incarceration and a few, including Eck himself, were destined for an ignoble end standing tied and blindfolded in front of a British firing squad.

After the destruction of the *Peleus* Eck managed to evade any enemy contact and worked at putting the whole torrid affair behind him. He had done his duty so there was no point in mulling over the matter. There were more important things to do and many ships which needed to be sunk. For over two weeks, however, as he worked his way slowly south along the west coast of Africa, Eck maintained a low profile. He was perfectly aware that by now the British might have found the wreckage of the *Peleus* and there could be many ships and aircraft out there hunting for him. Eck was actually in more danger than he thought. He had reported by radio on 15 March, advising his superiors at BdU (U-boat headquarters) of the sinking of the *Peleus* and the British had picked up the transmission on their radio direction finders. They did not know what had been transmitted but they now knew that another German submarine was definitely operating in the area. This transmission was passed onto the Royal Navy anti-submarine forces at Simonstown, the huge naval base near Cape Town, who were made aware that a German submarine was operating somewhere to the north-west of Cape Town.

An artist's impression of the sinking of a ship during the Atlantic War. Heinz Eck's war patrol did not have many such successes, testimony, perhaps, to his inexperience as a submarine commander. (*Catalogue Number NH-86699-KN, Courtesy of Navy Art Collection, Naval History and Heritage Command*)

On 1 April, 1944. Eck attacked his second (and final) merchantman, the SS *Dabomian*, the attack taking place just nineteen kilometres south-west of Cape Point. On this occasion Eck did not hang around to machine-gun wreckage or murder survivors. The *Dabomian* was a cargo ship with a crew of fifty-one men, two of whom were killed during the attack. Survivors were all subsequently rescued by two minesweepers of the South African Navy, HMSAS *Krugersdorp* and HMSAS *Natalia*.

Aboard the U-852 morale improved somewhat following the successful attack on the *Dahomian*. Eck had still to prove himself as a commander worthy of a crew's respect but this at least was a good effort.

However, the sinking of the ship stirred a hornet's nest in South Africa. The *Dahomian* was the first ship to be sunk in South African waters since August the previous year. This area was being heavily patrolled by British and South African warships and aircraft and any U-boat careless enough to operate so close to a major Allied naval base was courting disaster. The destruction of the *Dahomian* created a significant Allied response and a powerful anti-submarine group was dispatched to hunt down U-852. However, Eck managed somehow to evade them.

On 4 April, 1944, Eck radioed details of his successful attack on the *Dahomian* to BdU. It was a lengthy transmission which the British had no trouble intercepting. They were able to fix the position of U-852 as being approximately 240 kilometres east-south-east of Cape Agulhas (the Cape of Needles) which is a rocky headland at the southern tip of South Africa and the navigational dividing line between the Atlantic and Indian Oceans.

Eck may have suspected that there was a massive hunt underway for him but he could have no knowledge of its scope or extent. He remained in the Cape region for a couple of weeks seeking targets. This was a regular shipping route and he expected to find more ships but his constant searching proved almost fruitless. He did locate another large vessel and believing that it might have been a troopship fired three torpedoes at it. However, all three missed which was probably another indication to Eck's crew that they were being led by a submarine novice.

Yet Eck was wily enough to realise that by remaining in the Cape region he was inviting attack. He also reasoned that there were far too few ships in the area to warrant the risks involved. He decided to head north once again in the hope that the pickings might be richer.

It was at this point in the whole tragic story that the three survivors of the *Peleus* were found and the entire terrible saga of the massacre became known to the world.

The date was now 20 April, 1944. The Portuguese steamer, SS *Alexandre Silva*, unexpectedly came upon a raft drifting in the middle of the Atlantic Ocean. On board were three emaciated and desperate survivors. These were the chief officer of the *Peleus*, Antonios Liossis; Rocco Said, one of the

In what appears to be a moment of relative calm after all the violence, a merchant officer lowers his suitcase to a lifeboat before descending a Jacob's ladder to abandon his ship which clearly is very low in the water at this point. (*U.S. Office of War Information Collection, Control Number 90714118. U.S. Library of Congress*)

ship's greasers, and the seaman Dimitrios Argyros. The ship's third officer, (Agis Kephalas) who had been wounded during the massacre, had sadly not survived the long period adrift on the open raft. He had succumbed to a deadly combination of gangrene and yellow fever.

As we have seen, the three survivors were landed at Lobito in Angola a week after their rescue and it was there that the news was first heard of the destruction of the *Peleus* and the massacre of its crew. None of the survivors was able to state the identification number of the submarine (it had been dark), but it was now clear evidence, if any further evidence was needed, that a murderous German submarine commander was operating in these waters and he would have to be located and punished. The precise information about the attack and massacre, which was recorded by members of British Intelligence, was soon passed on to the British Admiralty in London.

Meanwhile, as Eck headed north, he should have been aware that he was heading into a storm of steel.

Orders were now issued to strengthen anti-submarine operations in the area and a hunter-killer group was assigned to find and destroy the German submarine. This powerful group consisted of no fewer than nine frigates and other warships and two escort carriers: HMS *Begum* and HMS *Shah*. Additionally, air defences were also improved dramatically. The regular shipping zones saw a significant increase in air-traffic as patrols were dispatched from airforce bases at both Addu Atoll and Diego Garcia.

Meanwhile U-852 managed to remain hidden, submerged by day and only travelling on the surface at night while recharging its batteries. U-852 had become a ghost, as Eck had been instructed. The Allied hunt for the submarine appeared to be going nowhere. And then on 31 April, 1944, British intelligence was able to advise that U-852 was in a position near Cape Guardafui, situated right at the tip of the Gulf of Aden. Clearly Eck had moved quickly out of the Cape Town region where he had intended to destroy a significant number of ships. From Aden several R.A.F. Wellington bombers were sent to hunt and destroy the submarine, no easy task in such a large area, but within a few days they located their elusive foe.

The date was now 2 May. Eck was being careless. The time was just after dawn and U-852 was then still on the surface when, for safety's sake, Eck should have submerged the boat an hour earlier. At that moment *Leutnant* August Hoffmann was duty officer on the bridge of the conning tower. It had been Hoffmann who had fired almost all the shots during the massacre and had also lobbed grenades into the rafts. Hoffmann and his two lookouts were taken completely by surprise as the Wellington bombers came out of the sun to release a storm of bullets, bombs and six depth-charges. With bullets splattering the conning tower, Hoffmann scrambled desperately to get the hatch down and dive the boat but it had already suffered terrible damage.

As the Wellingtons circled to come around for a second attack U-852 slipped beneath the waves. However, the situation on board the submarine was chaotic and every member of the crew was in deadly peril. Seawater was flooding into the vessel and when it struck the damaged batteries it created a deadly cloud of chlorine gas – one of the greatest hazards to submerged submarines. The vessel was able to remain submerged for only fifteen minutes before being forced to surface, coming up steeply at around a 60 degree angle. The steepness of its urgent surfacing caused the batteries to spill even more acid which further exacerbated the problems of chlorine gas. However, despite this, Eck ordered his gun-crews to their stations and the submarine's antiaircraft guns were soon pounding away at the Wellingtons as they swooped lower to press home their attack with savage sprays of machine-gun fire.

Both *Oberleutnant* Georg Colditz (who had also protested the slaughter of the *Peleus* crew) and *Matrosenobergefreiter* Josef Hofer were killed on the bridge at this time. The submarine was now completely crippled. Filling with water, it was well down in the stern and any attempt to dive the boat would have proved fatal.

Eck now made what was probably the most sensible decision of this entire war patrol. Realising that the submarine was doomed, his only hope, he believed, was to beach the vessel somewhere on the nearby Somaliland coast. It was to prove no easy task. With power still coming from the boat's diesel engines, U-852 limped towards the coast while at the same time fighting off repeated attacks from Wellington bombers. It was, at least, a brave and defiant ending. Over the following hours several of the crew were killed or wounded by gunfire from the Wellingtons but the submarine managed to keep going despite the almost continued strafing runs. By that afternoon, Eck was successful in beaching U-852 on the coast at Ras Hafun even while fending off the attacks. As the vessel ground onto the rocks and sand, Eck ordered his crew to abandon the boat and the survivors came scrambling up into the sunlight, wondering if they would have been better to remain within the protective hull of the submarine.

U-852 was beached, half in and half out of the water, leaning heavily to its port side. The bow was wrecked and the body of the vessel was peppered with bullet holes and shrapnel scars. Despite this the British aircraft continued to attack as the crew abandoned the submarine. Some were able to scramble out onto the sand while others dived into the water at the aft end of the boat in a desperate attempt to evade the strafing attacks. A few rubber rafts had been launched and there were several crew members on these but that was a decidedly dangerous position. *Leutnant* August Hoffmann, the principal machine-gunner during the attack on the *Peleus*, was attempting to get one of his wounded crew members onto a raft. At that moment a Wellington came down low and strafed the rafts and the men wading in the water. Hoffmann must suddenly have understood what it had been like for those *Peleus* survivors who had also been on rafts struggling to survive as he had murdered them with his machine-gun. Several men were killed in this strafing run and Hoffmann was wounded in the leg. Despite his wound he continued to help another crewman to wade through the surf to get to the beach.

Finally, all the surviving members of the U-boat's crew managed to get onto the beach. They were exhausted with the struggle to live, some were so badly wounded that they were obviously dying.

Meanwhile, as all these dramatic events were occurring, Heinz Eck had been attempting to destroy the submarine so that its secret equipment would not fall into the hands of the enemy. Even while the submarine had been under strafing attack he had attempted to destroy the boat using demolition charges but although the charges had exploded they had also failed to destroy U-852. Sadly one crewman had been killed. Eck also made another classic blunder at this important moment: he failed to destroy the submarine's war diary which contained a detailed account of the attack that had been made on the *Peleus*. This diary was to form a major document for the prosecution in the coming war crimes trial.

Details of the successful destruction and beaching of U-852 were radioed to British forces in the region and the following day a naval landing party supported by a unit of the Somaliland Camel Corps arrived at the scene. They came fully anticipating some kind of armed resistance but the surviving crew members of U-852 were completely defeated and gave up without a fight. When the boarding party examined the hulk of the submarine they discovered a wealth of information but not the war diary. The link to U-852 and the *Peleus* was not immediately established and this would only be made following investigations carried out by two naval intelligence officers, one British and the other American. These were a Lieutenant Burnett of the Royal Navy Volunteer Reserve and Lieutenant J.T. Rugh of the United States Naval Reserve. These two men were part of an organisation known as CSDIC – Combined Special Detachment Intelligence Collection.

The thirty-five surviving members of U-852's crew were taken into custody and transported to the British military base at Aden where they were interrogated by Lieutenant Burnett. At that time Burnett was in charge of the naval section of CSDIC. He decided that twelve of the men warranted further investigation including the submarine's doctor, Walter Weisspfenning.

At this time the American intelligence officer, Lieutenant J.T. Rugh, was unaware of Burnett's suspicions. In fact he had spent some time with Weisspfenning as a personal courtesy to the doctor, believing that as a non-combatant he would soon be repatriated to Germany to continue his medical work.

The twelve prisoners under suspicion, including Weisspfenning and Eck, were soon taken to Cairo and Heliopolis. Meanwhile Rugh began interrogating all twenty-two of the remaining prisoners, his suspicions growing every hour. He spent long periods questioning these men and writing extensive interrogation reports on their responses which finally told the terrible story of the *Peleus* massacre in some detail. Yet there was still a lot to be learned. Rugh wanted to delve even deeper. On 20 May he travelled to Heliopolis to collect nine of the submarine's crew, including Eck, and took them to Cairo. From there Eck and four members of his crew, at that time unnamed, were sent directly by air to England where they were to be closely interrogated. Rugh was still not quite certain what had happened as the boat's war diary had yet to be found, but he sent a telegram to intelligence authorities in the U.K. advising them that U-852 had been responsible for sinking the *Peleus*, although he did not inform them at that time that the surviving members of the crew had been machine-gunned in the water.

The intelligence officers in London at that time had no knowledge that they were about to be dealing with one of the worst crimes ever committed by a German U-boat crew – at least in this war, and were expecting only to be interrogating Eck on routine operational matters.

Meanwhile, Lieutenant Burnett decided to visit the wreck of the submarine where he was amazed to discover Eck's carefully written war diary. It was only now that the full truth began to come out. Burnett brought the submarine's chief engineer, Hans Lenz, back into his office for questioning. Until now Lenz had said nothing about the massacre. He had not wanted the shootings to take place and had attempted to prevent the massacre but he had also remained steadfastly silent on the issue during interrogation. Now, seeing the evidence before his eyes in the form of the war diary, Lenz made a full confession to Burnett, admitting that the crew of the ship had been machine-gunned in the water, that grenades had been used in an attempt to sink the rafts, and that it had all been carried out on the express orders of

Heinz Eck. Not only did Lenz make a complete confession, he also signed an affidavit which provided a full account of the massacre.

Lenz was placing himself fully in the frame as it was now a fact that he too had manned one of the machine-guns and had fired a short burst or two. What the investigators needed now was corroborating evidence to give firsthand testimony backing the evidence already discovered in the war diary, and in Lenz's testimony, and that meant at least one other person who had been on the bridge that night had to talk. Sadly, *Leutnant* Georg Colditz had been killed during the strafing attacks on the submarine or he would no doubt have corroborated Lenz's testimony as he too had protested to Eck before the massacre had taken place.

Lieutenants Burnett and Rugh now went to see the two lookouts who had been on the bridge during at least some of the period that the massacre had been taking place. These were *Matrosenobergefreiter* Johann Coirniak and *Obersteuermann* Wilhelm Schmidtz. Neither of these men had actually taken part in the shooting of the ship's survivors. Both men were quite willing to talk and both signed affidavits. When this information was passed to Cape Town the three surviving crew members of the *Peleus* were flown to Cape Town and there, on 7 June, 1944, they signed affidavits attesting to the facts of the case.

Meanwhile Lieutenant Rugh was tasked with a difficult mission. He was ordered to escort Coirniak and Schmidtz to London but he was also instructed to take Dr Weisspfenning with the other two prisoners. Weisspfenning did not know that Coirniak and Schmidtz had provided damning testimony to investigators and was under the impression that he might soon be repatriated as a non-combatant. It was one of Rugh's tasks to ensure that Weisspfenning never suspected why he was being sent to England and also to prevent him from becoming aware that the other two men had made their affidavits.

By 8 June, 1944, all the principal characters in this dark tragedy had been brought to London. These included Eck, Lenz, Hoffmann, Dr Weisspfenning and Schwender. It is almost certain that by now, having been intensively interrogated on the matter, they must have realised that war crimes charges might be brought against them. Even Weisspfenning must have been anxious that the interrogations had been so intense and that there was absolutely no discussion at all of his possible release. Yet at this time in the war no one was in a hurry to place these men on trial. It was now just two days after the Normandy landings and the focus of the entire British nation and also the Americans was getting their forces ashore and driving inland to defeat Hitler and bring an end to the war. All the suspects from U-852 were held in custody, their files were stamped top secret and they were allowed to stew for the remainder of the war.

*   *   *

What the five men must have believed as they were held in custody over the following months is not known, although they must have hoped that the war would soon end and that against a background of the monstrous atrocities of the Holocaust, for example, relatively minor war crimes such as theirs would fade into obscurity. By now it was becoming well known that Nazi Germany generally had been a festering sore of criminality for the entire period of Nazi control, commencing as far back as 1933 when Hitler had first come to power, so considering the masses of crimes committed by Nazi officials it seemed unlikely that too much time would be expended prosecuting what, by comparison, was a minor event on the grander scale of things. Yet Eck and his four companions were to be disappointed.

Five months after Hitler had shot himself and his bride, Eva Braun, in his Berlin bunker, the five suspects from U-852 were transported to Hamburg, where Heinz Eck had been born, and on 6 October, 1945, all five were formally charged with war crimes.

The first count was almost ludicrous as it charged the men with having sunk the *Peleus* 'in the violation of the laws and usages of war'. This charge was so outdated by events that it should never have been brought into court. It related to the original law that all merchant shipping, before being sunk, should be stopped, evacuated and the crews allowed to board lifeboats before the ship was sunk. It was a crime to torpedo a ship without warning. Of course few commanders had paid any attention to that rule during the First World War and it had never been applied by any sides of the conflict during the Second World War. If Eck and his men were to be charged with that crime then almost every submarine commander on both Axis and Allied sides would also have had to appear in courts of law to answer the same charge.

The second charge, however, was far more realistic and serious. The men were charged with, '… being concerned in the killing of members of the crew … by firing and throwing grenades at them'. As we shall see, Eck's defence against these charges was to assert that there had been no deliberate intention to kill anyone: he had been attempting only to sink the rafts and wreckage to prevent the detritus from being seen and pinpointing the scene of the attack. His second line of defence was that killing crew members in the water was justified as it was his duty as a commanding officer to protect his ship and crew and that by killing the men in the water he had been carrying out an 'operational necessity'.

The other defendants all relied on the defence that they had simply been obeying orders and that as serving members of the *Kriegsmarine* they had no choice in the matter.

The trial at Hamburg, which commenced on 17 October, 1945, was to last for four intense days. It was conducted as a British military court presided over by Brigadier C.I.V. Jones, C.B.E., commander of the 106 AA Brigade. The judge advocate was Major Aubrey Melford Steed Stevenson, K.C., who would later become one of the most controversial and outspoken High Court judges in modern British history. The prosecutor was Colonel R.C. Halse of the Military Department, Judge Advocate General's Office, while the jury was formed by three British army officers, two Royal Navy officers and two officers of the Royal Hellenic Navy, it being considered proper and diplomatic to have Greek representatives on the jury as the *Peleus* had been registered in Greece and many of its crew had been Greek.

It has to be said that despite the damning evidence and the provision of a very capable defence team it was unlikely that any of the accused would be found not guilty. The defendants were well represented by some of Germany's top legal experts led by Helmut Sieber, a *Kriegsmarine* judge who organised the defence team which included *Fregatten-Kapitän* Hans Meckel as a special adviser and Dr Harold Todson a well known Hamburg attorney who would both represent Heinz Eck.

The team also included two other attorneys: Dr Max Pabst and Dr P. Wulf. These men would both represent *Leutnant* Hoffmann. Pabst would also represent *Gefreiter* Wolfgang Schwender and Dr Weisspfenning.

Lenz selected his own legal representative. This was a Major Lermon, a barrister-at-law at the headquarters of the 8th Corps District.

Another attorney, Dr Albert Wegner, was retained to advise and present his opinions in regard to international law on behalf of all the defendants. As we will see later in this chapter, Wegner would make an emotional plea in defence of the five accused but his address to the court would frequently be interrupted if it was considered that he was wavering even slightly off the essential elements of international law.

The charge against all five men was:

Committing a war crime in that you in the Atlantic Ocean on the night of 13/14th March, 1944, when Captain and members of the crew of *Unterseeboat* 852 which sank the steamship *Peleus* in violation of the laws and usages of war were concerned in the killing of members of the crew of the said steamship, Allied nationals and throwing grenades at them.

These were difficult times for any German facing war crimes charges. The war had ended only months previously and by now people everywhere, right around the globe, were being made aware of the horror of Nazi oppression and murder on a scale that had never before been seen in the history of the world. War crimes had been the norm under Hitler's rule and they had been so massively omnipresent during the whole of the existence of the Nazi regime that it was difficult for anyone not to believe that almost everyone in Germany, military and civilians alike, must have known what was going on or have been complicit in it. Cinemas were now filled with people horrified at the *Pathe News* segments of emaciated bodies being bulldozed into communal graves at liberated concentration camps. War criminals were looked upon as being guilty until they were proven innocent, and even then, serious doubts remained.

One of the most profound aspects of the entire case was not that mass murder had been committed on the high seas. The war had already seen so much of that by all major participants: British, German, American, Russian and Japanese. They were all tarred with the same brush, although Allied war crimes were being kept secret at the time. What made this trial so newsworthy was the fact that a medical man, a doctor and non-combatant, was being charged with participating in the killing of innocent civilians when by all the international rules of war and by the rules of the *Kriegsmarine,* doctors, nurses and orderlies were prohibited from carrying and using firearms except for their own defence or in defence of their patients. The question on everyone's mind was: why would a doctor throw away his Hippocratic oath and begin taking lives rather than saving them?

The answer to that anomaly was complex and lies within the heart of the evidence and testimony that would be presented during the trial.

After some opening statements and the official checking that the names and ranks of the accused were correct, the charges were read and after some deliberation as to the precise meaning of the charges, particularly the term: 'In violation of the laws and usages of war' in relation to the sinking of merchant shipping, the men standing trial were asked to plead. All five stated that they were not guilty.

Over the course of that first day a number of witnesses gave damning testimony. The affidavits of the three men who had survived the sinking of the *Peleus* and the subsequent massacre in the water were also read to the court.

A number of the submarine's crew members, other than those charged, also described the events of that night. These included, for example, Able Seaman Wilhelm Schmidtz, the rating in charge of the small-arms on board the submarine. Schmidtz testified that he had been below decks during the massacre but had received Eck's order to bring up not only hand-grenades but also some small-arms including Mauser pistols and some machine-pistols. He had got the arms and five hand-grenades together and had taken them up on deck. It was about midnight. When he got there he found that one of the M.G.15 machine-guns had not been functioning and he had to check it. He testified that it had been fired at that time. He also testified that the following morning he did not check to see how much ammunition had been expended during the night but three of the five hand-grenades had been used. Additionally, he testified that the Mauser pistols and the machine-pistols had not been fired at all that night.

Weiner Hamesister had been the sick-berth attendant on the submarine that day. He testified that after the massacre he had treated *Leutnant* Hoffmann who had been suffering from a burnt hand. Hamesister asked Hoffmann what he had been doing and Hoffmann had replied that he had been throwing grenades. Hamesister had been on the bridge just before the massacre had commenced, although that was not his normal battle-station. One of his duties while in action was to act as a runner and, when surfaced, he was normally stationed at the foot of the bridge so that he could get to various parts of the deck quickly. However, just prior to the massacre he had been standing near the hatch on the bridge and therefore close to Eck but he claimed that there had been no direct order from Eck to any of his crew to target men in the water deliberately. He also claimed that none of the men on the rafts had been targeted although shooting at the rafts quite obviously meant that the men on them would also be shot. Hamesister also testified that during the five minutes or so that Lenz and Hoffmann had been interrogating the ship's third officer, Eck had impatiently told the sick-berth attendant to tell his two officers to hurry up with their questioning. He was evidently in a hurry to get on with what was to come next.

The next witness to present evidence to the court had nothing to do with the actual event. This was Mr John Coubro Mossop, a solicitor of the Supreme Court in London and commissioner for oaths who had been seconded to work as a civil servant at the Admiralty. Mossop had become involved in the case because he had been tasked with taking down a statement made by *Kapitänleutnant* (*Ing*) Hans Richard Lenz. He told the court that on 3 June, 1944, shortly after the prisoners had been transported to England, he had been asked to visit the London District prisoner-of-war cage to take Lenz's statement which was being made voluntarily in front of a witness who was an Admiralty intelligence officer. Even now, after the war, this officer's name was not to be released. The name was confirmed by Mossop after being passed to him on a slip of paper who nodded and stated that the name on the paper was that of the officer who had been present at the time.

Apart from having an opportunity to make an open, live statement in court, this was Lenz's best chance of saving himself from the firing squad and he was determined to make the best of it. During his statement he not only went into some of his own history in the submarine service but explained in detail why he had taken over the M.G.15 on that terrible night.

Lenz's statement demonstrated that he had been born at Hanover in 1917. He completed his final examination at Christmas 1935 and during the spring of 1936 had gone into the Labour Service before joining the *Kriegsmarine* at Stralsund that same year. He was then sent for training to the German Naval College at Flensburg. As part of his naval education he had served on board the training battleship *Schleswig-Holstein* (which would fire the first shots of World War Two by bombarding the Polish base at Westerplatte on 1 September, 1939. The ship would be bombed at Gotenhafen, [Gdynia] Poland, and sunk in 1944).

With the rank of midshipman, Lenz had also served aboard the battleship *Deutschland* after which he had been sent for further instruction to the naval college at Kiel. He was commissioned a *leutnant* (*ing* [engineer]) in October 1938. He was then appointed to a transport organisation at Wilhelmshaven and in December 1939 joined the U-boat service. The following year he was appointed to the Lehr Division at Neustadt. His first appointment as an engineer officer was aboard U-11, moving to U-453 in 1941. He subsequently served as an instructor at the Lehr Division before joining U-852 under the command of Heinz Eck.

Lenz's full statement was read to the court which explained how he had disagreed with Eck's decision to eliminate the evidence of the ship's sinking which, *ipso facto*, also meant killing the men who had survived the torpedo attack. Lenz was very careful to point out that he had been unable to prevent the massacre occurring by changing Eck's mind and therefore had gone below to write up a report about the conversation he had had with the freighter's third officer, Agis Kephalas. He was also very careful to point out that he had later taken over the M.G.15 to prevent Schwender from killing one of the men in the water or on a raft. Lenz stated that he had simply fired two or three short bursts of the machine-gun, '… with no result observed'.

During his time at the prisoner-of-war cage Lenz had not been in the least coy in showing a copy of his written statement to Eck. Three days after making the statement he had seen Eck in the cage and allowed Eck to read the statement, adding that other members of the crew had made similar statements. These statements very clearly demonstrated that everyone had simply been carrying out Eck's orders and that the entire concept of destroying the evidence had been Eck's. Upon reading Lenz's statement, Eck, apparently, had appeared unperturbed.

Three days later Eck made his own statement which was also read in court. The statement had been made before J.C. Mossop, commissioner for oaths, at the Number 3 Interrogation Centre. It was brief and to the point. In it Eck very clearly stated that neither before sailing from Kiel, nor at any time during the submarine's passage, had he received orders to shoot or in any other way eliminate survivors from any ships he might sink.

While this appeared on the surface to be quite a startling admission of guilt there were questions raised firstly about Eck having been cautioned before making the statement and also about the exact interpretation of his words. Eck was not fluent in English and his interrogators had been speaking in German with Eck's answers translated into English and then transcribed. These points were noted in the court and set aside for further deliberation.

Then however, the complete statement of the ship's chief officer, Antonios Liossis, was read to the court. Not one of the survivors appeared at the trial. By that time they were spread around the world on other ships but, as we have seen, they had made statements while at Cape Town shortly after being rescued.

Liossis statement as to his experiences were known to the court but in this full statement he made the startling claim that after the freighter's third officer, Agis Kephalas, had been interrogated by Lenz and returned to his raft, Liossis had heard someone on the submarine shouting the word 'Kill', or 'Kill them all', and immediately afterwards the machine-gun had begun firing. If this were true then Eck's entire defence of simply attempting to sink the rafts and wreckage would prove to have no meaning. If someone had shouted 'Kill them all' then the entire event became deliberate murder without any underlying excuses. Liossis also stated that, in contradiction to Eck's statement, the U-boat had, '… remained all night hunting out survivors who may still have been alive, using a search light', but Liossis and three other men had 'shammed dead'. He added that the U-boat had machine-gunned the rafts and wreckage all night, '… firing many bullets'. Liossis' statement had been made at Cape Town on 7 June, 1944.

This brought to a close the prosecution's case against the accused men. No statement had been made by Dr Walter Weisspfenning although while at the prisoner-of-war cage he had been given every opportunity to do so. The judge advocate, Major A. Melford Stevenson, now turned to the five accused men who were seated together in the courtroom. Stevenson advised them that they had three choices and that they should consider each choice carefully.

The first choice was for the men to give evidence on oath. If they chose this option then it was likely that they would be cross-examined on oath. The second choice was for each of them to make a statement without taking an oath. If they chose this option then no questions would be allowed. Not even the defending counsel would be allowed to question them. The third course of action they could adopt was to remain silent throughout the whole proceedings. However, as Stevenson very clearly pointed out, if they chose to give evidence on oath and thus opened themselves to cross-examination then considerably more weight and credence would be given to their testimony. Additionally, each of the accused was to be allowed to call witnesses for their defence.

Stevenson then asked each man in turn how they wished to proceed. Every one of the accused chose to appear as a witness and to give evidence in court, thus opening themselves to cross-examination. They all also stated that they would be calling witnesses in their defence. Some of these would be material witnesses while others would simply be character witnesses. Eck, Hoffmann, Weisspfenning and Schwender said they would call material witnesses while Lenz stated that his would be only a character witnesses. 'Is that right?' Stevenson asked, possibly a little surprised.

'That is quite right,' Lenz responded.

These events meant that each of the defending officers was now able to open the defence but there were already problems with this. Members of the defence team all claimed that they had been given barely enough time to prepare a proper defence for their clients and asked for a suitable adjournment in order to prepare for the trial. The defending counsel intended to rely on a defence of 'operational necessity' and particular German witnesses would need to appear in court. After considerable discussion it was decided to adjourn the trial until 14.15 hours (2.15 p.m.) the following afternoon. It

The commander and four other members of the crew of U-852 seen here during their war crimes trial at Hamburg in 1945. Left to right: Heinz Eck; August Hoffmann; Dr Walter Weisspfenning; Hans Lenz and Wolfgang Schwender. This photograph appeared in newspapers around the world at the time of the trial. (*Author's collection*)

was not nearly long enough but Stevenson, who just wanted to get on with the trial, gave them little choice in the matter.

The court reconvened on schedule for its second day when the judge advocate, Major A. Melford Stevenson, addressed Dr Harold Todson who would be defending Heinz Eck. Stevenson stated that as Eck was the first name of the list of those accused then Todson should have the privilege of making his opening statement. Major Lermon, defending Lenz, then stated that this issue had already been discussed among the defending counsel and that three of them wished to make opening statements: himself, Harold Todson and Dr Max Pabst. Stevenson granted these requests.

When Todson began his opening address he pointed out that his client, Heinz Eck, had not carried out the act of using a machine-gun on the rafts, and by inference the men in them, out of 'cruelty or revenge', but had merely been attempting to, 'eliminate all traces of the sinking'.

Professor Wegner, the international law expert representing all the accused, spoke about particular precedents, referring to a number of historic cases and made the point that destroying evidence in an attempt at self preservation had been used in the past on several occasions.

These details having at least been brought up, at this stage, the principal witness in the case, Heinz Eck, was called. This was the testimony which everyone in the room had been waiting to hear.

Questioned by his defence lawyer, Dr Harold Todson, Eck explained that prior to leaving Berlin to return to Kiel it had been impressed upon him by *Kapitänleutnant* Adalbert Schnee at BdU, and others, that submarine warfare was now of specific importance and that U-boats were at that time the only offensive weapon left in Germany's once powerful arsenal. Despite the 'secret' weapons being trialed by Hitler at that time this was a fairly accurate estimation of the situation during that period, with Germany unable to keep up its arms manufacture due to blockades and bombing and the fact that the German surface fleet was either captive in ports or rusting at the bottom of the sea. This was January 1944, six months before the Normandy landings when the situation would become a whole lot worse for the Germans.

Therefore Eck went away from that meeting in Berlin heavy with a sense of responsibility. The dangers and responsibilities had again been pointed out to Eck at Kiel, specifically the dangers of aircraft and the need for concealment. He had clearly been made aware of the Allied patrols coming from Ascension and Freetown and that a number of U-boats manned by highly experienced commanders and crews had been sunk in the vicinity.

The questioning went on to describe the location and sinking of the *Peleus* and why Eck had made the decision to attempt to destroy the wreckage. At one point Todson asked Eck, had it been clear to him, when he had issued the order to destroy the rafts, that in doing so the survivors would also be killed. Eck was unequivocal in his response: 'It was clear to me that the possibility of saving their lives disappeared,' he said. He added that it had not been possible for him to take survivors aboard the submarine because that had been specifically against his orders. He added that as the submarine still had a long war cruise to complete there would not have been sufficient provisions to feed everyone.

Eck was also asked to comment about the claim that the words: 'Kill them all' had been shouted on the bridge. Eck resolutely refuted the accusation. He stated that no person had used that term on the bridge and that it was impossible to believe anyone would have spoken those words, in English, which was the language reported as having been used that night.

When asked if he believed that any other submarine commander, having been placed in the same situation, would have acted in the same way and made the same decisions, Eck responded by telling the story of a U-boat under the command of Captain Hartenstein which had sunk the liner *Laconia* in 1942. Testimony subsequently presented during the trial provided further details of the sinking of the *Laconia* and its relevence to Eck's actions.

The *Laconia* had been carrying more than 1500 Italian prisoners-of-war, a Polish guard detachment and a number of English women. After the ship had been sunk Hartenstein had heard Italian voices calling for assistance in the water. When this had been established Hartenstein had contacted BdU headquarters and had begun efforts to take on board as many survivors as possible, including the women, and to tow the ship's lifeboats to a rendezvous with a French cruiser. However, the U-boat had been sighted by an Allied aircraft and despite the fact that it was now carrying Red Cross markings indicating that there were wounded or survivors on board, the aircraft had dropped a stick of depth-charges, damaging the submarine. Hartenstein had been forced to abandon the lifeboats and dive, although the U-boat had sustained some damage. Hartenstein had subsequently reported these events to BdU and orders had then been issued from BdU that rescue operations were not to be undertaken by U-boats.

In fact the order from BdU had been very specific:

No attempt of any kind should be made at rescuing members of ships sunk. And this includes picking up persons in the water and putting them in lifeboats, righting capsized lifeboats and handing over food and water. Rescue runs counter to the rudimentary demands of warfare for the destruction of enemy ships and crews. Orders for bringing Captains and Chief Engineers still apply. Rescue the shipwrecked only if their statements will be of importance to your boat. Be harsh, have in mind that the enemy takes no regard of women and children in his bombing attacks on German cities.

Eck told the court that the *Laconia* case and its subsequent orders had been drilled home to him before he had commenced his voyage aboard U-852 and that in his mind, '... military reasons go before human reasons before saving the lives of survivors. For that reason I thought my measures were justified.'

Eck was also questioned at this time by the prosecutor, Colonel R.C. Halse, who cut deeply into Eck's apparent coldness towards human life. From Eck, Halse ascertained that there had been about six rafts in the water at that time, at least that was the number he had been able to see in the darkness, each raft had been about 2.5 square metres. Halse evidently wanted to make the point that Eck had felt no compassion at all for the survivors. Halse asked if Eck had made any enquiry from the ship's third officer when being questioned as to the number of survivors in the water. Eck answered that he had not, adding, At that time it did not seem important to me.' When asked how many people would be left on the rafts, Eck had responded, 'I did not take any interest in that.' When questioned about taking any action to help the survivors Eck stated, 'I could not help them.'

Halse was unremitting in his questioning. He demanded to know the specific times that the machine-gunning had commenced and when it had ended. Eck attempted to ward off the questions claiming he did not know the times and stating for some unknown reason that the boat had been operating on Central European Time. Halse pointed out that it did not matter how the ship's chronometer had been set, he just needed to establish how long the firing had been kept up. Eck was finally forced to admit that it had been about five hours and that it had only been stopped at around 0100 hours (1 a.m.) because by that time it had become obvious that no matter what actions were taken none of the rafts were going to sink. 'I saw no further possibility to destroy the rafts,' Eck stated. 'I tried it with machine-gun fire, hand-grenades and also through ramming, but it was no good.'

Halse jumped in at that point: 'Was it not because there were no more survivors left?'

'I did not concern myself with that,' Eck replied coolly.

As we have seen, using the boat's loudspeaker system Eck had subsequently addressed the crew of the submarine about the incident, being aware that the killing of the survivors had affected morale. Colonel Halse was fully aware of this communication and its content and he questioned Eck about it now because it pressed home the fact that as far as the survivors were concerned Eck had felt absolutely no compassion towards them. Halse asked Eck to repeat a sentence that he had spoken to his crew that day. The sentence was, 'If we are influenced by too much sympathy, we must think of our wives and children who at home die also as victims of air attack.'

'Sympathy about the wreckage?' Halse asked.

'It was quite clear that the survivors would also die,' Eck responded.

'And you did not mind whether they died or not?' Halse pressed.

'In my remarks over the loudspeaker I had said that I did not care about it,' Eck answered.

'You realised that people would die as a result of the shooting?'

'Yes,' Eck responded without any further embellishment.

After a few more questions along similar lines the court adjourned. It reassembled at ten o'clock the following morning when Eck was again brought to the stand to complete his testimony. At this time Major Lermon, the officer defending Lenz, got straight to the point in establishing the case for his client. Lenz had objected to Eck's order to begin shooting at the rafts and by definition also the men on them but Lermon wished to establish that Lenz had no real choice in the matter. He had made his case and his objection had been brushed off by Eck.

'Is it a serious offence to disobey an order on active operations?' Lermon asked.

'For not carrying out an order in the face of the enemy one is punished with death,' Eck answered.

Lermon pushed the point, asking who would have the right to carry out that punishment and Eck replied that he, as the commanding officer, would have that right.

As the cross-examination proceeded a number of important points were made including the fact that Eck had ordered only three men to fire, Weisspfenning, Hoffmann and Schwender, although why Eck had ordered his doctor to fire remains a mystery, given that Weisspfenning was a non-combatant. Schwender's character was also put into question principally because Lenz had claimed he was a man of 'bad character' and that it was not right that the survivors should be killed by such a person. When asked about Schwender's character Eck replied that he had received many complaints about him.

There was also a clear case where Eck was attempting to confuse the issue. The previous day when asked what speed the submarine was capable of when surfaced Eck had responded that it could do five knots per hour. It's possible that members of the court, none of whom were submariners, could have let that one slide, although there were naval officers among the jury who would probably have noted the obvious inaccuracy. The implication here was that if the submarine did only five knots on the surface then Eck really had a better excuse for machine-gunning the rafts as it would have been almost impossible for him to get away from the scene of the sinking before being seen. However, the truth of the matter was that U-852 was easily capable of doing eighteen knots on the surface, it was actually rated for twenty knots, and if Eck had ordered full speed ahead immediately after he had torpedoed the *Peleus* then by seven-thirty the following morning he could, theoretically have been around 216 nautical miles or 400 kilometres

Adalbert Schnee with some of his crew on the bridge of his U-boat prior to taking up his appointment with *Befehlshaber der Unterseeboote* (BdU) in Berlin. He would later testify at Eck's war crimes trial. (*Bundesarchiv, Bild 101II-MW-4060-37, Bundesarchiv*)

away from the sinking. A distance of this kind was only theoretical and it would depend on a number of issues such as weather, sea conditions, engine performance etc. Yet that being the case, Eck's decision to destroy the rafts and the survivors was completely nonsensical. If the submarine could have achieved a distance of 400 kilometres from the sinking within twelve hours, or even only two thirds that, submerging at around 7.30 the following morning and then continuing at a slower pace underwater, it would have been unlikely for any Allied aircraft or surface ship to have found him. Eck deliberately misinformed the court when he said that U-852 was capable of five knots when surfaced. That was actually a little lower than its speed when submerged while running under battery power.

Yet it appeared for a while that Eck was about to get a major boost to his defence when his friend, Captain Adalbert Schnee, was called to the stand. As we have seen, Schnee had worked at the submarine headquarters BdU during the war and had met with Eck in Berlin where he had expressed his concerns over the vulnerabilities of the submarine type and had advised Eck to be extra careful to cover his tracks. During the trial Schnee backed up Eck's reasoning for his actions to the hilt, stating that he had specifically informed Eck of the dangers, that all four submarines sent into action in that particular area, despite being commanded by highly experienced officers, had been destroyed, and that it would be wise to destroy any evidence of a sinking before departing the scene in order to prevent being located by Allied aircraft or warships.

When Schnee was asked if it would have been wiser for Eck to leave the scene immediately and not bother about attempting to destroy the wreckage, Schnee very clearly stated that leaving the scene would have been a mistake and that what Eck had done was the correct action if he were to avoid being found by enemy aircraft. He also pointed out that in his opinion using a machine-gun would have been the best option to destroy the rafts as they presented a low, flat target which would have been very difficult to hit with any other weapon and that a machine-gun would pepper the target, destroying its buoyancy.

However, Schnee then also made the startling comment that the long and very arduous journey undertaken by U-852, travelling for lengthy periods submerged, and especially when it had reached tropical waters where the temperature in the submarine would have increased dramatically, would have been very difficult on the boat's crew and even more difficult on its commander. 'I can fully realise that the commander after such a journey may possibly lose his head,' Schnee told the court.

The official records of the trial do not indicate what the immediate reaction to that comment might have been, although if the trial had been held in an open public court rather than a closed military tribunal there might well have been gasps of amazement. Yet Schnee quickly realised that he had said too much. He was immediately questioned about his own war experiences and what he would have done under similar circumstances. He told the court that he had commanded four different submarines during the war and had sunk about thirty ships, mostly when he had been operating with wolf-packs in the North Atlantic but also hunting alone. In fact he had also patrolled the same area of the South Atlantic where U-852 had destroyed the *Peleus*. Schnee told the court that after the attacks he had personally carried out he had always left the scene as quickly as possible and not hung around to destroy wreckage. Yet he qualified this statement by adding that the situation in the North Atlantic was vastly different to that of the South Atlantic. In the north the Allies had been aware that German submarines had constantly been in the region so attempting to hide the evidence of a sinking would have been pointless. Whereas submarines operating in the South Atlantic had worked largely alone and with the utmost secrecy so attempting to destroy the evidence of a sinking made perfect sense.

The prosecutor jumped onto these points, asking Schnee what he would have done if he had been in Eck's shoes. Schnee now, however, became elusive as he apparently did not wish to open himself up to any kind of investigation into his own war background with any possibility it might have for him also to be charged with war crimes. His discomfort with the question was noted by Major Lermon who said that Schnee should be advised that he did not have to answer the question if he thought it might incriminate him. The judge advocate, Major Stevenson, then told Schnee, '… You can refuse to answer a question if you think it might expose you to prosecution for a war crime.'

When the question was again presented to Schnee he would only state that he did not know the case well enough to give an answer. Stevenson, who was now questioning Schnee as closely as Halse, responded that Schnee could do better than that as Schnee was completely conversant with the case. Schnee would now only mutter in German, words that were not translated for the court, and when asked again for his answer Schnee would only respond that it was very difficult for him to give an answer to that question. 'Now that the war is over I cannot possibly put myself in such a difficult position as Captain Eck was at that time,' Schnee responded.

'The fact that the war has ended has not deprived you of your imagination has it?' Halse asked rather querulously.

Schnee thought about that for a few moments before making an explosive comment: 'I would under all circumstances have tried my best to save lives, as that is a measure which was taken by all U-boat commanders; but when I hear of this case, then I can only explain it as this, that Captain Eck through the terrible experience he had been through lost his nerves.'

'Does that mean that you would not have done what Captain Eck did if you had kept your nerve?' Halse asked.

'I would not have done it.' Schnee replied.

Why Schnee gave this damning testimony is a moot point. During his meeting with Eck in Berlin prior to the departure of U-852 on its war patrol to the South Atlantic Schnee had very clearly advised Eck to destroy any wreckage and had even advocated such an action when he had first begun giving evidence. Yet now he was stating that he would not have done so had he been in command of the submarine at that time and that his friend had simply lost his nerve. What Eck must have been feeling when he heard this damning and conflicting testimony was never, of course, recorded by the court.

Schnee told the court that during his work at BdU he had never heard of any other German U-boat commander taking action that resulted in the machine-gunning of survivors in the water. He had actually been quite unaware of the fate of U-852 until he had read in the newspapers that Eck was being held in London pending a trial. Yet when asked once again, had he been in Eck's position, if he would he have destroyed the wreckage, Schnee surprisingly now responded that he would have attempted to do so because quite clearly any destruction of the rafts would have meant the probable deaths of the men on them, even had they survived the machine-gunning. This statement conflicted completely with the testimony Schnee had given only moments before.

Having heard this wildly confusing and conflicting testimony the cross-examination was now taken over by Dr Max Pabst who was representing both Hoffmann and the lower ranking Schwender. Pabst was keen to establish that his clients had simply been obeying orders when they machine-gunned the rafts and men and that they had no choice in the matter. Pabst established through his questioning that obedience on U-boats was total. Schnee stated that in all the years he had commanded submarines he never once had to deal with any kind of disobedience from his crews. He told the court that if disobedience had occurred and especially if that disobedience had endangered the boat he would have had no hesitation in resorting to the use of arms. In other words, he would have been quite willing to shoot anyone who disobeyed his command. This at least established for the court that Weisspfenning, Hoffmann and Schwender, all of whom had received a direct order from their captain to open fire, had no choice in the matter. Pabst did not, however, explore the possibilities of those men refusing to obey an order that was quite obviously illegal under international law because had he done so it would have weakened his case that the men were forced by military discipline to obey the order to fire. Only Lenz, and apparently one other man, Georg Colditz, who was now deceased, had attempted to reason with Eck before the murders but their attempts to save the lives of the survivors on the rafts had proved fruitless.

It now came time for *Leutnant sur See* August Hoffmann to give his evidence but before he was called to the stand Dr Max Pabst, who was defending Dr Weisspfenning, Hoffmann and Schwender, was asked if he wished to make his opening defence statement on behalf of the accused. Pabst addressed the court in German which was translated into English for the remainder of the court members. Pabst stated that not one of his clients had wanted to shoot at the men on the rafts. '… in their action they were lacking forethought', Pabst admitted. He added that the three men had been acting on orders and at the time had no idea that by doing so they would be opening themselves up to possible prosecution. Pabst added that had they disobeyed their orders they would have been placed, '… into imminent danger of life themselves'. Pabst told the court that Schwender did not kill anyone nor had he wanted to. He added that each of the defendants wanted to prove their innocence by giving their testimony to the court. Pabst then called Hoffmann to the stand.

August Hoffmann was just twenty-three years of age at the time he was on trial for his life. He had been born in Hamburg on 4 June, 1922. Prior to the First World War his father had served as an officer in the German Merchant Marine so it is rather surprising that Hoffmann would have wanted to serve in the submarine service, the precise objective of which was the destruction of shipping, particularly freighters and tankers. After the war his father had become a merchant. His mother was a teacher. Hoffmann had been brought up in a non-political environment and educated at a national school. He had made a decision to go to sea at a very early age and more specifically the decision to join the *Kriegsmarine* had come upon the outbreak of war and had been influenced by a cousin who had been the commanding officer of a submarine.

Hoffmann told the court that he had been eighteen years of age when he had first joined the *Kriegsmarine* in October 1940 and that at the time of the sinking of the *Peleus* he had been twenty-one. Under Pabst's questioning he stated that obedience was something that had been drilled into him as part of his training, adding, 'I have learned that when facing the enemy there was no such thing as disobedience and that it would be punished by death.'

Hoffmann confirmed much of what the court already knew of the tragedy. He had received a direct order from Eck, who had been standing close to Hoffmann at the time he had given the order. Hoffmann did not even think of questioning the order as he realised that by leaving the wreckage and rafts, the submarine would be in danger of discovery and that by disobeying his orders to destroy the rafts he would effectively be placing the boat in greater danger. Disobedience meant execution and he was never going to disobey his captain. He also admitted that this was the first time he had been in action and that as a result he had been excited by the events that were occurring. He confirmed that Weisspfenning had been the first to fire, Hoffmann had taken over after the machine-gun had jammed and had then continued firing at the rafts. He also admitted that it was he who had suggested to the captain that the 3.7cm cannon should be used but that Eck had told him it would not depress sufficiently to hit the rafts and that Hoffmann should try with the 2cm cannon. Hoffmann had used that weapon on the rafts but it too had achieved little or no results so the attempt had been abandoned.

When also questioned by Dr Harold Todson, the man defending Eck, Hoffmann very specifically stated that he had been on the bridge all through the events of that night and had never heard the words 'Kill them all', as had already been alleged during the court proceedings. Of course, even if he had heard those words Hoffmann would never have admitted to doing so as it would have been an admission of murder. 'I was on the bridge the whole time and I heard nothing,' Hoffmann stated. 'I would have heard it.' However, despite the fact that he claimed to having been on the bridge during the whole period, he also admitted that he had not been on the bridge to hear Lenz begging Eck to spare the survivors. This important point was not followed up by the prosecutor, Colonel Halse of the Advocate General's Office, who, through Hoffmann's admission, was given a golden opportunity to challenge the veracity of Hoffmann's statement. Hoffmann had just claimed that he had not been on the bridge at the time Lenz had begged Eck to spare the survivors but only minutes before he had stated that he had been on the bridge the whole time and had not heard the 'Kill them all' order. It was a classic opportunity for Halse to have been able to place pressure on the veracity of Hoffmann's testimony but it was not acted upon. If Hoffmann had admitted to hearing Lenz making his plea to Eck then it might have provided Hoffmann with just the germ of conscience that what he was about to do was both illegal and immoral. He would also not have wanted to admit in court that such a thought was on his mind at the time he began to pull the trigger of the M.G.15. On the other hand he would also not have wanted to admit that a 'Kill them all' order had been issued as that would have made him one of the principal perpetrators in the murders. Hoffmann was attempting to have it both ways.

He also attempted to act as if he believed that the rafts had been unoccupied at the time they were being fired upon and his testimony to the court was almost ludicrous, given the circumstances. He admitted that after the sinking when the rafts had been bobbing about in the water they had all displayed small lights. Then, for reasons Hoffmann would later not state, the men on the rafts had been ordered by those on the submarine's bridge to extinguish their lights. Almost immediately the lights on the rafts had been extinguished, firmly establishing that the rafts were then occupied by survivors and that the survivors were willing to obey the orders being issued by the Germans. 'You knew then that there were people on the rafts?' Colonel Halse questioned.

'We had to assume that,' Hoffmann responded.

'You fired at the rafts?'

'Yes.'

'Knowing there were people on them?'

'No.'

'How then were the lights put out?' Halse queried.

'By the people who were on the rafts in the first place, originally,' Hoffmann replied.

'Where had they gone between the time the lights were put out and the time you started to fire?' Halse continued.

'I thought they jumped into the water,' Hoffmann replied, without bothering to go into the fact that the men on the rafts would in no way have jumped into the shark-infested water before the firing had commenced and that if any of them had managed to jump into the water it would only have happened *after* they had come under fire.

Under slightly more pressure from Halse, Hoffmann later stated that now he was facing the court (and a possible death penalty) he did not think it was right that he and the others had fired, '… at helpless people in the water, or sitting on rafts', but at the time the implications of doing so had not entered his head. Clearly, the thought of an impending firing squad had managed somehow to realign his moral compass.

Soon afterwards Hoffmann again changed his testimony stating that he had been on the bridge when Lenz had made his protest to Eck. He had not heard the exact words but he had been close enough to know that Lenz had been in the process of begging for the survivors' lives. Halse now decided to press him on this. He asked Hoffmann to admit that when he realised that Lenz was pleading for the lives of the men in the water, had it not occurred to Hoffmann that what they were doing might have been wrong. Hoffmann responded, 'I did not think about it because at that moment the *Stabsarzt* [doctor] went to the M.G. and started firing, I believed that I could have stayed clear of the matter.' Hoffmann went on to explain, under more questioning, that when he used the term 'stayed clear of the matter' he meant that he had spoken to the ship's third officer and had advised him that he and the other men would be rescued the following day and that he felt sorry for him now that he was to be fired upon.

'If those thoughts had passed through your mind at that time it was quite clear to you then that what you were doing was wrong, was it not?' Halse insisted.

'No' Hoffmann responded coldly. He evidently realised that he had just admitted to having acknowledged to himself that murder was about to be committed and that he had every intention of assisting in the crime. He also admitted to throwing grenades into the rafts but on no account would he admit to seeing any men or bodies on the rafts nor would he admit to seeing bodies or survivors in the water. It was almost as if he had been functioning blind at the time. The inference that he had participated in the murders, knowing full well that he was committing murder, was poignantly clear. Hoffmann had taken the stand in an effort to defend his actions, having been warned that he would open himself up to penetrating cross-examination and while that examination itself had left much to be desired, Hoffmann had succeeded only in condemning himself and emphasising that he was suffering from a classic case of selective memory.

Hoffmann was also, later that day, to attempt to exonerate himself by stating that at the time of the shooting he really had had little time to think and he had not wanted to make himself guilty of disobedience. 'I had complete trust in the commandant and the righteousness of his orders,' Hoffmann said. 'I also know that he had orders and instructions of a secret nature which were not known to me. I thought the order was necessary on military grounds.' Then Hoffmann again contradicted his own previous testimony. Questioned by Halse, he admitted that he had taken over the machine-gun from Weisspfenning to clear the jam and continued firing at his own volition, having received no order from Eck to do so. Halse asked if he had been ordered by Weisspfenning to take over the gun but again Hoffmann stated that the doctor had not given him that order. 'So why did you take over the machine-gun?' Halse questioned.

'Because I had received a direct order from the commandant' Hoffmann stated.

No one now really knew what Hoffmann was saying.

'From the commandant?' Halse pressed, completely confused.

'Yes,' Hoffmann responded.

'When you took over that machine-gun was it working?'

'There was a stoppage – a defect.'

'Did you put it in order?'

'Yes.'

'And having put it in order did you continue to fire?'

'Yes.'

'Did the orders which you received directly from the commandant provide for putting it in order,' Halse continued.

'No,' Hoffmann answered.

'You did that on your own initiative?'

'Yes.'

This completely confusing evidence finally ended Hoffmann's testimony on the stand. Quite clearly there were issues he was not prepared to reveal and those he would talk about were both conflicting in content and confusing in their truthfulness and veracity.

The next person to take the witness stand was Dr Walter Weisspfenning whose testimony served only to assist the prosecution in their case. Questioned initially by Dr Max Pabst, his defence counsel, Weisspfenning would only admit to shooting briefly at a piece of wreckage and stating that he had not targeted any of the rafts. Under cross-examination he refused to admit that he had seen anyone on the rafts or in the water, nor would he acknowledge that there were any survivors despite the fact that when he had come up onto the bridge he had clearly heard the survivors in the water blowing their lifejacket whistles. He also refused, at first, to admit that, as a non-combatant, he was not permitted by law to use offensive weapons and that when Eck had turned to him and said, 'You shoot' he had obeyed the order immediately because, 'It was an order, it was during an action of battle, I had known the commander for a long period, and I did not have the impression that he would issue a wrong command to me.' Weisspfenning failed to point out when saying this that there was no battle going on at the time. No one was shooting back. He failed to acknowledge that the unarmed men in the water were principally non-combatant seamen who were simply struggling to survive under terrible circumstances. He did admit that he had been excited at the time as this was his first sinking, but would never admit that he had enjoyed firing the weapon, although this was the first time he had used a machine-gun. 'Everybody was excited,' he said. He also stated that he had never heard a 'Kill them all' order.

At first Weisspfenning attempted to deny any knowledge that the Geneva Convention prevented non-combatants from using weapons of war, despite the fact that it was pointed out to him, on two occasions, that he and other medical staff were only given the protection they enjoyed because they were prevented from carrying or using arms. Finally Weisspfenning was forced to admit that was the case but his elusiveness in responding to this simple and obvious question and the fact that he was evidently fully aware of the legalities of his personal protection in war as a medical man did nothing to assist his case in front of the court. If he could be so elusive on this simple matter, what else was he hiding and how much of what he was saying was actually the truth?

Now came what was obviously going to be one of the most interesting testimonies before the court: the statement of the one man on trial who had attempted to prevent the entire massacre: the submarine's engineer officer *Kapitänleutnant (Ing)* Hans Richard Lenz.

Hans Lenz was twenty-eight at the time of his trial for war crimes. He had been born in Hanover and came from a well respected family of lawyers. His parents were then living in Berlin but Lenz was very concerned about them because he had not heard from them for some time and Berlin had undergone massive Allied bombardment.

Lenz had attended school in Berlin and in 1936, upon leaving school, he had joined the *Kriegsmarine*. He had become a submariner in 1940, subsequently being promoted to chief engineer and serving in that capacity aboard three U-boats including U-852.

Unlike many of the men on board U-852, Lenz was a veteran. He had carried out a total of seven war patrols which was something of a rarity when Allied forces had largely perfected anti-submarine techniques. He had been decorated for his services receiving the Iron Cross First and Second Class. His reputation and war record were spotless and during his entire career in the navy he had never been disciplined for any reason.

Lenz came to the stand as something of a curiosity. By now the court was aware of the actions Lenz had taken in an effort to prevent Heinz Eck proceeding with his intentions of destroying the evidence of the sinking of the *Peleus* and *ipso facto* the killing of the survivors of that event. In fact, in an oblique way the court was also aware of Lenz's inherent character. There had been one point in the trial when *Leutnant* Hoffmann had been giving evidence and Hoffmann had inferred that he had not actually been able to hear what Lenz had been saying to the captain when he had been making his protest. However, Hoffmann had not been surprised to discover later that Lenz had been attempting to save the survivors' lives. Lenz was known among the crew as a caring and ethical man with strong principles and morality. Yet there was also the rather irregular connecting tissue of Lenz's actions and the court wanted to know more about this. If Lenz had so vehemently protested against Eck's murderous command, why then had he been willing to take over the M.G.15 from Schwender?

Until now the, at times, conflicting and confusing testimonies of the defendants had done little to assist them in their defence. Eck had been cold and precise with, apparently, little regret for his actions; Hoffmann had been elusive and contradictory while Weisspfenning had been elusive and obfuscatory. Now it was Lenz's turn to attempt to stem the damning evidence against him in relation to his having fired some of the shots that night. Major Lermon, representing Lenz, clearly believed that the best way for him to defend his client was to give a balanced opening address and then leave the rest to Lenz.

Lenz answered the questions put to him by Lermon with clarity and apparent honesty. Unlike all those who had gone before him he never attempted to obfuscate or avoid the questions. He went through the entire sequence of events, stating that he had been below decks at the time of the attack on the *Peleus* and had only come to the bridge after the ship had gone down. At that time he had been ordered by Eck to go forward and question one of the survivors to obtain the ship's name and other relevant details. When he had gone to the bows of the submarine he had not known what Eck had planned for the survivors and only learned of the coming massacre when he had returned to the bridge to give his report to Eck. That was the moment he had made his protest to Eck in an attempt to save the survivors' lives. Eck had told him that despite his protest it was his intention to have his order carried out. Lenz realised that there was nothing more he could do at that point. He had gone below to write his report of the conversation he had just had with the ship's third officer and to supervise the reloading of the torpedo tubes. Then the gunfire had commenced above.

'I heard the captain had decided to eliminate all trace of the sinking. I informed him that I did not agree, but since it was an order it had to be carried out,' Lenz said. His words were subsequently published in the world press.

Finally he had gone topside. He had seen pieces of wreckage in the water but no rafts. Then he heard someone on the bridge say that a 'shadow' had been sighted on one of the pieces of wreckage and that it looked like a human form. At that moment Lenz had looked towards Schwender who was manning the M.G.15 on the port side of the tower. Schwender was already swinging and aiming the weapon at what was, apparently, a human form and Lenz had roughly pushed him out of the way and fired a burst of the gun. 'I thought that if Schwender fired on those pieces of wreckage a human being who I had spoken to a short while ago might be hit and killed', Lenz told the court, '... and I did not want that man should be hit by bullets which a soldier, who, in my eyes, was considered bad, had fired.'

Lenz attempted to explain that during the training undertaken as the ship's workup for sea, he had experienced a lot of trouble with Schwender.

He also told the court he believed that Schwender was the father of an illegitimate child, although he later stated that in this instance he had been wrong about the child.

'Are you normally a person of excitable temperament?' Lermon asked.

'Yes,' Lenz admitted. 'I easily lose my temper.'

Lenz was cross-examined by several other members of the defendant's counsel. He stated that after he had snatched the weapon from Schwender he had aimed at a piece of wreckage but had not seen anyone on it before he had fired. He had not been on the bridge during the first part of the massacre therefore it was impossible for him to know if anyone had stated, 'Kill them all'. When questioned by Colonal Halse, Lenz admitted that he had never received an order from Eck to fire and that he had only fired to prevent Schwender from doing so. He had been hoping to save a life rather than taking one, or at least giving the man on the raft an honourable death. When asked if he would have taken the gun away from any other man but Schwender, Lenz responded that he would not have interfered. He only acted so that Schwender would not have the opportunity to kill the person who allegedly had been spotted on the raft.

Lenz's sole defence rested on his having protested the massacre to Captain Eck. His justification for taking the gun away from Schwender seemed a little confusing, given the fact that he had fired at the wreckage, and although he had been unable to see anyone on that wreckage, or nearby, the very act of firing a machine-gun into the water under those circumstances might have meant that some of the survivors could have been killed. This was an issue which would trouble the jury as they made their deliberations concerning the fate of the five men.

The next and final defendant to testify at the trial was Wolfgang Schwender himself, the man who had caused so much confusion in Lenz's actions on the bridge and for his defence. Schwender was being defended by two men conjointly, Dr Max Pabst and Dr P. Wulf.

Schwender was an inexperienced youth, just nineteen years of age at the time of the sinking of the *Peleus*. His inexperience and youthful brashness might have been the root of the hostility felt by other members of the crew, particularly the very experienced Lenz, a veteran of so many war patrols who knew the ropes and was well versed in the many problems associated with the operations of being on active service in the hostile conditions of a submarine at war.

At the time of his testimony Schwender was twenty years of age and was finding the stress of the criminal proceedings rather overwhelming. On the night before his twentieth birthday he had attempted to commit suicide in his cell but had failed. The method he had chosen in the attempt to take his life was not revealed in court documents but it must have been not too injurious because the following day the press was reporting on the suicide attempt while also adding that Schwender was, '... much brighter today'.

During his testimony Schwender admitted to firing the machine-gun and relied totally on the defence that he was simply obeying orders. 'Schwender, fire on the wreckage.' Eck had ordered. Schwender had done exactly that because, as he later testified, 'I realised that the commanding officer had the right of martial law at sea. If I would not execute his order he would make use of it.'

Schwender refused to acknowledge that the order to fire had been illegal but after being asked what sense the order might have had, he made the curious reply that he thought that: '... empty bodies were to be pierced'.

Schwender resolutely stated that he never fired on any people and that he had only targeted the rafts. By that time the moon had risen so he claimed that he could clearly see there were no people on the rafts which were only about thirty-five metres from the submarine. At the time he had been quite calm, or so he claimed in his testimony, although everyone else on the boat appeared to have been quite excited by the dramatic events. The cross-examination of Schwender also brought another interesting detail. He had once been a prisoner-of-war, although the details of that event were not revealed during the trial. Schwender himself only mentioned it because he stated that he had never failed to obey the orders of an officer even when he had been a P.O.W.

Schwender admitted that one of the lookouts on the bridge that night had called out that there appeared to have been a human form on or near one of the pieces of wreckage, but when the prosecutor, Colonel Halse, asked him if the lookout's call was basically an instruction that there was a human being to target with the M.G.15, Schwender became elusive. 'I only executed the order of the commanding officer,' he said.

Schwender's testimony failed to produce any new evidence other than that which had already been presented to the court. He left the stand without either strengthening or weakening his case, other than to demonstrate that he would obey orders totally, and that he really had no knowledge of the differences between right and wrong when it came to international law and orders that might have been illegal.

However, Schwender's ignorance of the law was fairly universal. As we have seen in literally thousands of cases since that time, ordinary people, soldiers and officials who served during the period of Nazi oppression, obeyed the orders of their superiors believing them to have been legal and correct even though in some cases those orders were resulting in the deaths of thousands and then millions of people. Schwender was no exception.

Yet the next man on the stand at least attempted to explain and deal with this vitally important issue. This was Dr Albert Wegner, a highly experienced lawyer, legal author, and expert on international law. It was his job to make the case for all five defendants. After Schwender left the stand the judge advocate, Major Stevenson, called for Wegner to make his case for the defence of the five accused. It was now the afternoon of the third day of the trial, Wegner was actually exhausted, having spent most of the previous night preparing for this moment, but did not want to make his case at that time. He asked for an adjournment, stating that he was far too tired to do the job effectively but Stevenson pressed him hard on the matter and Wegner reluctantly went on to make his case about international law in relation to this trial. His case started slowly and Wegner, perhaps because he was tired, rambled slightly, but Stevenson, who was known for his impatience, stopped him in his tracks and told him to concentrate on the essential points of international law. Wegner eloquently apologised and then went into the finer points of law that he felt he needed to make. These points are too complex, from a legal standpoint, to go into here, but one of the issues Wegner sited concerned the perceptions of legality in times of war and that legalities changed according to jurisdictions. What might be legal in one country, for example might not be legal in another.

Wegner also cited the case of the British Army in South Africa during the Boer War when a massive number of civilians had been interned behind barbed-wire under quite appalling conditions and the death rate had been staggering. There was a clear connection here to the German concentration camps. Was it legal for the British to have created concentration camps where a large number of deaths through starvation and disease had occurred while it was illegal for the Germans to have done the same thing? 'The individual knows the rules of warfare because they have been transformed into the law of his own country, and he had been taught by his national authorities what his international duties are', Professor Wegner stated, adding: '... international law ought to be the supreme law of the country, but national pride in all countries over-emphasised the dogma of national sovereignty, tending to deny or even to despise international law.'

Wegner went on to point out that historically it had often been stressed that force was an essential point of law and that while such 'heresay' prevailed among so many lawyers in so many countries, '… the individual must be excused to some extent for a confusion in his conceptions as to right and wrong.' Wegner was actually making a good case for the five accused. They had been brought up or had lived for too long in an age of Nazi immorality and violence where everything that had once been illegal had suddenly become the accepted norm. None of the accused had been trained in legal matters and their lives for many years had been steeped in violence, anger, hypocrisy and prejudice. He went on to state that the questions of right and wrong, guilty or not guilty, had been confused for years, even before the rise of National Socialism. He said, '… the way has been paved for the national-socialist contention that there be no universal truth and law, but that instead of it, the will and command of the nation have been a supreme and absolute and totalitarian value, claiming the individual whole and undivided loyalty, all that the state can enforce.'

In other words, the state of totalitarian rule negated any prior justification for what might previously have been the rule of law and that virtually everything that was once illegal was now legal under that totalitarian principle. Wegner pointed out that in history there had been many instances where right and wrong, the guilty and not guilty had been affected by the fact that uncountable violations of international law had been ordered by superiors including violations that had been made under English law.

Since then, Wegner said, it had become a well established rule in international law that men and women forming part of a military or public force, and acting on behalf of their government, were not to be held responsible as a 'private trespasser or malefactor'. He said that whatever an individual had done was actually performed as a public act by a person in 'Her Majesty's Service acting in obedience to superior orders', and that as a result the responsibility lay with the government. Wegner also pointed out, quite correctly, that there were very important differences between the old Imperial government that had existed at the time of the First World War, and the National Socialists of the 1930s and '40s. The king of Prussia had been a legitimate ruler with constitutional rules whereas Hitler had not been a legitimate ruler and that the people, including the servicemen, could be excused for being unable to distinguish between the two and therefore believe that a superior's order was also legitimate. Additionally, Wegner stated that those who lived in National Socialist Germany had been crushed by fear and that they would do anything and obey any orders which would prevent them from being sent to concentration camps or being killed summarily. 'There are questions of wrong and guilt', Wegner continued, 'being important to the defence of war criminals. … Here I will only mention that it is a grave danger to let one's mind be ruled by any mass mood of the moment.'

Wegner's statements had been well informed but not always to the point. He had quoted numerous instances in law where the defence of command had been used or at least implied but he had tended to wander off script somewhat from his brief, which was that of advising on international law on behalf of the accused. On occasion he had been distracted, possibly because he was so tired that day. The judge advocate, Major A. Melford Stevenson, had interjected rather irritably on several occasions in an attempt to bring Wegner back on track. The day closed when Wegner had completed his presentation to the court. He apologised for having wandered a little during his speech and said that, as he had stated beforehand, that he was particularly tired, having spent a great deal of time the previous night preparing for his presentation.

The following day the court reassembled. This was to be the fourth and final day of the trial. All the witnesses had now been heard, including the expert witnesses such as Schnee and Wegner, so it was time for the defence counsel to make their closing addresses. The first to address the court was Dr Harold Todson who went through all the important points of the case with a special focus on Adalbert Schnee's testimony as an expert witness. He pointed out that Schnee had stated that if he had been placed into that particular position after sinking the *Peleus* he would have fled the scene right away. Todson told the court that they should take into consideration that Schnee and the commanders who had lost their submarines in the area were all highly experienced and would probably have made the right decision but Eck was far from being highly experienced. This was Eck's first war patrol as commander of a submarine and it was possible that he had panicked somewhat, especially as so many submarines had been lost in the area and that anti-submarine warfare, tuned to such fine perfection during the Atlantic War, was now a highly effective killing machine capable of locating and destroying enemy U-boats with ruthless efficiency. Eck had simply made the wrong decision to stay and attempt to destroy the evidence rather than to flee and put a safe distance between himself and the site of the sinking.

Todson was sincere in his quest to defend Eck but the realities stared him in the face. Eck had been unable to defend his murderous actions by stating that he had never wished to kill the men, only destroy the rafts, because by destroying those rafts he was either killing the men outright with machine-gun fire or hand-grenades or condemning them to an almost certain death in the sea. Reading Todson's closing comments it appeared clear that he knew the men would be found guilty. The defence was so weak he was virtually clutching at straws.

The next defence counsel to speak was Dr Max Pabst who was defending Schwender, Hoffmann and Dr Weisspfenning. He began his closing speech by concentrating on the actions of Schwender. He said that Schwender had not deliberately shot at any humans but had only fired at a piece of wreckage and that as the moon had risen by that time he had been able to ascertain that there had been nobody on the wreckage. The short burst had jammed the gun, Schwender had cleared it and Lenz had then taken the gun from him. Pabst told the court that was the only time Schwender had fired and that he had not been involved in the killing of any of the survivors.

Pabst admitted that in the case of Weissphenning and Lenz it was impossible to state whether either of them had killed anyone when they had fired, and even if the court was able to establish that as fact, it would have to be decided whether they should be punished for murder, manslaughter or involuntary killing, the punishments for those charges varying greatly in severity. Murder would have been a case of killing deliberately and it had not been proven by the court that any of the shooting had been carried out with the deliberate intent to kill those in the water. In any case, Pabst stated, both men had acted on the basis of a 'binding order' which lifted the criminal responsibility from them. 'It is impossible to examine the superior's command for its admissibility,' Pabst stated. 'The soldier has not to examine whether an order given to him is appropriate, wise, just and permitted. In case he would be allowed such right of examination, every discipline in the army would be shaken.'

Pabst was the counsel who brought up a very good point of defence. According to German legal definition, if penal law was violated during an action undertaken as part of a man's service, the commanding officer was alone responsible for the crime. There was, however, a codicil to this. A subordinate who carried out a criminal act under orders would also be responsible if he was aware that the act he was carrying out was criminal. Pabst stated that the legalities did not end there, however. The subordinate would only be culpable if he had known at the time that the officer was ordering an illegal act. The superior must have known he was ordering a crime to be committed and the subordinate had to know that his superior was aware of that at the time. It was complex but basically it meant that under the circumstances, none of the men could have had a detailed knowledge of the law and if Eck had merely been ordering the destruction of the rafts then that was not a crime for which his subordinates should have been punished. 'As he is not bound to examine the matter, mere doubts as to the correctness of the order or a careless ignorance regarding the criminal purpose of his superior do not suffice to establish the penal responsibility of the subordinate,' Pabst stated, adding that if the purpose of the order given by Eck was to carry out murder, then Weisspfenning and Hoffmann were guilty if they had known what the purpose of the order was, and if it could be proved that they knew. The men had also known that Eck had been carrying out secret orders of which they had no knowledge and that it was possible Eck's actions were influenced by those orders.

Yet even more than these legal issues, Pabst made a solid case for the defence of all the men when he emphasised to the court a number of important points. Most of the men had been inexperienced. They had no knowledge of the legal issues involved. They were deeply inured to military discipline and the possibility of harsh, even capital punishments. Most were in action for the first time. They feared for the safety of themselves and their boat. They were in a state of excitement caused by the sinking of the *Peleus*. They had endured months at sea under difficult and dangerous conditions. All these points demonstrated that the crew had been stretched to the limit; they did not have all the facts and that they were easily capable of making what turned out to be the wrong decisions. Pabst stated, 'The accused deny to have known that the purpose of the order was only murder. They believed in military necessities. … The contrary cannot be proved to them. Therefore they cannot be punished. … I therefore ask the court to acquit the three accused. I ask them to acquit Schwender because no punishable act was done by him, and to acquit the other two because they cannot be made responsible for the order given to them.'

Dr Wulf, the second counsel defending Weisspfenning, Hoffmann and Schwender was asked if he also wished to make a closing statement but he declined, stating that he adopted what Max Pabst had presented to the court.

Major Lermon was next to present his closing address and he wasted no time in questioning why none of the survivors who had made sworn affidavits at Cape Town had been brought into the court to give evidence. It had been fourteen months since they had made those affidavits and while they were important it was even more important that such vital witnesses be presented to the court so that they could be cross-examined by the defending counsel. Relying on affidavits alone was hardly obtaining the full and impartial evidence needed by the court to reach a proper verdict in the case. Lermon also made the point that servicemen who were undertaking an action against an enemy were placed under law in an impossible situation. If they disobeyed their commanding officer they were liable to immediate summary execution. If they obeyed the order then they might be tried as war criminals on a capital offence and lose their lives anyway. Under pressure of action, how were they to react, especially when they were not fully conversant with the complex laws involved and at times decisions of life and death had to be made within seconds?

Lenz was in a particularly tricky situation. True, he had attempted to prevent the massacre by appealing to his commanding officer but basically that was his only defence. Four people had fired at the survivors or rafts that night and of all of those men only Lenz had fired without directly being ordered to do so. He had made his appeal to Eck and then gone below to let someone else get on with the killings. Had he not come up to the bridge when he did he would have saved himself from being charged with war crimes. It was his decision to take the gun from Schwender and his decision to fire, and although he professed a reason for doing so, members of the court were having difficulty in understanding that reason. 'What earthly difference does it make to a person who is shot at, whether the Archangel Gabriel himself or the Devil shoots at him?' Stevenson stated irascibly. Lermon, however, made a powerful comparison to try to make the court understand Lenz's motives in taking the gun that day. He asked the court to imagine that Lenz was about to face a firing squad (which in fact was now very possible) and while it did not matter much to anyone who formed the firing squad it would matter a great deal to Lenz if he knew that the squad was formed of men of honour or men who were, in Lermon's words, 'a band of ruffians'. Lermon asked the court to see the situation through Lenz's eyes. He did not have to involve himself and only did so out of a sense of honour. In closing, Lermon asked the court to bear in mind the good character of his client and to bring down a verdict of not guilty.

When Colonel Halse of the Advocate General's Office stood to make his closing address the men who listened to that address must have felt a deep dread forming within them. Halse was not mincing his words. One by one Halse went through the defence strategies which had been presented for each of the accused and one by one he shredded them with his interpretation of the law. His remarks were particularly strong when it came to Dr Weisspfenning who had been under the protection of the Geneva Convention and as a non-combatant had specifically been forbidden from carrying or using arms. Weisspfenning had, without any hesitation, upon the order of his commanding officer, taken up the M.G.15 and commenced firing on the rafts knowing full well that there were survivors on them.

Halse also very strongly attacked Lenz's defence of attempting to do the honourable thing. Halse called Lenz's defence 'absurd', particularly in that he had, apparently, strongly protested against the firing on innocent civilians and had been the only one to open fire without directly being ordered to do so.

When it came to Schwender, Halse refused to believe that the German rating had been unaware that there were survivors in the water and on the rafts when he had come up to the conning tower bridge. At that stage the firing had been going on intermittently for some considerable period and everyone in the boat must have known what was going on above. A ship had been sunk, there were obviously survivors and these were now being machine-gunned along with their rafts. Schwender had no excuse for obeying the order of his commanding officer when he should have known that by firing at the rafts he would also be committing a war crime.

When the judge advocate, Major A. Melford Stevenson, K.C., rose to make his summing up of the case he immediately pointed out to the court his feelings concerning the complexities of international law. He had already expressed his intolerance and impatience to the lengthy address given by Dr Albert Wegner on the subject and was keen to point out that despite its complexities the case against these five men came down to one basic element. He said that international law was only a set of rules expressed as treaties, customs or usages which were based upon the common sense of civilised nations and ordinary humanity. He pointed out that it was a fundamental fact that the killing of unarmed people was completely forbidden and had been forbidden for centuries. 'To fire so as to kill helpless survivors of a torpedoed ship is a grave breach against the law of nations,' Stevenson stated. He was implying that despite the complexity of whether or not any of the men were uncertain as to the legality of the orders they had received, they all should have known that to kill innocent civilians was a war crime. He added that obviously it was not possible for all soldiers and sailors to be conversant with international law but in carrying out Eck's order to fire, '... it must have been obvious to the most rudimentary intelligence that it was not a lawful command and that those who did that shooting are not to be excused for doing it upon the grounds of superior command.'

After a few more comments about his remaining impartial throughout the trial and that his role was now to advise the court in his summing up, Stevenson acknowledged that the defendants had been well defended by their various counsels and asked the court to use common sense when considering their verdicts. This completed the case and at 15.08 hours exactly (3.08 pm) the court closed so that the members of the jury could make their decisions.

It must have been considerably troubling to the accused men that exactly forty minutes later they were again ushered into the court to hear their fates. Such a short space of time to consider five independent cases appeared to be ominously brief, especially when this was a fairly complex legal case and there were five people standing accused. Yet at 15.48 all five men were brought back into the courtroom. As they stood before him, the president of the court, Brigadier C.I.V. Jones, C.B.E., commander of the 106 AA Brigade, read the verdicts for each of the men. They were all found guilty.

Each member of the defending counsel was then given an opportunity to speak in mitigation of his client. Some even called character witnesses. Dr P. Wulf, for example, called witnesses who testified to Hoffmann's character claiming that they had known him from his school days and that he had been a born leader with huge compassion for his fellow man and had never acted in a bullying way, either as a lad or as an officer. He had, additionally, even when in great pain himself from wounds he had received, managed to save the life of one of the submarine's crew when it had been under aircraft attack following its beaching on the coast of Somaliland.

Dr Max Pabst spoke on behalf of both Weisspfenning and Schwender, stating that they had had no choice but to obey orders, and that if the men involved had refused to act upon their orders it would have been tantamount to mutiny. 'The U-boat would have completely lost its character as a fighting force,' Pabst said.

After the mitigation pleas had been completed the court once again retired to consider what sentences to impose. The time was 16.35 hours (4.35 p.m). On this occasion the court remained out a little longer – an indication, at least, that they were considering each case reasonably thoroughly and not imposing a set sentence on all. They returned almost an hour later at 17.33 hours and the accused stood at attention to hear their fates.

The president of the court read the sentences to each man in turn. The sentences were read firstly in English by Brigadier Jones and then interpreted into German by the court interpreter. Heinz Eck, August Hoffmann and Dr Walter Weisspfenning were each sentenced to death by shooting. Hans Richard Lenz was sentenced to imprisonment for life – probably because he had fired the machine-gun without having been ordered to do so – while Wolfgang Schwender received a sentence of imprisonment for fifteen years.

As each man heard the sentences their faces remained quiet and impassive. The men were advised that the sentences had to be confirmed and the paperwork was soon completed to obtain this confirmation. Field Marshal Sir Bernard 'Monty' Montgomery confirmed the last of them on 12 November, 1945. At that time the three accused men had just eighteen days to live.

Sometime before dawn on 30 November, 1945, the condemned men were awakened in their cells at the Altona Prison in Hamburg. It was a cold grey day, bleak in every way. The men dressed in their *Kriegsmarine* uniforms and were marched through the prison's exercise yard and along a dull, tree-lined path towards the prison's firing range on Lüneberg Heath. There were no leaves on the trees and rain-heavy clouds were scudding across the sky.

At the firing range three strong wooden posts had been set into the ground. The prisoners were now firmly strapped to the posts, the military guards tying the men in regulation fashion so that after they had been shot they would not slump grotesquely, or fall to the ground, but remain in almost a standing position, knees bent slightly and head slumped. It was all fairly typical of British military precision which made the provision that a corpse should remain upright after execution. Once the men were thoroughly bound the sergeant of the guard checked the bindings once more before pulling black hoods over the men's heads. The members of the firing squad were ordered to take aim and, seconds later, to fire. Eck, Weisspfenning and Hoffmann slumped dead in precise military fashion. The time was now exactly 08.40 hours. The men murdered at the time of the *Peleus* sinking had finally been given their justice.

The funeral of Heinz Eck was supposed to have been kept a secret but word of the event soon leaked out to Eck's supporters, particularly former officers of the *Kriegsmarine* and especially those who had served in U-boats.

At that time Sefton Delmer, a British/Australian broadcaster and journalist, was traipsing around war-torn Germany looking for good stories. Delmer was one of those really interesting people who, during the war, had specialised in writing anti-Nazi articles and propaganda. He spoke German and several other languages fluently, having been born in Berlin to Australian parents. His father, Frederick Sefton Delmer, had been a professor of English Literature at Berlin University.

Before the war Sefton Delmer had even managed to wangle an interview with Hilter himself but throughout the war he had led a black propaganda radio and press campaign which had been so successful that Delmer's name had been placed into the now infamous 'Nazis Black Book'. After the planned

German invasion of England Delmer was to be be arrested immediately. Had that occurred he would almost certainly have been executed.

Yet it was now September 1946, about ten months after Eck had been executed. Delmer was writing a series of stories which were published in newspapers and magazines internationally. These described him as, 'A reporter tramping Germany as a German'. Delmer interviewed a number of young men who were living largely by buying and selling on the black market. He said that most of these men had to do so because they were unable to register for rations as they were on the run and did not want to draw attention to themselves. Among these men were a number of former navy officers whom Delmer described as, 'Young men with rucksacks loaded to bursting point with the contraband they were out to barter and sell.' Delmer pointed out that these ex-servicemen were in touch with one another despite the fact that the creation of any kind of association was illegal at that time. He described them as having, '… the past written on their faces, mouths turned down disdainfully at the correct Prussian officer angle', and that their uniforms had usually been dyed black. Delmer said that while no such post-war military associations existed, as they were banned, they survived on an informal level and this had clearly been demonstrated at the funeral of Heinz Eck. When Eck's funeral had taken place at the Ohlsdorf cemetery, several hundred German naval officers had suddenly arrived without warning. Delmer quoted one officer, Hans Dietrich, as stating, 'It was quite miraculous how quickly we all got the news. The funeral was only arranged four hours before it took place and was intended to be very secret. But we were all there.'

Yet since that time there has been a great deal of discussion as to exactly what kind of justice those crewman of the *Peleus* had received. Historians, legal academics, students and practitioners of law, especially military law, have often argued that Eck, Weisspfenning and Hoffmann had been the expedient victims of 'victor's justice', that their trials had been hurried through the legal system without precedents having been set. They had been executed, 'for example', just as the major war crimes trials were beginning at Nuremberg so in relation to war crimes that had been committed during the Second World War no legal precedents had been set. There was no legal point of reference compared to what might occur, and the legal arguments that might be used, during the defence and prosecution cases at Nuremberg. The guiding precedents had yet to be established.

There was also a certain degree of bitterness involved. Many German people believed that Eck and his men had committed no crime. How could one compare the deliberate killing of a few dozen seamen to the hundreds of thousands of civilians, including women and children, who had been killed by the British and Americans during the bombing of cities such as Hamburg, Dresden and Berlin? Everyone was confused. These were the early months and years of post-war Germany. The truth of the concentration camps was now just beginning to filter into the collective consciousness of the people. It was difficult to come to terms with any of it.

And then there were the mysterious deaths and the questions that followed the execution of the three men. Shortly after the trial Dr Max Pabst and Dr Harold Todson both died under unusual circumstances. As we have seen, Pabst had been defending Schwender, Hoffmann and Weisspfenning while Todson had defended Eck. Pabst's death was put down to suicide, although there were some doubts about that, and Todson was killed when he was travelling in a car that was struck by a British Army lorry. Naturally, conspiracy theories abounded, particularly in respect to revenge motives. Both deaths were investigated by the British military but the actual reports were never made public.

Had the trial been held before a German court it is likely that the result would have been very different. There is little doubt that the men would still have been found guilty, but possibly on a lesser charge, manslaughter, for example, which did not carry the death penalty. It is likely that if this had been the case all five would have been imprisoned but even that punishment would eventually have been reduced. In fact that is exactly what occurred in the cases of the two men who were sent to prison, Lenz for life and Schwender for fifteen years. Yet neither would serve anywhere near the sentences imposed.

Over time, attempts were made to have the sentences of both men reduced; members of Hans Lenz's legally trained family were relentless in pursuing the British authorities to have Lenz's sentence reduced and impassioned pleas were made through legal representatives hired by the family. Similar attempts were made to bring about a reduction in the sentence for Wolfgang Schwender.

Finally Schwender was released from prison on 21 December, 1951. Lenz served about another eight months of his sentence before being released on 27 April, 1952.

The precise number of men murdered by Eck and his crew at the time of the sinking of the *Peleus* has never been established because it was impossible to know how many of the crew had survived the actual sinking of the ship.

There is no doubt that the five men convicted of the killing of the *Peleus* crew deserved to be punished but at that time at least there was little discussion about the fact that charges were not being laid against Allied servicemen who carried out similar and even more deadly attacks on unarmed survivors. The captain and crew of the British submarine HMS *Torbay* were later listed as having killed enemy troops as they struggled in the water but those war crimes were then being kept strictly secret and no legal proceedings were ever instigated against the boat's captain or crew.

It is also worth considering the character and career of Major Aubrey Melford Steed Stevenson who performed the duties of judge advocate in this case. Stevenson would later become a particularly controversial member of the British legal system whose outspoken attitudes and strict sentences, once he had attained a position on the High Court, have frequently been critically commented upon in British judicial history.

As we have seen, Stevenson had been abrupt and forceful during the trial of these five submariners, even to the point of cutting off the testimony being made by at least one expert witness but this was fairly typical of Stevenson's opinionated character.

The very month before the opening of the *Peleus* trial Melford Stevenson had presided over the court-martial of a British subject named Theodore William John Schurch who has gone down in history as one of the most dedicated traitors of the Second World War. Schurch had served as a driver in the Royal Army Service Corps but had been captured by Axis forces at Tobruk and almost immediately began working for both the Italian and German intelligence services. He sometimes posed as a prisoner-of-war and was placed into P.O.W. camps in order to gain the confidence of Allied prisoners and glean important intelligence from them. He was arrested in Rome in March 1945, charged with treachery and desertion and tried by court-martial at the Duke of York's headquarters in Chelsea. He was found guilty on all counts and Stevenson sentenced him to be hanged. Schurch was executed at Pentonville Prison on 4 January, 1946, aged twenty-seven years. From this very significant case Stevenson was rushed to Hamburg to prosecute Heinz Eck and his four companions. It would probably be fair to say that Stevenson would have been buoyed by the successful conclusion to the Schurch case and looking forward to any other case which might also raise his prominence within the British legal fraternity. If nothing else, Stevenson was highly ambitious and would have seen it as a significant opportunity to be asked to prosecute such a high profile case as the *Peleus* defendants. Such cases were now beginning to come before the courts and the public generally was extremely keen to see justice meted out to those who had participated in the almost endless war crimes of the Nazi era.

Stevenson was actually an interesting man. His first wife, Anna Cecilia Francesca Imelda Reinstein, was the daughter of a German hairdresser. The couple had married in 1929 but Stevenson later discovered that Anna was having an affair with Maurice Buckmaster, a man who was to become famous in British intelligence history as head of Special Operations Executive (S.O.E.) during the war. When Stevenson discovered the affair he had, according to subsequent reports, promptly, 'turned his wife out'.

Stevenson would later go on to become involved in some very high profile cases including the unsuccessful defence of Ruth Ellis, the last woman to be hanged in England. He also represented Jomo Kenyatta in his appeal for having been imprisoned for being a member of the Mau Mau terrorists during the bloody uprising that had taken place in Kenya in the 1950s. Kenyatta lost that appeal but later went on to become the president of Kenya.

Throughout his entire judicial career Stevenson would court controversy and as a High Court judge he became infamous for imposing some of the harshest sentences seen in modern U.K. history. He died on Boxing Day, 1987.

Chapter Three

Tatsunosuke Ariizumi

The *Jean Nicolet* and *Tjisalak* Massacres

It was stiflingly hot in the cabin of Japanese submarine I-401. Captain Tatsunosuke Ariizumi could feel the sticky perspiration prickling in his hair and beneath the heavy collar of his now crumpled uniform. This was to be his last day on earth. He had decided that several days ago. In fact he had known that he would soon die since the moment he had received the imperial message advising of the national surrender. These last few days had been the worst of his life – the horror and humiliation of defeat, the sickening, almost vomit-inducing nausea in the pit of his stomach that would not go away. His beloved Japan was in ruins: Tokyo flattened by firebombing – Hiroshima where many of his friends and loved ones had once lived and also Nagasaki had now been blown into oblivion by some massively murderous American weapon. Right on the brink of being able to deliver what should have been a savage blow against the hated enemy, he had been chained like a dog, tethered by this almost incomprehensible national surrender. The Imperial Japanese Navy was now literally wallowing in defeat. There was nothing more he could do. He had spent his entire adult life working for victory, ruthlessly dedicated towards that one goal, and now it was over.

Ariizumi hefted the weighty, naval-issue, Model 94 automatic pistol in his hand, turning the weapon over and looking somberly at its dull metal. He had carried this weapon for years. In fact he had used it on numerous occasions to end the lives of many of those he had defeated. Men mostly, ships' crews or passengers, but also a few women. Yet he felt no remorse. Remorse was a weakness and in war there was no room for sentiment. War was meant for men who could act decisively and without fear. It was not enough just to obey orders. In war, orders had to be both obeyed and relished, even cherished, for in that holy partnership of obedience lay the path to total victory. At least he had always believed that to be the case.

The pistol was heavy in his hands, ugly, a pitted steel handgun made as a utilitarian instrument of death and destruction rather than a thing of beauty. The palms of Ariizumi's small hands were moist with perspiration as he turned the weapon over and cocked it quickly, injecting a round into its breech.

He leaned back against the chair, thinking back. They say that when you are about to die your whole life flashes before your eyes but now all he could think of was his career in the navy, beginning with his graduation ceremony at the Etajima academy all those years ago in 1923. Since then he had enjoyed an almost mercurial career, rising rapidly to his present position as the commanding officer of the 631st Naval Air Corps with simultaneous command of the deadliest submarine group ever assembled in the Pacific – a flotilla of unique submarine aircraft carriers tasked with delivering one mighty blow against the Americans – one they would never forget.

Sadly, that was now over and Ariizumi's mouth was bone-dry with the bitterness of defeat. He had not been able to reach his intended target at the Panama Canal or to fire a single torpedo or launch even one of his torpedo-carrying aircraft. In fact those aircraft were now at the bottom of the sea, jettisoned by the very catapults that had been designed to launch them into victory.

Tatsunosuke Ariizumi could not stand to think about it any more. Soon the captain of I-401 the second most senior officer aboard the submarine that day, would have to surrender. Hand command to the next American warship he saw. Ariizumi could almost hear the voices of an American prize crew coming along the passageway from the conning tower. American voices on a Japanese submarine! Happy voices. They would be exhilarated by total victory at taking such a prize, at winning the war. No doubt they would be chewing gum, smoking Lucky Strike cigarettes and talking about the many Japanese women they would take and the saki they would drink in celebration once they reached Tokyo. It was all just too much.

Ariizumi closed his eyes, placed the pistol into his mouth and aimed slightly upwards as his index finger gently touched the trigger. He could hear the water washing against the hull of I-401. He loved this boat, one of the most powerful submarines ever constructed. He regretted never being able to prove its worth as a hugely destructive fighting machine. Then his mind went blank for a few moments, almost as if he were living in some dark place – somewhere we go before we die, he thought. Then he realised that he just couldn't do it. Not then, at least. Gently, he eased the weapon from his mouth and carefully placed it onto the side-table. He noticed that he had stopped breathing. He sucked in the oily air of the submarine. It tasted of life. He looked again at the pistol, his black eyes seemed devoid of life, cold. *Later, perhaps*!

* * *

No one today really knows how many people Tatsunosuke Ariizumi murdered during the war years. He attacked and sank many ships, most of which, very unusually, had no survivors at all. This in itself was peculiar because although torpedoing and sinking a ship is in itself an extremely violent act, statistically there were almost always at least a few survivors. At times it was entirely possible for the entire ship's crew and all the passengers to survive such a terrible event. Given what we now know about Captain Tatsunosuke Ariizumi's murderous fanaticism, it would appear highly likely that the passengers and crews of many vessels he sank were actually finished off in the water with machine-guns or possibly brought aboard the Japanese submarine not only to be slaughtered in cold blood but also to provide a deadly kind of amusement for his crew. A murderous sport. While the actual events surrounding the sinking of most of Ariizumi's victims remains a mystery, we do know, however, that on at least two occasions Ariizumi was responsible for the most atrocious war crimes.

Basically, there is no other way to describe Tatsunosuke Ariizumi. He was a monster with a baby face. He came into this world in 1904, born into considerable privilege. His family was wealthy but they also had a long tradition of naval service and evidently this was how Ariizumi became interested in a life in the Imperial Japanese Navy. He graduated with the 51st Class at the Japanese Navy Academy based at Etajima in Hiroshima Prefecture in 1923, after which he was posted to several surface ships including the aircraft carrier *Akagi* (Japanese for *Red Castle*). The *Akagi* would later take part in the attack on Pearl Harbor, the bombing of Darwin and the invasion of Rabaul before being attacked by U.S.

Infamous Japanese submarine commander Tatsunosuke Ariizumi. (*Wikimedia Commons*)

aircraft during the Battle of Midway and sunk on 5 June, 1942, with the loss of 267 lives.

It is not known why Ariizumi subsequently joined the submarine service although he would certainly have known that he stood a better chance of obtaining his own command at a relatively young age. In April 1931 he was posted to the rather antiquated Type L submarine RO-64 where he commenced his practical training in underwater warfare. The RO-64 was hardly the pride of the Japanese fleet. It had been constructed by Mitsubishi Heavy Industries, being laid down in October 1923 and launched in April 1925. It carried a complement of just forty-eight men.

Ariizumi was subsequently posted as the torpedo officer to a number of submarines including I-51; I-56 and I-70. This period was largely a long training session for the young man as he accumulated the knowledge and experience necessary for him to be commissioned as a commanding officer. In July 1937 he graduated from the Naval War College and the following month was posted to Sasebo as chief of staff to the 3rd Submarine Squadron. From there and from the experience he gained at the squadron, Ariizumi's rise to power was almost guaranteed. As war clouds were gathering over Europe at the end of the 1930s he was posted to the bureau of the first section of the Naval General Staff and placed in charge of general planning. In November 1940 he was promoted to the rank of commander. He now became one of those officers responsible for the detailed planning for the midget submarine attack on Pearl Harbor. Yet Tatsunosuke Ariizumi's particularly brutal role in the war was still some years away and would not wholly come into being until he was appointed the commanding officer of the Japanese submarine I-8.

The I-8 was famous in Japan at this time and in fact the vessel was to carry both fame and infamy into history. It was a Junsen Type J-3 submarine, one of the largest constructed in Japan prior to the war. Both the I-8 and its sister submarine, the I-7, would participate in the attack on Pearl Harbor although Tatsunosuke Ariizumi would not be in command of either at the time.

By the standards of the day the I-8 was a bit of a gargantuan although it would be dwarfed by the now well known submarine 'aircraft carriers' produced by Japan during the war, the design and construction of which would be closely associated with the work of Tatsunosuke Ariizumi.

The I-8 was built by Kawasaki Kobe and laid down on 11 October, 1934, being completed in December 1938. It was capable of a range of 26,000 kilometres at sixteen knots and could dive to 330 feet. It carried a complement of one hundred officers and men and was armed with six forward torpedo tubes, a 14cm naval gun, two antiaircraft guns and a Yokosuka E14Y seaplane which could be launched from the bows of the submarine and was capable of carrying either a torpedo or a bomb load.

The submarine was held in awe not only because of its size, armaments and its capacity to carry an aircraft but also because it had taken part in one of the most daring missions ever undertaken by a Japanese submarine up until that time.

The 'Yanagi Missions' as they became known, formed part of a plan arranged under the Axis Powers Tripartite Pact to provide for an exchange of important resources such as strategic materials, manufactured products, weapons and many other items between Germany, Italy and Japan. While this was a feasible and sound concept to begin with it soon became evident that it could never work effectively. At first cargo ships were used to transport the exchanges but as the war progressed it became increasingly more difficult and dangerous to send these goods to the Axis countries so submarines were used instead. Yet such a trans-oceanic voyage for the fairly basic submarines of that period was a particularly difficult task. In fact only seven submarines attempted to undertake these voyages including two German U-boats. Of these submarines the Japanese I-30, the first to attempt the voyage, was destroyed by a mine off Singapore while returning to Japan; the I-34 was sunk by a British submarine, the *Taurus;* the I-29 was sunk by an American submarine, *Sawfish,* and the I-52 by a U.S. Navy aircraft. The I-8, however, then under the command of an officer named Shinjo Uchino, was successful not only in travelling to German-occupied France but also of returning safely to Japan.

The I-8, in company of the I-10 and a submarine tender, the *Hei Maru,* left Kure on 1 June, 1943. The cargoes included two Type 95 oxygen-propelled torpedoes – then considered to be the most efficient torpedoes ever invented, plus torpedo tubes, drawings of an automatic trim system and a new reconnaissance aircraft, the Yokosuka E14Y. All this Japanese technology was being offered as part of the Tripartite Pact to aid the German war effort.

A second crew of submariners was also taken on board for transport to Germany. It was intended that these would man a German submarine, the U-1224, a new type IXC/40 U-boat, and take it back to Japan where it could be reverse engineered.

The vessels arrived in Singapore nine days after departing Kure. There I-8 took on board a cargo of quinine, tin and raw rubber prior to departing for Penang which was then, of course, under Japanese control.

The Kure naval base in Japan from where the Yanagi missions departed. This was a major military facility. (*Catalogue Number 80-G-351898 (U.S. National Archives) (Above) and 80-G-351901 (U.S. National Archives) (Below). Naval History and Heritage Command*)

In the Atlantic the I-8 experienced particularly powerful storms but managed to survive. On 20 August the I-8 successfully rendezvoused with a German submarine, the U-161 which was then under the command of Captain Albrecht Achilles. As the submarines came alongside each other two German radar operators and a new radar unit, the Metox 600A, were transferred to the I-8 and the Metox was installed on the Japanese submarine's bridge. I-8 then proceeded on its way towards the coast of France, a German Ju 88 aircraft providing air-cover. The submarine arrived at Brest two days later.

In German-occupied France the arrival of a large Japanese submarine carrying a wealth of innovative designs and a cargo of raw materials was more than welcome, the captain and crew of the submarine were greeted with considerable enthusiasm and invited to parties and other welcoming functions in both Paris and Berlin. It must have been a particularly happy time for the crew of the submarine, possibly the last such festivities they would enjoy.

The I-8 departed Brest on 5 October that year for the return journey to Japan. No one was under any illusion that with the war in the Atlantic at its height and with Americans dominating the Pacific the chances of arriving safely back in their homeland after such a long and dangerous journey were not too good. On board the submarine was an exchange cargo of machine-guns, bomb-sights, a torpedo boat engine, marine chronometers, radar equipment, antiaircraft gun-sights, electric torpedoes and penicillin. There were also several important personnel on board including Rear Admiral Yokoi, the naval attaché to Berlin, a Captain Hosoya, naval attaché to France, three German officers and several radar and hydrophone operators.

The dangers of the return voyage could never be overstated. Once again striking rough seas, the I-8's arrival in Singapore was delayed which prompted its captain to radio the vessel's position to Germany. However, that single message was intercepted by the Allies and an attack on the I-8 was launched. Yet this attempt to destroy the submarine failed and the I-8 arrived at Kure to a heroes' welcome on 21 December having travelled approximately 30,000 nautical miles.

The prestige won by this vessel, at least within its Axis circle of operations, was not to last and it would be Captain Tatsunosuke Ariizumi who would be astonishingly successful in turning the submarine's sound reputation into an infamous trail of bloody historical infamy.

* * *

The SS *Tjisalak*, victim of the Japanese submarine I-8 and its commander Tatsunosuke Ariizumi. This photograph was taken in 1917, shortly after its construction and twenty-seven years before it would be sunk and its crew murdered. (*Wikimedia Commons*)

The SS *Tjisalak*, was a 5787 tons Dutch freighter and passenger vessel which had been constructed in 1917 for the Java-China-Japan Line. By the Second World War it was a relatively old vessel, restricted in speed but still capable of transporting goods and passengers safely to various destinations. It was at that time taken over as an Allied transport and used to ferry supplies and passengers from Australia to Ceylon, although its route across the Indian Ocean placed the ship in frequent danger from roaming Japanese submarines. It was almost inevitable that one day it would be attacked.

On 26 March, 1944, the *Tjisalak* was en route from Melbourne to Colombo carrying a cargo of flour and mail. The vessel was under the command of Captain Hen. There were about one hundred people on board. These were comprised of eighty crew members including English, Dutch and Chinese nationals plus five passengers including an American Red Cross worker named Mrs Verna Gorden-Brittain. There were, additionally, twenty-two Laskar seamen who were returning to India after their own ship had been torpedoed. Bad luck, sadly, was about to give them a second taste of that kind of devastating attack.

The time was now 5.45 a.m. on the morning of 26 March, 1944. A single torpedo fired by Tatsunosuke Ariizumi aboard I-8 struck the ship which very quickly began to list to port. One man was killed during the explosion, this was an Australian, Lieutenant Dawson. The captain of the ship realised immediately that the vessel was doomed and gave the order to abandon ship. It was a fairly safe and successful evacuation and almost everyone was immediately taken on board the ship's boats. Only a handful of men remained on board the *Tjisalak* and these were the British gunners who had been placed on the vessel to operate the gun which had been installed on the foredeck as some kind of defensive weapon in the event of just such an attack. The gun-crew was being led by a very experienced commander, a Dutch officer named Jan Dekker who was actually the ship's second officer. Dekker and his team were determined to wait on board the stricken ship for as long as possible in case the enemy submarine surfaced nearby and could be engaged. When I-8 did appear the gun-crew immediately brought their weapon into action and the submarine's crew was quick to respond. Under intense fire from the Japanese and with the ship rapidly going down from beneath their feet, the gun-crew was also forced to abandon ship.

There were now 105 survivors scattered around in boats and rafts. The I-8 nosed amongst them as if seeking further victims. A Japanese officer who spoke excellent English shouted across to the survivors ordering them to come to the submarine. Once there everyone was placed on the submarine's deck while Tatsunosuke Ariizumi looked on from the conning tower. Captain Hen was taken to the conning tower where he was seen in conversation with the Japanese officers. He was heard to shout, 'No, no. I don't know.' At that moment one of the Chinese sailors from the *Tjisalak* managed to slip quietly into the water in a vain attempt to escape. Being Chinese he would have had a better understanding than the Europeans about what was now probably going to happen. The Chinese had been brutalised and murdered in their hundreds of thousands by the Japanese since the invasion of Manchuria in 1931 and the even more brutal Rape of Nanking in 1937-38 during which around 300,000 men, women and children had been massacred. However, the Chinese sailor in the water did not last long. He was simply shot out of hand by members of the submarine's crew and his body allowed to drift away.

That first murder must have shocked and horrified the passengers and crew of the *Tjisalak*. What it essentially meant was that they no longer had any rights as prisoners or innocent civilians and that their captors intended to give them only the most brutal forms of treatment.

The survivors of the attack were now roughly tied together in pairs and led aft around the submarine's conning tower where they were immediately set upon by a group of Japanese seamen wielding a variety of weapons including knives, bayonets, guns and sledgehammers. Four men were immediately successful in surviving this horrific attack by jumping or falling into the sea. Japanese sailors on the submarine's deck quickly poured gunfire into the water but the men in the sea miraculously managed to survive. These were the chief officer of the *Tjisalak*, Frits de Jong; the second officer, Jan Dekker, who had commanded the gun crew; the second radio officer James Blears, and the third engineer, Cees Spuybroek.

Dekker later stated:

Japanese ratings came on deck armed with tommy-guns, rifles and Samurai swords. We were told not to look behind or we would be shot. One man fell overboard and the Japs began shooting at him. They started plucking out the Europeans whom they ordered to remove their lifejackets. Then they shot them. I was ordered to go aft. When abreast of the conning tower of the submarine I felt a terrific blow on the side of my head. As I fell I saw a Jap with a big sledgehammer preparing to hit me. I ducked but was struck a glancing blow on the right temple. As I fell I saw another Jap pointing a rifle at me. I rolled over the submarine's side and stayed underwater as long as possible. Bullets splattered the water.

Meanwhile the killings on the submarine's deck continued unabated and it was clear that the Japanese would have no mercy, even for the solitary woman on board, Mrs Verna Gorden-Brittain. Mrs Gorden-Brittain had been in Singapore at the time of the Japanese capture of the island and had been taken prisoner and interned. However, she had subsequently been repatriated to Australia where she remained for some time until her husband, who was then in Calcutta, had been able to send for her. Delighted to be once again on her way to see her husband, Verna Gorden-Brittain had boarded the first available ship, the ill-fated *Tjisalak*. Now on board the Japanese submarine she watched as the men were being ruthlessly butchered, knowing that her turn would soon come. When it did she faced death courageously. Just before she was killed she called out, in Japanese, 'Goodbye.'

When there were only about twenty people left alive these were tied together with a long rope and pushed overboard to drown. The last man on the rope, a Laskar named Dhange, was able to free himself but the remaining people on the rope stood little or no chance of surviving.

The I-8 now departed the scene of the massacre believing that they had killed everyone who could later bear witness against them. However, the four men who had jumped or fallen overboard as the massacre was taking place had all managed to evade the Japanese. They were able to swim back to the location of the sinking of the *Tjisalak* and climb on board an abandoned life-raft. It saved their lives. Three days later the survivors spotted a ship approaching their position. This was an American Liberty Ship, the SS *James O. Wilder.* For some reason the crew of the Liberty Ship opened fire on the raft in error, although they quickly realised their mistake and took the survivors on board for passage to Colombo.

*   *   *

Tatsunosuke Ariizumi's next victim was the SS *Jean Nicolet* which he attacked on 2 July, 1944.

The *Jean Nicolet* was one of America's 'Liberty Ships', constructed at Portland, Oregon, in October 1943. It was operated by the San Francisco based Oliver J. Olson Company for the War Shipping Administration. Its captain was David Martin Nilsson of Oakland, California. Its first officer was Clement Carlin.

On that fateful day the *Jean Nicolet* was steaming in the Indian Ocean on a long voyage that had begun at San Pedro, California, bound for Calcutta. The ship was loaded with a large cargo of war materiel destined for the Burma/India theatres of conflict. The ship had already visited Fremantle in Western Australia where it had bunkered and taken on more stores and discharged some of its cargo.

On 21 June the *Jean Nicolet* had departed Fremantle, bound initially for Colombo, Ceylon, where it was destined to receive further orders prior to steaming to Calcutta. On board the vessel was a significant cargo of steel plate, steel mooring pontoons, heavy machinery, landing barges and a large amount of general military cargo.

There were one hundred people on the ship at that time which included the crew totalling forty-one men, plus twenty-eight armed naval guards and thirty-one passengers, mainly military personnel. These included six U.S. Army officers, twelve U.S. Army enlisted men, eight U.S. Navy technicians, four civilians and a solitary U.S. Army medical corpsman.

Steaming alone, the *Jean Nicolet* was always going to be a target for Japanese submarines which were prevalent in the Indian Ocean during that period. Speed, zigzagging and being blacked out at night helped enormously but few merchantmen could outrun the modern Japanese submarines when they were travelling on the surface.

The time was now 19.07 (7.07 p.m.) on 2 July. The *Jean Nicolet* was steaming through the dark evening at a position approximately seven hundred miles south of Ceylon. Suddenly two massive explosions rocked the vessel as torpedoes fired by Tatsunosuke Ariizumi aboard the I-8 smashed into the starboard side of the ship. The explosions were so great that the ship lurched alarmingly to port before listing back to starboard. The first torpedo detonated somewhere between number 2 and number 3 holds, blowing the hatch covers off number 3 and beginning a fire, while the second struck around numbers 4 and 5 holds. The ship very quickly began to list heavily to starboard and, fearing that the vessel would capsize, Captain Nilsson ordered the crew and passengers to abandon ship. The ship's crew immediately ran to their stations, began to lower the lifeboats and all the boats were got away successfully.

Everyone on board the vessel at that time managed to get away safely. They were able to leave the *Jean Nicolet* without any sense of disorder or panic. Prior to leaving his post the radio officer, Augustus Tilden, was able to send out a distress call advising that the ship had been torpedoed and gave the vessel's accurate position. The message was immediately acknowledged by operators in both Calcutta and Ceylon so Tilden was able to advise the captain and other survivors that help would soon be on its way. They had no way of knowing, of course, that they were to be the victims of a psychopath who had the full intention of murdering everyone on board the ship.

Only one person had been injured during the process of abandoning ship: this was an army officer, Lieutenant Miller, who had fallen into one of the boats and had broken an arm.

The last people on the ship included Captain Nilsson, a naval gunnery officer, Lieutenant Deal, two naval gunners and two merchant mariners, George Kenmore Hess and a seaman named McDougall. Captain Nilsson decided that this small group would leave the ship using the number 2 for'ard raft. McDougall raced to the raft, released the sea-painter (rope) and allowed the raft to drop into the sea. He immediately jumped into the sea to try to control it. The two naval gunners then jumped into the sea and scrambled onto the raft. Meanwhile Captain Nilsson and Lieutenant Deal decided to undertake another round of the ship to ensure that there were no other people on board. This was completed within a few minutes and when both men were sure that no one had been injured or trapped in the ship they too joined the other survivors on the raft. The sea-painter was cut and the raft immediately began to drift astern of the ship. As the raft drifted, a lifeboat in charge of the chief officer came alongside. Captain Nilsson went on board, taking charge of the boat. As the raft had been drifting he had seen a light on board the *Jean Nicolet* and wanted to go back to check one more time that no one had been left on the ship. As the boat headed for the *Jean Nicolet* the I-8 suddenly surfaced on the boat's starboard side. Although it was dark at the time the submarine could clearly be seen and it was obvious that the vessel's guns were being manned. Captain Nilsson cut the lifeboat's engine so that it would not give away their position and the men manned the oars, rowing as silently as possible to get clear of the enemy submarine and to get to the drifting raft on which were Lieutenant Deal and the small group of men who had been the last to leave the ship. However, luck was not with the survivors that night. The Japanese sighted the boats and turned menacingly towards them.

What happened immediately afterwards has gone down as one of the most abhorrent acts in modern maritime history. A powerful searchlight on the vessel's conning tower was switched on. It scanned the survivors quickly. It was also clear to those survivors that the machine-guns on the conning tower had now been manned. Seaman McDougall was still on the drifting raft at this time. He later testified that as the Japanese submarine nosed towards the survivors all those on the raft had slipped over the side into the sea. The Japanese penchant for machine-gunning the crews of torpedoed ships was by this time well known and there was every reason to distrust the intentions of the Japanese submariners. For a while it was difficult in the darkness to see exactly what the Japanese were doing. The survivors saw the submarine stop and go astern, then the men clinging to the sides of the rafts heard machine-gun fire and their worst fears were confirmed. The Japanese were either murdering some of the crew or passengers in the water or they were sinking wreckage to hide the fact that a submarine was operating in the region. Either way it did not look good. Soon afterwards the submarine turned again towards the raft and the other boats and turned the searchlight on. Then some person speaking excellent English ordered everyone to come alongside the submarine. This person also demanded to know the name of the ship that had just been torpedoed. Charles E. Pyle, then in one of the boats, shouted across that the ship's name was the *Jean Nicolet* and, lying to protect the senior ship's personnel, added that all the ship's officers were still on board the burning vessel.

Those men in the water were ordered to climb back onto their raft. Meanwhile several more took advantage of the semi-darkness to slip into the water and hide behind their boats.

William M. Musser was just seventeen years of age at the time; he came from Lancaster, Pennsylvania, and worked as a mess-man on board the ship. In fact this was Musser's first trip to sea. He was ordered to swim to the submarine which he did and when hauled aboard was escorted by Japanese seamen towards the bows of the submarine. As he walked for'ard, however, one of the sailors pulled Musser around and struck him savagely over the head with a piece of steel pipe. Musser staggered backwards and as he did so the sailor, laughing, drew a service pistol and shot the unfortunate youth in the head. After Musser had fallen to the deck the sailor kicked his body into the sea.

The survivors in the boats now had no illusion of how they would be treated once they had climbed onto that submarine's deck. They were all extremely apprehensive. The ship's first officer, Clement Carlin, turned to the man seated beside him. It was one of the crew, Charles Pyle. 'If you come out and I don't,' Carlin said to Pyle, 'I want my brother to have all my property.'

Another young man, nineteen years of age, Richard L. Kean from Kennewick, Washington, was ordered to climb out of the lifeboat onto the submarine's casing. There he was roughly searched, his lifejacket was taken from him and his arms were tied behind his back. He too was taken for'ard but suddenly the Japanese seaman leading him turned with a bayonet in his hand and thrust it into Kean's stomach. Kean doubled over in pain and as he did so was struck over the head with a rifle butt and kicked into the sea. Only a few minutes had passed since the submarine had surfaced and two men were already dead.

The remaining survivors were now brought on board. When everyone was on deck the abandoned lifeboats and rafts were sunk with machine-gun fire. Each of the survivors was searched, their lifejackets were removed, and any valuables they owned such as watches or rings and also their shoes were stolen from them. Seaman McDougall later testified that the Japanese would only allow one person at a time to get on board the submarine. When McDougall climbed onto the deck he was made to put his hands in the air and as he did so a Japanese sailor saw McDougall's watch. He pulled McDougall's hand down and pulled the watch from his wrist. He also saw that McDougall was wearing a ring and attempted to get it off McDougall's finger but the ring was a tight fit and would not move. The Japanese sailor pulled out a knife and was about to slice off McDougall's finger but McDougall was able to pull back and with some difficulty managed to get the ring off his finger. The Japanese seaman snatched it away.

All but three of the ship's survivors were brought on board. The Japanese attempted to kill the last three by machine-gunning them but fortunately those men were able to reach one of the rafts that had not been sunk by gunfire.

Meanwhile the submarine returned closer to the sinking *Jean Nicolet*. All the prisoners on the deck of the submarine were bound securely, their hands tied tightly behind their backs. They were made to sit on the submarine's deck with their heads bowed between their knees. Anyone who raised their head or made a noise was beaten with iron pipes or jabbed with bayonets.

The *Jean Nicolet's* radio officer, Gus Tilden, Captain Nilsson, and another man, Francis J. O'Gara, a representative of the War Shipping Administration, were taken to the submarine's conning tower and pushed below. This accorded with orders that Japanese submarine commanders had received which stipulated that captains of ships, or senior officers or anyone who might afford valuable intelligence was to be taken prisoner, while all others might be killed.

Meanwhile, Captain Tatsunosuke Ariizumi was enjoying his success enormously. Standing in the conning tower he began to harangue his captives: 'You are now my prisoners,' he shouted enthusiastically. 'Let this be a lesson to you. Americans are all weak. You must realise that Japan will eventually rule the world. You Americans are stupid for allowing your leaders to lead you into a war you can never win. Don't you know that the entire American fleet is rusting at the bottom of the Pacific Ocean?'

As this entire terrible drama was unfolding aboard the I-8, the *Jean Nicolet* could still be seen, not too far away, burning furiously. Contrary to Captain Nilsson's fears, the ship had not capsized, and although listing alarmingly to starboard, it had refused to sink. The I-8 now continued to cruise slowly around the scene of destruction looking for additional survivors or those who might be attempting to conceal themselves behind lifeboats. Tatsunosuke Ariizumi now ordered his gun-crew to shell the *Jean Nicolet* and they opened fire almost immediately. As this was happening a wave came over the hull of the submarine washing three of the bound men into the sea. These were Carl Rosenbaum, Able Seaman George Kenmore Hess and Lieutenant Morrison R. Miller of the U.S. Army. Rosenbaum and Hess would survive the ordeal, although how they managed to remain afloat without the use of their arms is something of a miracle. However, Lieutenant Miller, as we have seen, had broken an arm while abandoning the *Jean Nicolet* and he was not to survive.

Captain Tatsunosuke Ariizumi now ordered his crew to form a gauntlet on the deck of the submarine aft of the conning tower. Those survivors on the for'ard part of the vessel could not see the preparations that were being made to torture and murder them. The sailors who now formed the gauntlet were armed with bayonets, rifles and steel poles or stanchions. At the far end of the gauntlet was another seaman, reported to have been a monster of a man, armed with two bayonets. The survivors on deck were now brought forward, one by one, to run through the gauntlet. As they did so they were beaten brutally or stabbed until they staggered out of the other end only to be greeted by the large seaman and his twin bayonets who would thrust the weapons into the victims before heaving their bodies over the side. It was brutal, bloody and calculated not only to deliver the utmost pain and humiliation to the victims but also to provide an entertaining sport for the crew of the submarine. The ship's carpenter became the first person of those still hidden behind the conning tower to realise what was happening to the men who were being taken away. He was able to peek around the conning tower and saw Ordinary Seaman King being murdered. King was just eighteen years of age. The carpenter watched in horror as King was bayoneted several times in the stomach and then kicked overboard.

Three men managed to evade the worst of it. These were Charles E. Pyle, the ship's 1st assistant engineer; Harold R. Lee, another mess-man, and Robert C. Butler. These men managed somehow to jump or fall overboard while going through or having gone through the gauntlet, despite the fact that their arms were bound behind their backs.

This game of death continued for some time as the ship's survivors were led sequentially to their brutal deaths. Charles E. Pyle one of only a handful of men to survive the massacre later testified that it had been around midnight before the Japanese had come for him on the foredeck, leading him aft to what should have been his execution. He noticed that the deck guns were now being secured, so evidently the Japanese had finished using them for the night. There were at that time around thirty-five survivors still bound on the foredeck apprehensively awaiting their turn at the gauntlet. When Pyle saw what method of execution he faced he stopped in shock. At that moment he received a stunning blow to the base of his head. He was then pushed through the gauntlet while the Japanese sailors rained blows to his head and body with various objects. When he was later examined by a doctor it was discovered that his head had been split open from ear to ear. When Pyle reached the end of the gauntlet, barely conscious and in great pain, he had simply fallen into the sea. He later only recalled that the water had been, 'white' and 'foamy'.

As we have seen, Robert C. Butler, a ship's mess-man was one of those who managed to survive the gauntlet. He later testified that he had been sitting quite far forward on the submarine and had been unable to hear what was going on behind the conning tower. All he knew for sure was that people were being treated cruelly and he was frightened by what might be in store for him. He said that he was afraid to look back. Then suddenly it was his turn at the executioners' line and when Butler was brought to them he was horrified to see that they were holding swords, clubs and lengths of bloodied lead piping. Butler was kicked in the stomach and struck around the head several times. A sword slashed down and opened a terrible gash over his eye. Yet somehow Butler managed to break free when he had only just been thrust into the gauntlet, and jumped overboard. He sank and tried to kick away from the submarine as much as possible and when he came to the surface the submarine was still in sight but now some distance away.

Suddenly an alert was sounded on the submarine. By that time around thirty survivors remained on the foredeck awaiting their fate. These people had been able to hear the torture that was going on at the aft end of the submarine and were fully aware of the horrors that awaited them there. The sudden sounding of the alarm immediately put an end to the Japanese' murderous game. An aircraft had been spotted on radar and it was heading directly towards the Japanese vessel. The submarine's crew was immediately ordered below to take up their stations ready to submerge. The diving alarm sounded, Captain Ariizumi cleared the conning tower, pulling closed the hatch, sealing the vessel. Those left on the foredeck were unable to help themselves as their hands remained bound behind their backs. As the submarine dipped beneath the waves all those remaining survivors slipped into the sea. Seventeen of them were to drown or be taken by sharks. The others, thirteen in number, were able to keep themselves afloat even while bound. One of the men who had slid into the water that night was George Kenmore Hess, a seaman who had been working diligently during the entire period to saw his way through the ropes that held him using nothing more than his fingernails. In this endeavour he had been extremely successful. By the time the submarine had slid underwater, the rope had been so frayed that Hess was able to break it. Yet this was not the end to his good fortune and determination. Secreted in his shirt was a seaman's knife. Fortunately the

Japanese had failed to find it while searching the survivors when bringing them on board the submarine. With his hands now free Hess was able to reach the knife and he used it to cut the ropes of several of the other survivors – all those he could reach in time as the submarine was disappearing beneath the waves.

George Kenmore Hess, Seaman McDougall, and sixteen other men managed to survive the atrocities inflicted upon them by Tatsunosuke Ariizumi and his murderous crew. After escaping from the submarine or having been ditched into the water when it submerged these men had swum around all the remainder of that night, moving closer to the *Jean Nicolet* which could still be seen burning in the distance.

The submarine had fled the scene but it had been in little danger of attack. The solitary aircraft its radar operator spotted that night had been one of those sent to search for survivors. The distress call sent by Gus Tilden before the *Jean Nicolet* had been abandoned had resulted in a search being immediately instigated. That aircraft had not, of course, been able to locate the few remaining survivors of the sinking. Members of the aircrew were looking for lifeboats and believed that the survivors would be in properly equipped boats and rafts which would have had a plentiful supply of distress flares. When no flares were seen the search aircraft returned to its base. This was not, however, the end of the rescue attempt.

Meanwhile the survivors in the water had managed to close with what remained of the ship. By the time they reached the position it was fairly clear that the *Jean Nicolet* would not survive much longer and soon afterwards the vessel slipped beneath the waves. However, the survivors managed to find one of the life-rafts which had become jammed in the ship's rigging and had never been launched. When the ship had gone down the raft had floated free and this was to be the salvation of the men in the water. They managed to scramble aboard and although overcrowded they were at least able to keep away from the sharks.

The following morning the survivors saw a Liberator bomber approaching their position. They had no flares or any other method of signalling their position but the crew of the Liberator was obviously up to the task for they were able to see the men on the raft. Another small rubber dinghy was dropped, sufficient to hold just four people. About an hour later another Liberator appeared over the scene but soon flew away without taking any action whatever. Confused and angry, the survivors could only hope and pray that more substantial assistance was on its way.

The following morning, 4 July, 1944, another Liberator flew overhead. This was evidently working as a marker in cooperation with a surface vessel because soon afterwards a ship appeared in sight. This was the Indian warship HMIS *Hoxa* which had been dispatched to locate survivors.

All the survivors were given food, drinks and medical attention as soon as they were taken on board the warship. They were subsequently taken to Addu Atoll in the Maldives Group, landing the following day. There they were interrogated by members of British Intelligence and the whole bloody drama of the mass murders was revealed. When news of these events finally filtered back to Britain, Captain Tatsunosuke Ariizumi would become widely known as 'The Butcher' and marked for arrest and trial at the end of the war.

The survivors were allowed to rest and recuperate on the Addu Atoll for a week. On 12 July they were placed aboard another Indian warship, HMIS *Sonneti*, for passage to Colombo where they arrived two days later. From there, on 27 July, they were flown to Calcutta where the American service personnel were assigned to duties while the remaining crew members and ten naval armed guard unit members were transported by train to Bombay. From there they were transported aboard the USAT *General William Mitchel* to San Diego, landing back on U.S. soil on 6 October that year.

Only about two dozen men from a total of one hundred survived the butchery aboard the I-8. One of these was Francis J. O'Gara, the representative of the War Shipping Administration who had probably been saved because of his association with that organisation and the intelligence that might have been extracted from him. After the war O'Gara was found alive at the Ofuna prison camp near Yokohama. It was quite an astonishing discovery because O'Gara was considered to have been killed by the Japanese after he had been taken prisoner. So sure were the authorities that this was the case that a Liberty ship had been named after O'Gara. This was the only Liberty ship ever named after a living person. O'Gara was an interesting character. Before the war he had worked as a sports writer but in 1942, after the beginning of hostilities with Japan, he had joined the merchant marine as a seaman. He had worked at this highly dangerous profession for around two years after which he had gone to work for the War Shipping Administration, a position which should have afforded him better protection than that of a seaman aboard any of the American ships that were constantly coming under Japanese or German attack.

After being hustled below decks, and following the massacre of his friends and associates on the I-8, O'Gara had experienced a particularly unpleasant voyage aboard the Japanese submarine. He had been beaten, brutally interrogated, starved and often denied water. He had been allowed no communication with either Captain Nilsson or the radio operator Gus Tilden, although he did see them briefly from time to time and we may assume that both Tilden and Nilsson were treated in exactly the same manner.

After the massacre of the *Jean Nicolet's* crew the I-8 with its three captives travelled to Penang in Malaya where it arrived on 15 August that year. O'Gara and Captain Nilsson were taken ashore but what became of Gus Tilden remains a mystery. Some later time O'Gara was again placed aboard the I-8 and transported to Yokahama where he was incarcerated at a prison camp. Captain Nilsson's fate is also unknown but it is believed that he may have been placed on board another Japanese submarine which was subsequently sunk by the Americans.

Three months after the sinking of the *Jean Nicolet* the comment made by the first officer, Clement Carlin, to another crew member, Charles Pyle, concerning the distribution of his property in the event of Carlin's death, later formed part of a Superior Court case. Clement Carlin did not survive the massacre aboard the I-8 but the man who had been seated next to him, Charles Pyle, did. He later testified in support of the 'oral will' he had been given by Carlin only a short time before Carlin's murder. Pyle confirmed that Carlin had entrusted that oral will to him, quoting Carlin's exact words and adding, 'The Japanese took aboard all the men and subjected them to beatings and fettered everyone's hands except mine. They thought I was dead.'

*   *   *

The principal questions now, of course, are what became of Captain Tatsunosuke Ariizumi and did he ever pay for his many war crimes? The answers are not simple. In fact there are a variety of theories as to what finally happened Ariizumi but to get to that point we must deal with events immediately prior to the end of the war. Actually we have to go even farther – back to the Japanese attack on Pearl Harbor.

It was Admiral Isoroku Yamamoto, the commander of Japan's combined fleet, who originally came up with an astonishing concept which, had it been successfully carried to its fruition, might conceivably have altered the terms of the final Japanese capitulation from an unconditional surrender, as demanded by the Allies, to a conditional ceasefire which would have made a massive difference to the American occupation of Japan and possibly even to its administration of war crimes justice.

Before the war Yamamoto had travelled extensively in the United States and had realised that America, with its massive industrialisation, would be a difficult, almost impossible foe to defeat. If ever Japan was to go toe-to-toe with the U.S. then it would be necessary to demoralise the American people to such an extent that they would finally sue for peace. Yamamoto's plan to achieve this goal was through the construction of massive submarines. These were to be larger than any submarine previously built and so powerful that they could wreak enormous destruction wherever they went. Just three weeks after the successful raid on Pearl Harbor Yamamoto ordered the construction of the I-400 series of submarines. These were to be used in a second, even more devastating attack on Pearl Harbor and also on many other American targets including the bombing and shelling of New York and other major coastal cities. The Panama Canal was also to be targeted. If this could be destroyed, or at least closed for the duration of the war, this would disrupt very seriously American shipping movements – both warships and merchant vessels – thus not only strangling supplies but also affecting American sea-power. Yamamoto envisioned that these massive submarines, capable of carrying three aircraft, would be able to rain bombs on U.S. targets to such an extent that the American people would lose their will to keep fighting.

The I-400 series went immediately into production and if they had been completed earlier they might have played a significant role in the fight to control the Pacific. No one had ever dreamed of a submarine so large or so powerful. It was more than 400 feet long – as long as a football field – and capable of travelling 40,000 nautical miles (more than 78,000 kilometres) without refuelling – that was about four times the range of most submarines then in existence. The submarines would carry four months of food and other supplies for a crew of around 150. The attack aircraft, each capable of speeds up to 220 miles per hour and with a range of 600 miles, could deliver bomb-loads on cities, military targets and shipping.

Yamamoto ordered the construction of eighteen of these top secret 'underwater aircraft carriers', as they became known, however, he was not to live to see his dreams come to fruition. On 18 April, 1943, in retaliation for the attack on Pearl Harbor, the transport bomber carrying Yamamoto was deliberately targeted and attacked by American fighters over Bougainville Island and shot down. In effect the Japanese admiral was assassinated. His death brought about significant changes to the design and output of his pet submarine project. As the war progressed and Japan lost its dominance in the Pacific region it became clear to the Japanese military that following the loss of Guadalcanal the way lay open to the Japanese heartland. Every effort now turned to defending Japan rather than taking the fight to American shores. Plans to attack cities such as New York were dropped in favour of attacking the Panama Canal in an effort to disrupt U.S. Navy shipping. If that could be achieved then it might buy enough time for Japan to regroup its forces.

Yet all this was taking a massive amount of time, money, scarce resources and planning. By early 1945 not one of the new submarines had been completed and there were major problems with the production of the specially designed aircraft. A massive Allied blockade around Japan was preventing the production of much needed steel and eventually it was decided to cut the production of eighteen super-subs to just five – plus two more which would actually be of a smaller design. The first of the super-subs, the I-400, was

This is the I-400, sister ship to the I-401, seen here after its surrender with members of its Japanese crew on deck. These submarines were designed to take the war directly to American shores and wreak terrible damage. (*Catalogue Number NH-111806. Naval History and Heritage Command*)

Japanese crew members under guard aboard the I-400, sister ship to the I-401, following their surrender. Note: Rails to launch aircraft running from the cone-shaped hanger. (*Catalogue Number NH-111822. Naval History and Heritage Command*)

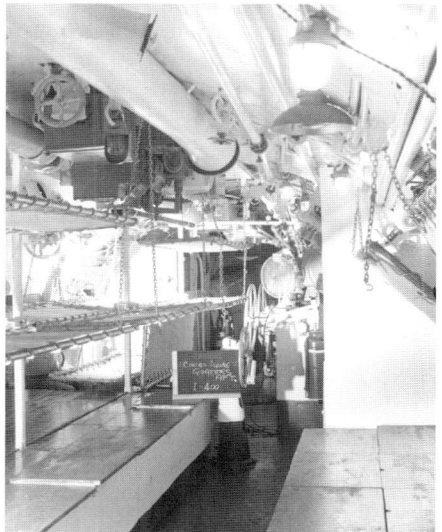

The galley and crew's quarters aboard the Japanese submarines I-14 and I-400 respectively. (*Catalogue numbers NH-111805* (*galley*) *and NH-111816* (*crew's quarters*). *Naval History and Heritage Command*)

completed towards the end of 1944 followed by the two smaller submarines. The I-401 in which Captain Tatsunosuke Ariizumi would subsequently sail was completed in early January 1945. The I-14, the final massive submarine, came into service by March that year.

Even at this relatively late stage in the war these issues demonstrated the fanaticism that then existed within the minds of the Japanese military hierarchy. Japan had almost certainly lost the war but the Japanese firmly believed that significantly disrupting the Panama Canal traffic might just convince the Americans to give up their demands for an unconditional surrender and instead accept some form of conditional ceasefire.

Another even more sinister element now also crept into the overall concept. Vice Admiral Jisaburo Ozawa, then the vice-chief of the Naval General Staff, suggested using the new submarines to deliver a devastating biological weapons attack against one of the major population centres along the west coast of America. For years the Japanese had been testing biological weapons at their notorious Unit 731 in Manchuria so Ozawa's suggestion was a concept that interested the war planners in Tokyo. Dr Shiro Ishii, the equally notorious head of Unit 731 and an expert on viral weapons, was consulted on the issue. He quickly stated that to carry out such an attack effectively the aircraft launched from the I-400 submarines should carry a large number of plague-infected fleas. Such a plan had already been tested successfully in China. Ishii, who would be executed after the war, stated that to be most effective the attack should be made against San Francisco, Los Angeles or San Diego. For a while it looked as if America was about to be decimated but then the head of the army's general staff decided against the proposal, claiming that

Admiral Jisaburo Ozawa. At six-feet seven-inches in height, Ozawa was considered by his contemporaries to have been rather ugly. His men nicknamed him the 'Gargoyle'. Yet he was a highly efficient officer and well respected for his naval capabilities but had he got his way he would have unleashed a devastating biological attack on the United States from the I-400 series of submarines. Ozawa died in Japan in 1966 at the age of eighty years. (*Catalogue Number NH-63425. Naval History and Heritage Command*)

it would be completely unacceptable on 'humanitarian grounds'. It was a decision possibly made with the realisation that Japan might just lose the war; deploying such a devastating and internationally illegal weapon of mass destruction against civilian populations would later be counted as a major war crime and those responsible held to account.

Meanwhile, plans to attack the Panama Canal proceeded and training of the submarines' crews took place as quickly as possible. This training period revealed major defects in the designs of the submarines and the requisite skills of their crews, all of which had either to be rectified or otherwise resolved or worked around. Finally it was decided to use huge 1760 lb bombs in the attack, each of the aircraft carrying just one of these weapons. The pilots were also instructed that as this was a 'do-or-die' mission which simply could not fail they were to crash their aircraft into the canal's locks, flooding and blocking the canal and thus effectively rendering the waterway inoperable for many months to come. How the pilots really felt about this new directive is unclear although it has been recorded that they accepted the decision 'quietly'.

Then in March 1945 Iwo Jima fell into American hands and Okinawa was attacked. American forces were now so close to the Japanese mainland that the end seemed close and inevitable. All the years of planning to carry out the submarine-launched air attack against the Panama Canal was abandoned and it was decided instead to attack the American aircraft carriers at Ulithi, a staging area near Truk in the Caroline Islands that was then being used by the Americans. Truk itself was still under Japanese control and had been used for several years as a submarine base to attack shipping along the east coast of Australia. (See chapter one).

When Captain Tatsunosuke Ariizumi was informed of these changes in the plans he was devastated. His dream was to strike a mighty blow against the enemy, one that would have a major impact on the Americans' ability to wage its war against Japan. Any attack against the American carriers at Ulithi, even if successful, would not create the disruption that an attack on the canal would achieve. However, Ariizumi was under orders and, dutifully, he obeyed. The two large submarines were instructed to travel independently to Ulithi and then rendezvous close to the target.

Meanwhile the two smaller submarines, the I-13 and I-14 were ordered to go to Truk. The base was now just a shell of what it had once been, its power and influence as a major base having been largely destroyed following Operation Hailstone of February 1944 when the port had been subjected to a massive air and sea attack made by American forces. The American attack on Truk may be likened to the Japanese attack on Pearl Harbor. In fact Truk was such an important naval base that it had often been referred to as the Japanese Pearl Harbor.

From Truk the submarine commanders were ordered to send their aircraft on a mission over Ulithi to confirm that the American carriers were still in port.

What became of I-13 is unknown. The submarine never arrived at Truk and it was presumed to have been lost. The I-14, however, reached the rendezvous successfully and its aircraft were launched as instructed to carry out a reconnaissance mission over Ulithi. Yet it was now far too late. Soon afterwards the news was received that an atomic bomb had destroyed Hiroshima followed by a second bomb which had largely destroyed Nagasaki, and on 15 August the 'Jewel Voice Broadcast' from Emperor Hirohito was heard, announcing to the Japanese people that the government had accepted the Potsdam Declaration and that the Second World War therefore had come to an end.

Yet for many fanatical military commanders like Captain Tatsunosuke Ariizumi there was still some 'wriggle room'. Hirohito's broadcast, which was actually the first time he had ever considered communicating directly with his subjects, was not only self-delusional (he spoke about the Japanese having wanted only to emancipate East Asia) but was also spoken in classical Japanese which many ordinary Japanese people could barely understand. Hirohito also made no reference to an actual surrender, stating only that the Potsdam Declaration had been accepted. Many commanders were left confused. Had Japan surrendered or not?

At this time Captain Tatsunosuke Ariizumi was not technically the commanding officer of I-401. That role was being filled by Commander Nobukiyo Nambu. Ariizumi was the officer in overall charge of the submarine group – what was left of it – and whatever happened next would be his call. He was already severely disappointed that the attack on the Panama Canal had been called off and although the planned attack on the American carrier force at Ulithi was a poor substitute he was determined to carry it out. Emperor Hirohito's ambivalence seemed to present the perfect opportunity. However, the following day, 16 August, 1945, the submarine group received specific orders cancelling the attack on Ulithi. The order came just a few hours before Ariizumi planned to launch the strike. Very specifically, Captain Tatsunosuke Ariizumi was instructed to raise the dedicated black flag of surrender, to destroy the group's aircraft by jettisoning them into the sea, to destroy the logs and secret code books, and to return to Kure. The

The American submarine USS *Segundo*. After the I-401 had surrendered to the *Segundo*, the American crew was unable to determine exactly what had become of Tatsunosuke Ariizumi. This photograph of the *Segundo* was taken in 1966. (*Catalogue USN 1115253 U.S. National Archives. Naval History and Heritage Command*)

group was also ordered to fire off all their torpedoes which was the easiest way of jettisoning them. One torpedo, however, malfunctioned and circled around, heading back towards the submarine but this too just sank to the bottom of the sea without causing any damage.

On 24 August, 1945, the image of I-401 was picked up by a radar operator aboard the USS *Segundo*, a Balao-class submarine of the U.S. Navy that had been commissioned in May the previous year. The *Segundo* was then under the command of Lieutenant Commander Stephen L. Johnson, just twenty-nine years of age at the time. The *Segundo* was his first command position.

The *Segundo* was a well equipped and battle-hardened vessel which had seen its own share of action. It had worked as part of wolf-packs that had attacked many Japanese convoys in the Pacific. It was now undertaking what would be its fifth and final war patrol and had been assigned to the Tokyo Bay region. The image of I-401 came onto the *Segundo's* radar screen when both vessels were approximately one hundred miles off the coast of Honshu.

All of which brings us back to the fate of Captain Tatsunosuke Ariizumi. There are at least two versions of what happened to him at this point in the war.

The first, and probably the most accurate is that after receiving his orders to surrender, having struck the black flag and jettisoned all his log books, codes and weapons, Ariizumi ordered his submarine to return to Kure. Having been spotted by the *Segundo*, Ariizumi's instinctual reaction was to take evasive action and his manoeuvres immediately after the contact had been made raised significant suspicions aboard the *Segundo*. Their caution was warranted because the I-401 was massively larger than the *Segundo*, three times larger, in fact those on board the American submarine could hardly believe what they were seeing. No submarine was supposed to be this large – it was the size of surface ship, and what armaments might this monstrous vessel be hiding? Its deck was bristling with weapons including a huge 5.5 inch gun that would have been quite capable of blowing a destroyer out of the water. It would make mincemeat of a relatively tiny vessel like the *Segundo*. Additionally there appeared to be three triple-barrelled anti-aircraft guns on the Japanese submarine's bridge and an astonishing array of torpedo tubes in its bow.

Bringing the *Segundo* to full alert, and displaying as much caution as possible, Lieutenant Commander Johnson brought the *Segundo* closer, moving at a snail's pace. The black flag on the submarine's bridge indicated that the vessel was surrendering in accordance with the national Japanese surrender but one could never be too sure what would happen and different Japanese military commanders had placed very different interpretations on Emperor Hirohito's Golden Voice speech. Additionally, the Japanese had frequently displayed untrustworthy characters and it was always possible that the *Segundo* was being lured into a deadly trap. The situation was made even more suspicious because the I-8 was still also flying the Rising Sun flag from its mast.

However, after manoeuvring themselves into more advantageous positions both submarines ended up facing each other, their torpedo tubes apparently ready to fire, although Johnson could have had no way of knowing that the I-8 had already jettisoned its entire load of twenty torpedoes. Johnson had now also received orders allowing him to attack and destroy the Japanese submarine should it display any hostile intent. Johnson was reasonably sure that a battery of Japanese torpedo tubes aimed specifically at his submarine was a fairly hostile indication of belligerence but he wanted to be sure before he launched any kind of attack on this enemy vessel. He was now keenly aware that he was in the centre of historic events. This was no ordinary submarine. What he was seeing was quite evidently some kind of secret super-submarine and its capture intact would not only be an astonishing achievement but also a technological coup. Who could say what kind of modern wonders such a machine might reveal? Johnson had no way of knowing that he was facing a machine that could act as an underwater aircraft carrier, and that this particular submarine also carried Commander Tatsunosuke Ariizumi, the very person who had been responsible for the development of this Leviathan and a man already on the list of most-wanted war criminals.

Yet Johnson also did not realise that he was now dealing with Lieutenant Commander Nobukiyo Nambu, the captain of I-8, who was a well disciplined and combat-hardened submarine commander. Nambu had a tremendous amount of experience behind him. He had been present during the attack on Pearl Harbor and had managed to survive the entire war in the Pacific. Neither Nambu nor his superior, Captain Tatsunosuke Ariizumi, had easily accepted the emperor's bland instruction to surrender and since

The 5.7" deck gun aboard the I-401. This photograph was taken following the surrender of the submarine and the mysterious disappearance of Tatsunosuke Ariizumi. (*Catalogue Number NH-111803. Naval History and Heritage Command*)

that time various radio messages from Tokyo had caused only further confusion including one which had clearly stated that although peace had been declared the projects then under way were to be completed as planned: 'execute predetermined missions and attack the enemy if discovered' as the message had stated in no uncertain terms.

The I-401, however, allowed itself to be boarded by a small American crew who would act as guards during the voyage back to Japan. According to a U.S. Navy report, at 0400 on 31 August, 1945, while the I-401 was in the process of entering Tokyo Bay, Captain Tatsunosuke Ariizumi placed a pistol into his mouth and shot himself. His body was taken topside by members of his crew and placed into the sea. This version has been disputed by some who state that the Americans on board heard no pistol-shot, nor had they witnessed any bodies being thrown overboard. All they knew was that Ariizumi had disappeared.

It was also subsequently reported that while entering the bay the submarine had come close to land at Sendai where Ariizumi might easily have been able to slip into the water and swim ashore, his escape probably being aided by members of the submarine's crew. Dead or alive, Captain Tatsunosuke Ariizumi was never seen again, at least not under his real name. In a country teeming with residents of all kinds, and particularly a country experiencing post-war social and economic difficulties, where the establishment and its bureaucracy went out of its way to protect those men who had served during the conflict, locating one man who really did not want to be found would have been almost impossible. In any case, no one was looking for Ariizumi. He was a war criminal but as far as the authorities were concerned he was already dead.

After the war one man who went in search of Captain Tatsunosuke Ariizumi was actually one of Ariizumi's intended victims. This was Francis J. O'Gara who had been located emaciated but alive in a prison camp in Japan. O'Gara was convinced that Ariizumi was still alive and desperately wanted him brought to justice. However, despite researching and working for years towards that objective, O'Gara was unable to prove that Ariizumi was then anything more than an enigma.

The Japanese submarine I-8, which Ariizumi had commanded at the time of the two massacres, did not survive the war, nor did any of the crew who were aboard the vessel at the time of its destruction. It was sunk off Okinawa on 31 March, 1945, during an encounter with two American warships, the USS *Morrison* and USS *Stockton*.

The USS *Stockton*. (*Catalogue Number NH-99598. Naval History and Heritage Command*)

The *Stockton*, a Gleaves-class destroyer, was the first American warship to locate I-8 on radar that day. The ship and its crew had been through significant action during the war. After an overhaul at Seattle the vessel and crew had been assigned to Pearl Harbor for refresher training. The destroyer was then sent to act as a carrier screen for the landing at Iwo Jima (Operation Detachment). On 21 February, 1945, just a couple of days

The USS *Morrison*. (*Catalogue Number USN 243852 (U.S. National Archives). Naval History and Heritage Command*)

after the landing, the group of ships to which the *Stockton* was attached experienced a determined suicide attack by four Japanese aircraft. The escort carriers USS *Bismarck Sea* was sunk, after blowing up, (with the loss of 318 lives) and the USS *Lunga Point* was damaged. From that time the *Stockton* was utilised to provide escort for replenishment units working to bring fuel and supplies in support of the Okinawa campaign. On 31 March, the I-8 pinged alarmingly on the ship's radar and the *Stockton* launched a solid depth-charge attack which failed to destroy the enemy submarine. Meanwhile the USS *Morrison* arrived just in time to see the I-8 surfacing very briefly before almost immediately diving again. The *Morrison* launched its own depth-charges, forcing the Japanese submarine to the surface where it was sunk by gunfire. There was just one survivor who was subsequently rescued by one of the *Morrison's* boats.

The *Stockton* managed to survive the war but the *Morrison* did not. On 4 May, 1945, only slightly more than a month after sinking I-8, the destroyer was attacked by kamikaze aircraft, four of which crashed into the ship. The ship sank very quickly, although a landing craft, the LCL(L)-21, (later often referred to as a 'pallbearer') was able to pluck 187 men from the water. The cost in lives had been great, a total of 155 American seamen had gone down with the ship.

Harold Jiro Nakahara, had been the radio officer aboard the I-8 at the time of the attack on the *Jean Nicolet* and it was he who had acted as the interpreter. After the war he came forward and gave detailed accounts of the massacre to war crimes investigators, identifying several of the perpetrators. Nakahara was fluent in English, having been born in Hawaii. Upon the outbreak of war with Japan he had been studying in Japan and had been unable to return home. He had subsequently been forced into joining the Japanese Navy as a radio officer and interpreter.

Three members of the I-8's crew were however, subsequently charged with war crimes and brought before a war crimes tribunal. Jiro Nakahara decided to give evidence against the other two and was acquitted while the two convicted men received only light sentences which were later commuted. In effect, for the hundreds of lives callously taken by Ariizumi and his men – mass murder on the high seas on far too many occasions – no one was properly punished.

In January 1949, five years after the destruction of the *Jean Nicolet* and *Tjisalak*, Admiral Soemu Toyoda was placed on trial at Yokohama. Two of the cases presented to the military court were those of the *Tjisalak* and *Jean Nicolet*. Of particular interest to the court and highlighted by the prosecution was the murder of Mrs Verna Gorden-Brittain. 'Mrs Brittain, who was married to a British flying officer during the war was on her way from Australia to India to join her husband,' the press subsequently reported. 'Survivors of the Dutch ship *Tjisalak* and the American steamer *Jean Nicolet* gave evidence of how several persons including Mrs Brittain were taken aboard a Japanese submarine and stabbed to death or machine-gunned on its decks.'

Admiral Toyoda was famous in Japan. He was a former member of the Supreme War Council and later the commander-in-chief of the Japanese Combined Fleet. Yet he was no strategist and many of his grand plans had failed miserably including the Battle of the Philippines Sea, the Battle of Leyte Gulf and other disasters including ordering the massive Japanese cruiser *Yamato* into an action it could never win. Despite these setbacks Toyoda became the final supreme commander of the Japanese Navy from 25 May, 1945. He was later arrested by SCAP (Supreme Commander of the Allied Powers) authorities and placed into Sugamo Prison in Tokyo charged with violating the laws and customs of war. He pleaded not guilty before the Military Tribunal for the Far East and was subsequently acquitted. He thus achieved the distinction of being the only member of the Japanese armed forces who was acquitted after being charged with war crimes.

Chapter Four

Alexander Marinesko

The *Wilhelm Gustloff* Disaster

That morning the sea was the colour of Welsh slate. The Baltic was a turmoil of wind and waves, ice-cold and somehow depressing. Captain Friedrich Petersen leaned against the bridge bulkhead, wiping condensation from the glass and peering into the early morning. The sea was rolling against the harbour walls in wind-driven, white-topped waves. A few gulls wheeled away, their wings caught momentarily in a sudden down-draft. Petersen watched for a moment, feeling uncharacteristically morose. He had always loved this ship. From the moment he had stepped aboard the *Wilhelm Gustloff* it had been a love affair. During those first few years of peace, the calm before the storm, Petersen had taken his ship to European and exotic ports carrying the banner of a youthful National Socialism – the ideal of statehood rising from the ashes of war, depression and despair. It had carried chosen passengers around the globe, receiving, at least in the beginning, warm acclaim, even from the most searching and critical of press commentators. The *Wilhelm Gustloff* had been beautiful – like a white cloud floating on the surface of a deep blue sea. It was a vision. People saw it and fell in love.

Friedrich Petersen had always looked forward to getting away from shore, going to sea, even in his younger days as a mere deck officer, but to take the *Gustloff* to sea was somehow special. And to be taking such a ship to sea as its commander, that had been extremely special, one of his greatest joys.

Yet it was over now. The *Wilhelm Gustloff* was still here. Petersen himself was still here. But everything else had changed.

Gone were the rich trappings of luxury, the ornate dining saloons, the richly draped and furnished cabins, the deck-hockey and smoking-rooms and the shaded promenade where white-liveried stewardesses once served *Dom Perignon* with smoked salmon and cucumber sandwiches. That kind of life was now so far in the past that even Petersen had trouble remembering

The *Wilhelm Gustloff.* This photograph was taken in Danzig in September 1939. (*Bundesarchiv Bild 183-H27992 Bundesarchiv*)

it clearly. The past was like some kind of dream. A life lived before it had moved into the greyness before death.

The once gorgeous *Wilhelm Gustloff* now seemed somehow to hug the wharf for safety. It had become a bleak ship, painted dull grey, berthed in a bleak grey dockyard where any semblance of colour or warmth or sea romance had long since dissolved into a background of broken cranes hanging limply over bomb-smashed harbour walls, half-sunken ships, tugs and lighters, the ruins of burnt-out buildings and the constant movement of thousands of half-starved, bitterly cold refugees, wounded and grey-clad military personnel, moving in a seemingly haphazard, listless formation beneath a dawning sky pregnant with the promise of snow.

The war was drawing to a close. Everyone knew that but not a single person was brave enough to voice the words. There were already too many corpses in the world. The Russians were closing in from the east and soon there would be nothing left of Hitler's so-called Thousand Year Reich. Even now, if one listened carefully, it was possible to hear the low rumble of the Soviet guns in the distance as General Konstantin Rokossovsky's 2nd Belorussian Front moved inexorably east and north towards Danzig and Gdynia which the Germans, in a fit of nostalgia, had renamed Gotenhafen. Death was coming to Gdynia like a steam-train and the thousands of refugees flooding onto the docks in search of a ship to take them somewhere – anywhere – were wide-eyed, terrified testimony to that.

It was time to get away. Boarding had been going on for days. Peasants, wounded soldiers, nurses, even a large group of pregnant women had come aboard, cramming themselves into the cabins and passageways, going deeper and deeper into the once grand liner, seeking out every nook and cranny in which to roll out a blanket or two. Whole families had come aboard. Hundreds of families, Baltic Germans, Lithuanians, Poles, all desperate not to be entangled fatally in the hugely destructive machinery of the flailing Soviet military. All along the wharves grey ships were boarding tens of thousands of refugees – a mass of humanity, all desperately seeking a way to survive.

Captain Petersen walked to the port side of the bridge and looked down to the wharves directly below. The sight simply deepened his depression. It was still early morning. Grey light lay on the harbour of Gdynia like an undertaker's shroud. Refugees in their hundreds were huddled in groups all along the wharves, some still asleep, rolled in snow-covered blankets, shivering. The harbour was coming alive after another bitterly cold night. January in the Baltic could be a killing month. It was so easy to die, and now, the first month of 1945, with death everywhere, with the entire German army folding like playing cards, dying seemed almost a natural thing to do.

Two officers at the gangway were at least attempting to maintain some kind of order as the refugees came aboard. Some even had boarding passes but in reality the time for such frivolities was long past. They came aboard, those depressingly tired, slack-eyed people, huddled in their shawls, their old blankets, moth-eaten coats, carrying suitcases and parcels of food, a chicken or two; a dead rabbit slung around the neck of one old woman looked much like a fur stole.

A young radio officer came onto the bridge, ashen-faced, tired after a full night seated at his post. He saluted briefly and handed Petersen a pink message slip. Petersen nodded curtly, taking the slip and holding it up to the pearl of light coming through the salt-encrusted windows of the bridge. He read the few words briefly, his lips compressing. There were to be no warship escorts. Nor would there be any air-cover for the ships about to leave for Kiel. The weather was going to be too bad and, in any case, every aircraft that could fly was being pressed into service in a desperate but futile attempt to stem the crimson tide of sovietism that was washing rapidly across Europe from the east.

Petersen crumpled the paper in his hand and looked once more at the seething mass of grey humanity on the wharves below. Two measly torpedo boats. That's all that could be spared! Just two puny boats to protect some of the largest evacuation ships in the whole operation, ships that would soon be leaving with tens of thousands of people on board, including countless thousands of children, all desperate to get away.

Petersen nodded to the deck officer, leaving him in charge of overseeing the boarding, and went to his cabin. He looked down and saw that the crumpled signal was still in his hand. Sitting in one of the luxurious armchairs he smoothed the paper on his knee and read it again. It was all damned madness. The whole thing was insane. The ship wasn't ready, none of the ships were, but the *Wilhelm Gustloff* was now a lame old lady. It hadn't been to sea for years. The comfortable cabin accommodations had been gutted to make room for thousands of U-boat recruits who had trained at the port for most of the war. The engines were stiff with rancid grease, flanges needed repacking, engine parts replaced. It had all been a nightmare fuelled by the constant threat of an invisible enemy, a great horde of them like the mongols of Genghis Khan, there, just over the horizon, guns and rockets thundering.

*   *   *

Alexander Ivanovich Marinesko's entire body was taut with nervous tension. Peering through the periscope of Soviet submarine S-13, he could see little in the half-light of half-dawn but somehow he knew the German torpedo boats were still out there somewhere, hunting him. Some people would call it a gut feeling but to Marinesko it was more an ache, a dread in the core of his bones brought into play by years of ice-cold, knife-edged tension.

The S-13 had left Hanko on 11 January, 1945, for what would prove to be its most successful and murderous war patrol. Marinesko knew these waters like the back of his hand. He'd seen service in the Black Sea Fleet and also in the Baltic Fleet as the commanding officer of the Soviet submarine M-96, considered in its time to have been one of the best submarines in the fleet. Had not alcohol got in his way, Marinesko's career in the navy would have been meteoric, despite the fact that he came from a poor background, his father having been a Romanian sailor and his mother a Ukrainian – not exactly the background one would expect of a naval officer with high ambitions. But then Marinesko's ambitions were modest. Promotion was welcome but the only success he was interested in was that of killing Germans, any Germans. It didn't really matter who they were.

These are scenes from the *Wilhelm Gustloff* at the time it was being used at Gdynia as accommodation for submarine training crews. (*Reproduced courtesy of the* Wilhelm Gustloff *Museum, www.wilhelmgustloffmuseum.com*)

Twice, early in this patrol, the S-13 had been sighted and attacked by German torpedo boats and then again, shortly afterwards. The Germans never stood much chance of success, especially against a submarine capable of diving so quickly and under the command of a highly experienced captain who had spent almost the entire war fighting from beneath the waves.

Marinesko slammed up the periscope handles and stood straight, rubbing a hand back through his thick forest of brown hair. The control tower was almost in darkness, the men's faces eerily illuminated by the glow of their instruments. Everything was silent. There were no words, no sounds apart from the whisper of the two 550 horsepower electric motors which were now pushing the S-13 through the freezing waters of the Baltic Sea at a steady nine knots.

Marinesko looked at his gold watch. It always gave him a certain thrill to see it there on his wrist, his award for having captained M-96, the best submarine in the Baltic Fleet. The time was now 08.20 and the submarine was en route to the Stolpe Bank on the Pomeranian Coast where, with luck, Marinesko would lie in wait for a rich prize, one of the huge transports carrying refugees, troops and wounded Germans to Kiel.

If Marinesko had anything to do with it, they would never reach their destination alive.

Not one of them!

*   *   *

Captain Friedrich Petersen suddenly felt as if he alone had to save the world. He couldn't shake the feeling that everyone in Poland was somehow converging on the *Wilhelm Gustloff*. He stood on the port bridge wing looking down to the wharf where a long convoy of army vehicles was in the process of drawing up close to the ship. They were not ambulances, nor were they marked with the international Red Cross, but they were carrying nothing but wounded men, some evidently desperately wounded, as they began to climb down from the rear of the trucks, or were lifted down on stretchers. There were not just a few. Dozens of trucks were disgorging hundreds of wounded. An avalanche of pain, blood and suffering. The *Gustloff's* seamen supervising the loading were visibly shaken by the sight of all these injured men, some of them in their fifties, or sixties – old men, hustled into any kind of uniform and ordered to fight or die. They found that the dying part of that equation came easily.

More trucks arrived, moving towards the hulking grey mass of the *Hansa*, also scheduled to leave for Kiel with the *Wilhelm Gustloff*. They too were carrying wounded, some supplies for the journey, munitions for the anti-aircraft guns.

Civilians traipsed after them, hoping for a berth on any ship. They were exhausted, dazed by war, by lack of sleep, by hunger, but largely by the terror of what was to come. The Russians were preceded by a wave of terror, real or imaginary, no one really knew, but the rumours were there and they were bloodily persistent. Rape, torture, brutality, humiliation, mass executions, especially for Nazi party members or those involved in organisations such as the Gestapo, any kind of police or the many German organisations used as instruments of mass murder. Indeed, Petersen knew for a fact that Gestapo agents were already on board the *Wilhelm Gustloff.* Narrow-shouldered men with mean features and bulky pistols beneath their coats, rats running scared now that the rat-catchers with strychnine baits were rapidly approaching from the east.

Petersen turned and looked aft. The lifeboats were strung along the port side all the way from the bridge superstructure almost to the stern deck. The same number of boats were hanging from the davits on the starboard side but it was quite obvious that should anything happen and the passengers and crew needed to take to the boats then there would be nowhere near enough for those on board, not even with all the rafts Petersen had ordered to be brought onto the ship. The *Wilhelm Gustloff* was a big, beautiful, solid liner and Petersen loved her, but if she sank, thousands of people were definitely going to die.

*   *   *

Kraft durch Freude, 'Strength Through Joy', was, like all National Socialist propaganda, the complete antithesis of actuality. Promoting health, happiness and prosperity, the Strength Through Joy organisation was a subsidiary of the German Labour Front and promoted the concept of a working class utopia where everyone was gainfully employed, fit, well and happy.

The 25,000 tons liner which was now berthed at the chillingly cold, overcrowded Gdynia docks had once been among the more well known public-relations tools of the Strength Through Joy organisation. Built in 1936 at a cost of 25 million *Reichsmarks*, the vessel had been launched the following year. It had originally been intended to name the ship *Adolf Hitler*, after the Fuhrer, but Hitler himself decided to name the liner after Wilhelm Gustloff, a former leader of the Swiss branch of the National Socialist Party who had been assassinated in 1936. Hitler was reported to have made the decision to change the proposed name of the ship during the memorial service being held in Wilhelm Gustloff's honour. Intended originally as a liner, the ship's civilian career – providing cruises, concerts and other cultural offerings to German functionaries and workers, was to be spectacularly brief.

The *Wilhelm Gustloff* served its original purpose largely as a propaganda vessel until the spring of 1939. By that time the whole world had finally realised that war was almost inevitable. The ship's first military role was to bring home the Condor Legion from Spain after the legion had assisted in bringing General Francisco Franco to power following two years of bitter and particularly bloody civil war.

On 1 September, 1939, the day Germany invaded Poland to ignite the Second World War, the *Wilhelm Gustloff* was requisitioned by the German *Kriegsmarine* and given the official title of *Lazarettschiff D* (Hospital Ship D). Clearly, Hitler had known when he first commissioned the construction of the vessel that he would soon be in need of large hospital ships.

Powered by four, 8-cylinder MAN diesel engines, driving twin, 4-blade propellers, the *Wilhelm Gustloff* was capable of 15.5 knots with a range of 12,000 nautical miles carrying almost 1500 passengers in relative comfort.

Painted white with the internationally recognised green band and red crosses around its hull, the *William Gustloff's* career as a hospital ship was to be even shorter than its life as a liner. In November 1940 all the hospital and medical equipment was removed from the vessel and the ship was painted in the standard drab grey of the *Kriegsmarine*. However, its seagoing career was almost over. Due to the superiority in numbers of British surface vessels, then blockading German ports, the *Wilhelm Gustloff* was transformed into a barracks and used to accommodate trainee submariners at the port of Gdynia. The ship would go to sea just one more time.

It would be its last.

It was now January 1945 and the evacuation of German troops, civilians and wounded was well underway, a mass of bloodied, tired, cold, dispirited humanity flooded onto the Gdynia docks, all searching desperately to escape. The Germans had even given the evacuation a designated title. It was called 'Operation Hannibal'.

There was a gentle knock on his cabin door and Captain Friedrich Petersen looked up from his desk. He knew that sound. It would be his first officer. Two taps, followed by two more, almost softly.

'Come.' Petersen smiled thinly as his first officer came into the cabin. He looked worried. 'It's not going well, captain.' He paused for moment, uncertain. 'I mean, the numbers. The boarding passes, we should not have bothered issuing them. People are just flooding on board. We can't stop them.'

Petersen looked at his watch. It was a little after 4.30 in the afternoon. The light creeping softly through the brass-lined scuttle was like age-faded pearl. He looked up at his first officer.

'I have some news that's not so good. When we leave, we'll have only the *Hansa* with us and two torpedo boats.'

'Just two?' The first officer looked crestfallen.

Petersen nodded, grimly. 'How many are aboard? Do we have numbers yet?'

From farther down the passageway came the sounds of children crying. A baby was wailing hungrily.

The first officer sat in a deep leather chair and lit a cigarette. Smoke curled around his eyes. He looked tired – and somehow haunted. 'We're attempting to get the numbers together now, captain, but it's too many. If anything should happen it's going to be a disaster, worse than anything we could possibly imagine.'

Petersen nodded. 'But you must have some idea?'

The first officer shrugged. 'Closest calculations right at the moment are that we have around 170 crew, almost a thousand officers and U-boat crew, more than 370 female auxiliary helpers, 160 wounded men and more than eight thousand civilians.'

Petersen looked shocked. 'Eight thousand!'

The first officer looked defeated. He slumped deeper into his chair. 'More than five thousand of them are children, captain.'

Petersen closed his eyes and leaned back in his seat. He could feel a solid lump of dread beginning to form in the pit of his stomach. 'So that means there are what … more than …?'

'More than ten thousand souls on board, captain,' the first officer finished for him. 'And that's just a rough guess. There could be a couple of thousand more. It's impossible to say. They're crammed everywhere, on top of each other. It's like hell out there.'

Petersen blinked in the softened light. His face was pale. 'Dear God!'

*   *   *

In the fading light the *Wilhelm Gustloff* looked almost menacing, its grey, rust-streaked paint was illuminated by the pale shore-lights strung on poles along the wharf but also by the fires of those refugees who were cooking evening meals, crouching in the lee of the wharf buildings in an almost impossible attempt to get out of the biting wind.

Captain Petersen came out of the port saloon onto the first deck. Even here it was severely overcrowded. He had just completed an inspection of his ship and never wanted to do another. Just walking along the passageways was a task not easily undertaken. People were everywhere, crowded along the bulkheads of every passageway, in every cabin, filled to capacity, in all the offices, the saloons, canteens, access hatchways to lower decks and machinery spaces, the ship was like a beehive, a moving, throbbing mass of noisy humanity. There were foreign smells too, the stench of backed-up toilets unable to cope with so many people and the human waste they generated. There was the stink of stale bodies, of people who had slept rough for weeks, possibly months. The wounded had their own peculiar smell – blood, old dressings, gangrene, iodine, urine and vomit. Some had already died so they were beginning to smell too.

Petersen was glad to get back onto the upper deck. He sucked in fresh air but at that moment the sounds of shelling in the distance seemed to intensify. Were they closer or had the wind suddenly changed direction? He opened the port bridge wing door and stepped inside, glad at least to have this sanctum away from the crowded decks and passageways.

He was alone for a few moments. Darkness had fallen. He paced back and forth, thinking hard, just waiting for the signal to come from base H.Q. giving him permission to leave. He stepped to the starboard wing and looked up at the dark, clouded sky. When they were eventually allowed to leave harbour he would be completely absorbed in dodging Soviet submarines and getting his ship safely to Kiel, but at least he would be at sea, with room to manoeuvre. Here, tied up to some Polish wharf in the middle of a war zone, the *Wilhelm Gustloff* was a sitting target for Russian bombers or even those damned British Lancasters which had already wreaked so much havoc, death and destruction on the harbour and its shipping.

Petersen walked through the rear of the bridge and went down to his cabin, pouring himself a small whisky to help soften the frustration that was growing like a cancer in his belly.

The hours dragged by as if time somehow had slowed. Petersen sat quietly listening to the new sounds of his ship. The vessel was alive with them, alive with the hustle of people and the cries of the wounded, the slap of the sea against the grey hull, but there was no peace in these sounds, it was as if the ship was stirring with anguish and concern, almost as though everyone on board was somehow hovering between this life and the next. Petersen washed his face in cold water, took his hat from the hook behind the cabin door and went up to the bridge.

*   *   *

The *Wilhelm Gustloff* was finally released to leave harbour and the mooring lines were cast off at around 12.30 on the afternoon of 30 January, 1945. Leaving harbour with the former liner was the *Hansa*, also loaded to capacity with refugees, wounded, military personnel and Nazi Party officials and their families. Two small but very fast torpedo boats were to act as escorts, ostensibly providing at least some kind of protection against Soviet submarines. Additional protection had been provided in the form of anti-aircraft guns with trained crews, but the weather was expected to be unsuitable for air operations and during the relatively short trip to the canal port of Kiel they would probably not be required.

Petersen had already decided on his course. There were two principal options, both with an almost equal amount of advantages and dangers. He had discussed his plans with no fewer than three other ship's captains who were travelling as passengers on the vessel. There were two merchant marine captains on board and also an experienced German U-boat captain named Wilhelm Zahn. However, there had been some disagreement regarding the proposed ship's course to Kiel – particularly from Zahn. Captain Petersen, who, in any case, had the final say on the matter, wanted to take the *Wilhelm Gustloff* well out to sea into deep water where it was known to be clear of mines. However, Zahn argued that it would be safer to remain closer to shore, to hug the coastline and travel without any lights as it would make a submarine captain's task of finding and attacking the ship so much more difficult. There is little doubt that Zahn was correct in his assumption.

When the *Wilhelm Gustloff* cast off its mooring lines that afternoon and headed into the Baltic it would be almost completely unprotected from the vengeful Soviet submarines that were inevitably circling somewhere out there like sharks. Zahn argued forcefully, attempting to change Petersen's mind, but in the end the chosen course would take the ship out into the deep waters of the Baltic and there she would die.

The *Wilhelm Gustloff* cast off its mooring lines and tugs nosed its massive hull away from the wharf's stone walls. Those refugees still shivering on the docks that night were watching history unfold before their eyes. Some regretted not being able to get on board. Later they were to be eternally thankful.

The sun goes down early in the Baltic in winter, although in truth the sun is rarely seen through the almost constant layer of thick grey cloud. With night quickly falling, the *Wilhelm Gustloff* steered south-west, churning up the sea at a steady rate of nine knots. In the blackness of the night not even the wash of the ship's two massive four-bladed propellers could be seen.

The *Gustloff* was a grey ghost sailing on a grey sea, shrouded in a cloak of darkness.

Petersen remained on the bridge, with the duty officer and lookouts, ever watchful, scanning the night for any signs of danger. The first cause for concern came with a brief flashing signal that one of the escort boats was experiencing engine trouble and was turning back to Gdynia. Petersen cursed beneath his breath. The torpedo boats were all but useless but at least they were there. If a submarine suddenly put in an appearance then they at least might be able to do something – anything – to protect the two ships or to rescue survivors.

Then another blow fell. The *Hansa* was also experiencing engine trouble and was forced to abandon the run to Kiel. It too was turning back to Gdynia. The *Wilhelm Gustloff* would be alone in the night with just a single torpedo boat to protect it against whatever the Soviets had decided to throw at them.

The *Wilhelm Gustloff* was now heading for Kiel on Petersen's preferred course through the areas clear of minefields. The ship was still darkened when Captain Zahn came onto the bridge in an attempt to urge Petersen to return to shallow waters. Petersen was having none of it. At around that time one of the radio officers also came onto the bridge, a message slip in his hand. Petersen took it quickly and scanned the radio officer's hurried scrawl. A German minesweeper convoy was on a course that could intercept with the *Wilhelm Gustloff*. In the darkness of the night it could prove catastrophic. As a precaution Petersen decided to turn on the ship's port and starboard navigation lights. Moments later the red and green lights blinked on. All four captains on board were now becoming extremely concerned that they were dangerously exposing the ship. If a Soviet submarine was lurking out there, the *Wilhelm Gustloff* would make an irresistible target. The intensity of the dangers facing the liner were even further heightened because the submarine detection equipment aboard the sole remaining escort vessel was now frozen solid and had become completely inoperable. If a Soviet submarine was anywhere in the vicinity it would be completely invisible.

*   *   *

The war patrol aboard Alexander Marinesko's Stalinets-class submarine S-13 was going well, despite the fact that Marinesko had already had to dodge several attacks from German torpedo boats. At more than seventy-seven metres in length and carrying twelve torpedoes, the boat was capable of speeds up to nine knots when submerged. The submarine had already proved its worth in the Baltic war against the Germans. Commissioned in July 1941, its first commanding officer had been Captain Pavel Malantyenko. Under Malantyenko's command the boat had previously sunk three vessels in the Baltic totalling more than four thousand tons. These had been two Finnish freighters, the *Hera* and the *Jussi H.*, both of which had been torpedoed, followed by a small German freighter which the S-13 had sunk with gunfire. These relatively small actions were to serve only as an 'appetiser' for the carnage that was soon to come under the command of Captain Alexander Marinesko.

Submerged that night at periscope depth, S-13 was a wraith. Running almost silently on its twin electric motors, its presence in the vicinity remained completely undetected. With his face glued to the periscope lens, Marinesko could hardly believe his luck when the red and green navigation lights of the *Wilhelm Gustloff* suddenly winked at him from across the darkened waves. At that distance, and largely blacked out, it was impossible for Marinesko to know how large the ship was, or its name, but this was evidently a German vessel and possibly a large one. Without doubt it would be filled with refugees, wounded and German troops but it was not a registered hospital ship and therefore fair game.

Marinesko sucked in the stale submarine air and closed his eyes for a few seconds, gathering his thoughts.

Plotting a successful torpedo attack is a tricky business, especially when there was the very real possibility of German anti-submarine boats being in the vicinity, hidden by the night. Most German merchantmen were also armed with anti-aircraft weapons which could quickly cut swathes into the relatively delicate hull of a submarine making submerging impossible. Marinesko had no way of knowing that aboard the *Wilhelm Gustloff* the ship's guns had also been rendered inoperable by the intense cold. They were frozen solid and could not have damaged S-13 in any way.

For the following two hours S-13 shadowed the *Wilhelm Gustloff* while Marinesko made his plans. Finally he decided that his best chance of success would be to surface the submarine and under the cover of night to steer around the stern of the *Wilhelm Gustloff*, to position the S-13 between the far shore and the ship itself with his bows pointing to the vessel's port side.

Finally, S-13 was in position and ready to attack. The time was 2100 hours (9 p.m.) about nine hours after the *Wilhelm Gustloff* had departed for Kiel. The crew of the submarine went to battle-stations, the torpedo tubes were already loaded. The *Wilhelm Gustloff* and around nine or ten thousand people, including approximately five thousand children, had just minutes left to live. This was not going to be just another tragedy of war or 'acceptable collateral damage' – the sinking of the *Wilhelm Gustloff* was to become the deadliest shipping disaster of all time.

Marinesko wasn't even thinking about the casualties now. The death toll, whatever it was to be, would be just another statistic of war. A hundred dead: two hundred ... five it made no difference. These people were Germans. Contrary to their own beliefs they were not born to be racially superior. If Marinesko had anything to do with it they were born to die. They had come to Mother Russia like a plague, killing everything in sight, slaughtering in the hundreds of thousands, massacring whole towns and villages. Now it was their turn.

A large slab of ice bumped suddenly against the hull of the submarine, one of many floating past in a sea that was well below freezing that night. Marinesko watched the pale glow of the ice as it floated astern and a cold chill ran through him. In a few minutes time he would be launching a deadly attack on a merchant ship filled to overflowing with people. Anyone who found themselves in the water after the torpedoes struck would have only twenty or thirty minutes to live, if that. Marinesko realised that tonight the sea would be the murderer. More people would die of hypothermia than the explosives that were about to hit the ship. There was nothing he could do about that. It was just war.

He put the Zeiss binoculars to his eyes and scanned the darkness, adjusting the focus as his target's navigation light came suddenly into view. He checked the luminous dial on his watch, waiting for the second hand to reach twelve. 'Fire tubes one and two,' he said softly. The duty officer repeated the order into the microphone he wore around his neck. He was shivering so badly that he could hardly say the words.

'Fire one and two.'

Seconds later the submarine jolted in the water as the first two torpedoes spat into the sea.

'Fire three and four,' Marinesko ordered. Seconds later a third torpedo plunged from its tube and began its deadly journey towards destruction. Marinesko turned to his duty officer. 'What happened to four?'

The duty officer was listening to a voice in his earphones. He nodded unconsciously, turning to Marinesko. 'Four has become stuck in the tube, captain. They are trying to dismantle it now but the tube won't be ready for use for an hour or so.'

Marinesko was only half listening. He raised the binoculars to his eyes once again, straining to see through the darkness. There was nothing, just the sounds of the waves slapping against the hull of the boat and the two red and green navigation lights bobbing about, seemingly on the very surface of the sea. Marinesko was now counting off the seconds. They dragged by so slowly. More ice began scraping against the hull.

'Clear the conning tower, prepare to dive to periscope depth,' Marinesko was still counting as he spoke, hardly breathing. When his count reached sixty seconds there was still nothing. Five more seconds passed. Marinesko was now alone on the conning tower, rigid, almost frozen himself.

When the first two torpedoes struck the *Wilhelm Gustloff* it seemed, from a distance, to be almost an anticlimax. Two brief orange glows, mere flickers, like dim light bulbs far away, followed seconds later by another dull glow and then, almost immediately following that third explosion came the sound, the crump-crump-crump as the high explosive charges in the heads of the torpedoes detonated against the steel plates of the ship's outer hull. Marinesko scrambled for the conning tower hatch, climbed down and slammed the hatch shut behind him.

On board the *Wilhelm Gustloff* the detonation of three massive explosions in the middle of the night, striking the ship in its most vital areas, could not have been more devastating.

The first torpedo struck the ship for'ard, smashing into the bows of the vessel killing initially an unknown number of passengers and many of the crew who had been asleep in the crews' mess at the time. The blast virtually sealed off the bow section from the remainder of the ship. Alone, this one torpedo cause significant damage but may not have sunk the massive liner had the remaining members of the crew been able to implement effective damage-control measures. However, moments later came the second blast. This struck the *Wilhelm Gustloff* amidships, blasting a massive hole in the ship's steel plates. The principal force of the explosion was centred right in the liner's commodious former swimming pool which had been emptied and was now being used as sleeping space for hundreds of women, members of the Women's Naval Auxiliary. The blast turned the deep pool into an instant bloodbath. Ceramic tiles, steel rails and other fittings were transformed instantly into thousands of pieces of deadly shrapnel. Many of those not killed by the blast of the torpedo exploding were either killed or wounded by the flying fragments of steel, ceramics or glass. It was subsequently reported that of the 373 women who had been asleep, or attempting to sleep, in the drained pool that night, only three survived. The scene of carnage in and around the pool has been described horrifically in many ways since that bloody night – screaming young women, some of them not so young, hysterical with fright, covered with the blood of their friends and comrades, dead civilians everywhere, dead children like toy dolls, broken on the decks, bloodied, tragically dismembered. The ship was filled with shock and horror, the questioning confusion of what was happening. How had all this death suddenly appeared right in their midst? Incongruously, while all this destruction was taking place, amid the turmoil of blood and smoke and the cries of the wounded, the ship's alarm klaxon continued to wail its now obsolete warning.

At that moment Marinesko's third torpedo struck the ship, smashing into the engine room, killing almost everyone there and completely disabling the liner. Communications on board the vessel failed instantly as did the lights. The four massive MAN diesels were largely obliterated. The *Wilhelm Gustloff* began immediately to lose headway. A massive volume of water flooded into the ship and the doomed liner began quickly to list to port.

Between decks on the *Wilhelm Gustloff* that night everything was in a state of panic and confusion. Many of the passengers and crew were already dead, killed almost instantaneously by the blasts of the explosions, but thousands more were still alive and all of them now wanted desperately, somehow, to get to their lifeboat stations and survive.

For many of the passengers it was difficult to imagine what was going to happen next. Some even believed that the ship could still be saved, they could survive this, but others knew that the *Wilhelm Gustloff* was doomed, that it would soon be on the bottom of the sea and that most of the passengers and crew would be down there with it.

The passengers particularly had been completely unprepared, both for the attack and the ordeal they would soon have to face once the sea had claimed the ship. It had been hot between decks. Even in this cold weather it had been steamy. Thousands of people generated a lot of heat; the ship had been locked down and battened up for the weather and for security, and people had quickly shed much of their clothing. Now, in the darkness, illuminated only by the dim, emergency lighting, and amid all the confusion, panic, suffering and death, it was almost impossible for the refugees, wounded, nurses and military personnel to find their clothing and the lifejackets that had been issued to them upon boarding the liner. Officers had repeated Captain Petersen's orders that life-jackets were to be worn at all times but too many people, stifling in the heat, had abandoned the only piece of safety apparatus that might have given them at least a slim chance of life.

Minutes were now counted in lives as the terrified surge of people struggled through the hellish, smoke-filled darkness to the lifeboats on the upper decks. Many people were dying in the rush. When people realised that the ship had been hit, when they managed somehow to recover from the initial shock, then an almost instantaneous need for survival kicked in, overruling in many cases all thoughts of common decency, of unselfishness, or any tendency to look after others who might be in need of assistance. Hysteria simply bred more hysteria; panic created panic, and when thousands of people are panicking simultaneously, in a situation of death and imminent destruction, then the scene quickly descends into utter chaos.

There was no time for any kind of damage-control. Those members of the crew who had been detailed to carry out emergency repairs in the case of attack were nowhere to be seen. They should now have been carrying timber supports to the breaches in the hull, shoring them up with mattresses or whatever materials they could find in a desperate attempt to stem the flow of seawater. Damage-control under such circumstances would always be treacherously difficult, the men struggling to hold back a tide of water under almost impossible conditions, but in the darkened confines of the *Wilhelm Gustloff* that night the task would have been all but impossible, largely because of the enormous volume of people who now surged out of the cabins and every available space within the ship, clogging every stairwell and passageway in a desperate attempt to get successively up each deck, one after another, while every deck was choked with both the maniacal living and the quiet dead.

The people formed human wedges in every passageway, a solid throng of men, women and children, crushed, shoulder-to-shoulder, carried along by their own panic and the weight and momentum of those around them. Those who fell were trampled underfoot. Even if some of the passengers had wanted to save those who had fallen it would have been an almost impossible task. They would be unable to lend assistance as they had no power of their own. They were simply being impelled forward by the crowd, squeezed through bulkhead doors and up stairs – a terrified mass of humanity with little or no independent will of their own other than survival.

*   *   *

On the main upper deck, at least during the early minutes of the tragedy, there was *some* semblance of order, despite the obvious fact that the ship was almost certainly going to sink and many people were probably going to die. In the heavy seas the ship was rolling sluggishly under the influence of the dark waves but it was quickly apparent to all that the vessel was tilting alarmingly to port. Crew members and anyone free to lend a hand struggled to get the lifeboats ready so that they could be loaded and lowered. However, it was quickly discovered that many of the davits had become hopelessly frozen and would not move. Men attacked the davits with an array of tools: axes, hammers, even wheel-spanners, smashing away the ice in a desperate attempt to get the davits to move so that the boats could be got out and lowered.

Those passengers who had been closest to the main deck were now coming out into the snow, wind and ice, leaving behind the warmth of the ship to be confronted immediately by conditions that were evidently highly dangerous, even to people who were well dressed and prepared for such weather. Yet most were still in relative states of undress, wearing only light clothing and far too many were not wearing or even carrying their lifebelts. Despite this they were hurried to their lifeboats by those members of the crew who had been fortunate to survive the triple torpedo blasts, and as the davits were in the process of being de-iced, they formed orderly queues with women and children taking precedence.

The good order on deck, however, lasted only momentarily. As that fear-crazed mass of humanity came from the lower decks onto the frozen main deck the people were already in a state of complete panic. The situation was made immediately worse by the fact that although they had escaped from between decks with all its inherent dangers, confusion, death and fear, they were now confronted by even more dangers. Whipped by snow and wind, the decks covered with ice and the ship tilting alarmingly to port, the people came out in a crush and began slipping and sliding about, desperately attempting to save themselves from either sliding into the sea or being forced overboard by the crush of those around them.

One boat was now about to be lowered and a mass of people, men, women and children, simply launched themselves at it, ignoring the orders of the crew and the protests of those who had been waiting patiently to be allowed to board the lifeboat. It was immediately filled to overflowing, some people even throwing themselves down into the boat as it was being lowered. When the boat touched the surface of the sea, however, it very quickly capsized throwing all its occupants into the freezing waters of the Baltic.

Meanwhile, on the bridge, Captain Petersen was attempting to think through every major problem as they rapidly presented themselves. The *Wilhelm Gustloff* was a big, robust, fairly modern ship. If trained damage-control crews could be brought into action quickly, shoring up as much as possible of the breached hull and pumping out water with the portable pumps, then vital time might be bought while an orderly evacuation of the ship could take place. At least that was the original emergency planning when such an eventuality had been anticipated. However, the reality was now far more complex. Firstly, Petersen knew that only a fraction of the passengers and crew would be able to get into the lifeboats, even if the boats could be launched. The remaining passengers would have to take to the rafts – more easily launched, admittedly, but so precarious and unprotected from the elements that it seemed unlikely many people on them would survive for long, especially if they were soaked by seawater as they would almost certainly be.

Petersen paused, rubbing thick granules of salt from his eyes. He was finding it difficult to think, perhaps it was the intense cold. He shook his head in an attempt to clear his mind. It seemed to work. He realised immediately that somehow he had to control the widespread panic that was evidently sweeping throughout the ship. Passengers were swarming on deck, screaming in terror, wild-eyed, clinging to relatives, the infirm, the children, all seeking ways to escape the death that loomed so close. Petersen leaned over the bridge rails, shouting to make himself heard above the wind and the cries of frightened passengers. He ordered his crew to take control, to stem the flow of passengers from below, to bring order to the flow of people coming on deck and to prevent the remaining lifeboats from being rushed. However, the panic had firmly set in and despite every effort of Petersen and his crew, little could be done to quell the rising hysteria that was emanating from the surging mass of people in a solid wave of fear.

Petersen realised that with so few places in the boats and so many passengers scrambling to fill them, there were soon going to be thousands of people in the sea where their survival might be counted in just minutes. It was essential to get rescue vessels to the scene as quickly as possible and radio officers were working to send distress calls on their emergency transmitters, the main transmitters having been badly damaged during the torpedo blasts. The trouble with this situation lay in the fact that the emergency transmitters were only low powered units and so far there was no indication that anyone was hearing the distress signals. Time after time the signals went out accompanied by all the essential details. The *Wilhelm Gustloff* had been attacked by a submarine. Thousands of people were on board. Help was urgently needed. SOS SOS. Time after time. There were no replies. Petersen paced up and down on the bridge, issuing orders calmly, a man in control of himself while many of those around him were in a state of complete confusion, fear and panic. Silently, inside, he screamed out to hear a response to the distress calls.

* * *

The davits on the starboard side of the ship were even more useless than those on the port side, if that were possible, because the badly stricken vessel was increasingly listing to port and the boats on the starboard side were pressing against the hull of the ship, preventing them from being launched. Those boats that were able to be dropped from the davits, filled with terrified survivors, were often dashed against the side of the ship while being lowered, spilling their occupants into the sea. Hundreds of passengers who were unable to get into lifeboats simply jumped into the freezing water. With slabs of ice floes bobbing around in the darkness, it was evident to all that those who were forced to jump would have only minutes to live if they could not get into one of the few lifeboats that had been launched successfully. It was a heartbreaking sight of terrified, shouting men, women and screaming children, jumping for their lives, knowing that they were really just jumping to their deaths.

Meanwhile, below decks, a thousand mini-dramas – deadly mini-dramas – were being enacted every minute and the minutes themselves were stretching out, it seemed, into hours as the thousands still trapped between the decks attempted desperately to escape. Captain Petersen had sent crew members below in an attempt to help the passengers clamber up through the tilting decks but they were very seriously hampered by the condition of the ship at that time and also by the continuous rush of panic-stricken people.

Lifeboat davits aboard the *Wilhelm Gustloff*. Getting the lifeboats away after the ship had been torpedoed proved to be murderously difficult. (*Reproduced courtesy of the* Wilhelm Gustloff *Museum, www.wilhelmgustloffmuseum.com*)

Petersen had no way of knowing exactly what was going on below but he could imagine. The damage-control parties, whose job it should have been to assess the damage to the hull and interior of the ship, and then report that damage to the captain and the designated damage-control coordination officer, had been unable to get to those sections where they were most needed. Additionally, communications were down and even if the damage-control parties had been able to report they would have had no way of doing so apart from sending a runner. Yet with the passageways and stairs clogged with passengers they also had no way of getting the messages to the bridge. It was a hopeless, uncontrollable situation from the very beginning.

On every level of the ship people were attempting perilously to climb upwards, deck-by-deck, and the personal tragedies occurring everywhere throughout the ship were both uncountable and often unimaginable. Husbands were torn from their wives and children who were being ground beneath the wild stampede of thousands of feet. Men abandoned their families in a cowardly attempt to save their own skins. Whole families were trapped in cabins or compartments either by steel doors that were so badly damaged by the explosions that it was impossible to open them or by doors that would no longer move because of the pressure of the rising water. As the cabins and compartments filled rapidly, so the dying continued.

In the damaged radio room the ship's communications officers continued to send out their pathetically weak distress messages, unsure whether or not anyone was receiving them. Like Captain Petersen and the other officers and crew on the bridge that night they were praying that somewhere out there in the icy darkness at least one person was listening to the urgent calls for assistance and that help was already on its way.

In fact this was actually the case. The Germans were utilising what they called a 'corridor' in their plans to evacuate all the refugees, wounded and military personnel from Poland to Germany and the corridor that night was relatively well populated with German shipping ranging from trawlers, torpedo boats, minesweepers, a mine-layer, several merchant vessels and at least one major German warship, the *Admiral Hipper* which had left Gdynia soon after the departure of the *Wilhelm Gustloff*.

The *Hipper*, as it was more generally known, was under the command of *Kapitän* Heningst a well respected and highly experienced officer who maintained a genuine concern not only to ensure that he carried out his orders but also to ensure the wellbeing and survival of his crew and passengers. On this occasion the *Hipper* was being used not to track and attack Allied convoys, the task for which it had originally been designed, but was now involved, like the *Wilhelm Gustloff*, in ferrying passengers from ports such as Danzig and Gdynia to Kiel. The *Hipper* was escorted that night by several minesweepers and the relatively small but fast and modern torpedo boat destroyer TZ 36 under the command of a rather youngish captain, Lieutenant Commander Hering.

On board the *Hipper* that night were approximately 1700 passengers, all of whom had been rather miraculously crammed tightly between decks, warships generally being designed as weapons platforms rather than vessels where space might be used to carry cargoes or passengers. It was a tight squeeze.

Having somehow received the weakened distress signals from the *Wilhelm Gustloff*, Captain Heningst immediately turned the *Hipper* and his escorts onto a course that would bring the ships to the reported position of the stricken vessel. Heningst's mind was racing with the new problems that now confronted him. How was he to rescue thousands of men, women and children, half-frozen, struggling in the wild seas, while also attempting not to make a target of his own ship? Submarines may still be lurking nearby waiting for just such a rescue attempt to give them another opportunity to sink a second ship, especially a warship like the *Admiral Hipper* which would be a major prize for any submarine commander to claim.

Additionally, Captain Heningst was grappling with the logistical problem of where to put everybody. He had no way of knowing how many people were actually on board the *Wilhelm Gustloff* – no one at that time knew that exact figure, but Heningst knew that there were several thousand people on board. How many would still be alive by the time the *Hipper* arrived at the scene was a question no one wanted to think about.

As the *Hipper* raced to the scene, its bows slicing a clean wave through the icy sea, Heningst stood on the bridge, a tin mug of hot chocolate in his fist, his fingers thrumming on the steel bridge rail at his side. Every minute now counted. Every minute those survivors were in the water meant that more people were dying somewhere out there in the icy darkness.

There were other vessels too, now racing to the scene of the disaster, having learned of the event from radio signals relayed by a small minesweeper which had been closer to the scene of the disaster and had been able to pass on the terrible cry for help. It was said there were six thousand people on board, but it was just a guess. Yet no one listening to the Morse signals that night could believe the number. There must have been some kind of mistake. They were correct. It was indeed a tragic error. The number was wildly inaccurate. There were not six thousand souls on board the stricken vessel but closer to ten thousand. Had anyone voiced that opinion at the time they would been regarded as being on the fringes of lunacy. No ship, not even the *Wilhelm Gustloff*, could carry that many people. It was an impossible number.

Having relayed the distress signal, the minesweeper turned on a course to bring it to the *Wilhelm Gustloff's* last known position. It was about two hours away. By the time the *Hipper* and its escort vessels arrived many of the passengers and crew of the *Wilhelm Gustloff*, who were then in the process of throwing themselves into the sea, would be both dead and frozen.

Captain Heningst ordered full speed ahead and the officer of the watch rang down the command on the engine order telegraph. Heningst went to the bridge side window and looked back into the night where he could just make out the bow-waves and several darkened outlines of his ships. He realised that most of his escorts could never hope to match his speed of around twenty-eight knots. Only the destroyer under the command of Lieutenant Commander Hering could hope to match that speed and on board that ship, as on the *Hipper*, preparations were almost immediately being set in motion to take on board a large number of survivors assuming, of course, that there would be any survivors to rescue from the frozen sea.

*   *   *

On board the *Wilhelm Gustloff* the situation could hardly have been more dangerous. Getting the lifeboats away was proving to be far more difficult than had ever been imagined when the ship had been designed. The ice-bound davits were locked solid and crew members were working frantically to release them in time before the entire ship toppled onto its side and crushed or drowned everyone. The increasingly sloping deck was like some kind of rough skating rink on which passengers slipped and slid uncontrollably. Some slipped right into the waiting sea. Seamen and male passengers were desperately hacking at the frozen ropes which held the rafts in place but even these seemed unwilling to release their rafts. People were literally fighting for places on the boats. Even murder was taking place as men fought to get themselves or their families to safety. Social values had all but broken down. Self-preservation was the dominant factor that drove people on. Selfless acts were few. The term, 'every man for himself', had taken on a whole new and very personal meaning. The only way to survive this catastrophe was to fight for it. The strong would live, the weak would perish.

The boat stations were now being swamped. Seamen with their petty officers were desperately attempting to prevent the boats from being rushed. Boats filled to overcapacity were difficult to lower safely and highly dangerous once they hit the turbulent water. Yet no one was really thinking of these issues as the blind struggle for survival continued with thousands of frantic people crowding on deck and thousands more squeezing up behind them.

Petty officers were shouting warnings. One even fired a shot from his revolver in an attempt to calm the crowd through the sudden shock of fear. However, the panic was beyond control, beyond fear. The frenzy of imminent death was upon almost everyone. That single pistol shot went almost unnoticed. As the boats continued to be swamped the petty officer was forced to issue a final warning. Even though he was wearing a seaman's glove, the pistol felt ice-cold in his hand. His mind seemed frozen too. He could hardly believe that it had come to this. He pointed the revolver at the chest of the closest man and shouted hoarsely, 'Stand back or die.'

If anyone heard him they did not react. The man whose life was threatened looked at the petty officer for what seemed a long moment then pressed forward again, struggling to make way through the crowd.

With the boat now almost impossibly filled with struggling men, women and children, the petty officer lost both patience and control and, fearing for his own life, turned again to the pressing wall of people and fired twice in rapid succession. Two passengers fell dead in the throng.

It was the signal for murder to commence.

The scene was now almost impossible to describe. Fear has an indescribable energy. It has an ugly face, a face that can haunt dreams and blunt caution. Captain Petersen was standing on the bridge wings, shocked by the sudden pistol shots and uncertain what they might have meant. In the darkness he was unable to see that two passengers lay dead. Had he been able to see the decks more clearly he would have had great difficulty in distinguishing those who may have been shot from those were were being trampled to death by thousands of feet. Suddenly there came an ominous stutter of machine-gun fire. Petersen leaned over the rails, struggling to see what was happening, but was also unable to see that aft of the bridge someone had managed to find a machine-pistol and had begun killing several members of the ship's crew who had been attempting to control the boarding of the lifeboats. The gunfire ceased as abruptly as it had begun. Nothing had changed. The fear and panic was still all-pervasive, only now there were bloodied bodies also lying on deck and the wild boarding of lifeboats was continuing unabated. Terror had taken command. Petersen could see it in their eyes.

He turned to the white-faced duty officer standing behind him on the bridge. 'We've got to bring this situation under control.' He paused, gripping the bridge rail tightly. He felt suddenly nauseous, sickened by what he was about to say. 'Issue small-arms to all hands. Cordon off the passengers into sections, by force if necessary, and prevent them from rushing any more of the boats.'

The officer nodded and rushed off the bridge as Petersen shouted to the radio officers. 'Any response to our distress calls?'

A radio officer shook his head. 'Not yet captain, apart from a weak message that might have been something from the *Hipper* but we can't be sure.'

Petersen turned away, his face a mask of pain.

Meanwhile, on the upper decks, armed seamen led by officers and petty officers were beginning to put in an appearance. The bloodied bodies of their comrades lent them a steely determination to become hardened to the needs of the passengers. Using the threat of their weapons and itching to use them now that some of their own had been ruthlessly gunned down, they forced wedges into the crowds, pushing them back, segmenting them and at the same time bringing some semblance of order. The crowd, despite the frenzy, quickly recognised the very clear threat of violence and reluctantly responded. Better to calm down, to await developments rather than simply being shot out of hand and tossed into the sea like dead meat.

Slowly, access to the boats was cleared. Order, however tenuous, was somehow restored. In the biting wind, in darkness, in pounding hail, with the ship now tilting alarmingly, the passengers and crew waited for what would happen next.

Yet even as all this was happening, elsewhere on the ship the tragic mini-dramas were continuing. Boats were being lowered, sometimes in good order, only to be washed away or overturned the moment they hit the water. Hysteria and calm sanity seemed to coexist everywhere. When passengers saw that boats were being overturned in the heavy seas many of them experienced a sense of terrible, almost suicidal hopelessness followed by a strange acceptance of death and its accompanying quiet listlessness. They sat on the decks, on chairs, on ventilation housings and looked around disinterestedly, almost as if the scene were not real, as if it existed in another world or in a dream. Petersen, standing on the bridge, saw it happen. He remembered reading of exactly the same effect that had overtaken passengers and crew aboard the stricken *Titanic* in 1912: people had seated themselves quietly while others had been raging at impending death. Now it was exactly the same. Some were listless, emotion having drained from their faces, while others were galvanised into action at the sight of the lifeboats dropping to their destruction loaded with screaming passengers. They tore around the ship looking for any way to escape this nightmare. If the boats could not be lowered successfully then there must be other ways to get off the ship and still survive – life-rafts, wooden doors, mattresses, anything that might float and keep them at least partially out of that freezing water until help could arrive.

By now the upper decks were literally choked with people yet even more were flooding up from below, pushing, shoving, unaware of the freezing horrors that awaited them on the exposed decks. One man turned and was surprised to see that, from that hatch at least, he was the last to climb the steel steps. When he looked back and down into the gloom of the darkened passageway he understood why. There were no more people behind him because the stairwell was filled with rising water and the water was filled with corpses, many of them children, just swirling around as though caught in a whirlpool. He turned and hurried up the last few steps into the icy night and hail. Almost immediately the wind began to buffet him badly and he pulled up the collar of his coat. At least he had been wise enough to keep the coat close and when the panic had begun and the lights had gone out he had been able simply to reach out in the darkness and grab it quickly. He had already been pulling it on when the emergency lighting had flickered reluctantly into life. Now he looked around at the chaos of the promenade deck. Seamen were loading the boats with passengers, women and children, he noticed, but there was some kind of order now, at least here. Wounded soldiers were also being allowed onto the boats but only a few of them. Some nurses were tending to several injured women, bending over them, their faces pinched with fright and cold. Not far away a minister of religion was on his knees praying, his hands held high. Then the light seemed to drift out of the minister's eyes. He was not a young man. His face was creased. It was grey with fright. Suddenly he fell onto his side, shook violently a few times, almost as if he were shivering in the cold, and died. Nobody took any notice as the body slid down the angled deck and rolled almost casually into the sea.

From the aft deck now came the sounds of a few more gunshots. Some believed that drowning was a quiet, peaceful death but it wasn't true. Drowning was a choking, horrible, gagging, desperate death. Those who were capable of thinking about it in those vital minutes realised that. A pistol was easier. It was quicker.

*   *   *

Two ships now led the pack in a desperate attempt to get to the scene of the disaster before all those on board the *Wilhelm Gustloff* could become ice-stiffened corpses. The cruiser *Admiral Hipper* and the destroyer TZ 36. On board both vessels preparations were in full momentum to receive survivors. Moving at a speed of around twenty-eight knots in heavy seas was hard on the ships and also on their passengers and crews. Lunging and plunging through the ice-heavy waves, the ships were gyrating almost drunkenly, their sharp bows smashing relentlessly into the waves as they forged their way to the scene of the tragedy.

On board both ships conditions could hardly have been worse as the crews and passengers prepared to receive survivors. Preparing hot food and drinks under such conditions was not only difficult it was positively dangerous. Bedding had to be dragged out of storage compartments deep in the bowels of the ships – compartments that were usually accessed only when in harbour and even then they would be entered reluctantly as they were often wet, mouldy and claustrophobic places inhabited by rats and cockroaches. Clothing had to be found, sandwiches cut and made with knives and ingredients that somehow seemed to take on a mind of their own as the ships plunged like monstrous rocking horses. On the bridges of both vessels their respective captains and their watch-keepers and lookouts had their eyes glued to binoculars as they strained to see ahead through the swirling sea-spray and hail.

These two ships, and the escort minesweepers now far behind, were not the only ships now racing to the aid of the *Wilhelm Gustloff*. The stricken liner's weakened distress calls were being picked up by numerous ships and ports all along the coast and had created a frenzy of activity as ships and small vessels were now gearing up to race to the scene of the rapidly unfolding tragedy. Minesweepers, patrol boats, motor-launches and even smaller vessels were now heading out of their various ports and into the biting wind and waves on their urgent humanitarian missions. It was only a matter of time before at least one vessel arrived to begin plucking survivors from the water. But time now seemed to compress significantly. What had been hours now seemed like minutes because that's how long a human being could last in that frozen sea. Most of those in the water were already dead. If the living could stay out of the water long enough they might stand a small chance of survival, but that chance was slim indeed. People everywhere prayed.

*   *   *

Boats were getting away, a few here and there amid all the massed confusion and panic. They dropped from the davits loaded to capacity and if they were not immediately crushed by the strength of the waves then they would float off, bobbing about madly, their terrified passengers holding grimly onto the thwarts, frightened of being tossed into the water by the violence of the waves. Many were immediately seasick, adding further to the suffering of all. A few of the boats were without oars, an oversight which one of the sailors immediately described as, 'A cock-up of monumental cock-ups.' An old man shouted angrily wondering how on earth they were going to survive in a sea like this without oars. A hundred people in a boat designed to carry less than half that number.

Other boats nearby were in much the same state of confusion, overloaded to the point of complete instability, people white-faced and wet, eyes black with the horrors of everything they had seen and heard during the last half hour – things they never wanted to see again but would haunt their dreams for the remainder of their lives.

Looking back from the boat the survivors could just make out the shape of the *Wilhelm Gustloff* where thousands were trapped in a wailing frenzy of fear. From across the water came the sounds of gunfire, the crackle of automatic weapons and the screams of the wounded. People in the boats wondered what was going on over there. But it was fairly obvious. Dying was going on and it was now beginning in earnest.

*　*　*

The *Wilhelm Gustloff* was dying too and it was not going gently. From deep in the bowels of the liner came the low rumbling of explosions. The explosions frightened the passengers even more, if that were possible. Then panic broke out on the promenade deck and suddenly the gunfire started again, more intensely this time, and prolonged, as the seamen fought not only to keep the half-demented passengers under some kind of control but also to save their own lives. Men were fighting back now. Some were battle-hardened soldiers, fully armed, and they knew how to fight. They had been fighting the Soviets for years. People were dying on the decks like stranded fish. It was wet and bloody and rather than succeeding in keeping a check on the crowd, the gunshots and the dying created even more havoc and confusion, more bitterness, more murder.

Captain Petersen knew now that there could be no hope. The ship was almost in its final stages of existence. The rapidity and intensity of the gunfire was clear evidence that the situation was completely out of control. It was no longer a case of simply abandoning ship in any kind of orderly fashion. It was now every man for himself. He closed his eyes, lowered his head, breathed deeply, trying to control that terrible feeling of inevitable horror that was rising darkly from somewhere deep within him. There was nothing more he could do. If this was his time to die then he had better get on with it.

The last boat was pulling away but from the intensity of the crowds still on deck it might appear that the *Wilhelm Gustloff* had been carrying no boats at all. So few people had managed to get away that they had hardly put a dent in the numbers now churning around the blood-sodden decks, all terribly aware that there appeared to be no way off this ship.

The angle of the icy deck was also increasing alarmingly and people were either falling into the sea or simply allowing themselves to slip overboard. And they were not going in their twos or threes any more. Now they were going in their dozens, silently too, most of them, quietly aware that death was waiting close at hand and they just needed a little quiet space in which to die. But although many went to their deaths with an almost ethereal silence, the overall scene was still one of noise and confusion and screams of terror rising sometimes to hysterical shrieks.

Seated precariously in the stern of one of the overcrowded lifeboats, one woman was able to twist her body slightly to watch the last few minutes of the *Wilhelm Gustloff's* existence. The sea all around was now littered with debris – boats, floats, people, bodies, wooden planks, lifebelts without people, oil. 'She's going', someone said in the bows of the boat, his voice had a note of almost unbelieving awe, and the woman in the stern twisted her head to watch. Years later she was to describe it to her grandchildren. She never forgot even a second of what she saw that night. When the *Wilhelm Gustloff* died, it did so in grand style, an epic performance filled with every single element of deadly operatic tragedy.

How many people were still alive and trapped on the ship at that moment is impossible to calculate accurately. Many thousands, certainly, a number that made the sinking of the *Titanic* thirty-three years earlier seem somehow almost insignificant by comparison. The ship's emergency lights were still on, yellowed by distance as the survivors, huddled in the lifeboats, watched the tragedy unfold before them. Yet those lights were bright enough, even through the snow that was now falling, for the spectators to this tragedy to see the ship's death agony in all its horror. Low in the water now, and listing badly, for a few moments it almost appeared that the ship might survive for it suddenly righted itself, and although still low it was fairly even with the heaving sea. Yet the illusion of any apparent safety was quickly dispelled. Within a few minutes the *Wilhelm Gustloff* began to go down by the bows and the thousands on deck let out a collective scream of terror as the ship's stern began to rise, quickly exposing its massive twin bronze propellers. Within moments people were falling forward towards the bows, as out of control as the ship itself. They were caught by the tide of gravity and the waves of people who tumbled on top of those in front and then those farther back, also tumbling forward so that thousands of people, men, women, children, babes torn from their mother's arms, were either falling forward as the ship began its juggernaut dive or were simply thrown over the side, dropping into the sea like rice pouring from a sack.

And then it was gone. The people too, most of them. The ship had left a massive vortex in the sea, the waves were flattened momentarily by a vast pool of oil in the centre of which were hundreds of bodies and what seemed like some kind of heaving rubbish dump of debris – tables, chairs, deck-cupboards, ropes, canvasses, bottles of wine and beer, crates of food from the galleys, children's toys, luggage, officers' hats – there seemed to be no end to the variety and intensity of the flotsam.

The other flotsam, of course, was far more tragic. Thousands had gone down with the ship, either trapped between decks before the ship had gone or sucked down by the vessel itself as it had plunged to the sea-bed. Yet there were still well over a thousand people, maybe two, struggling to survive in the freezing water.

Those in the water were ferociously attempting to get onto rafts or boats. Those in the overcrowded boats and rafts were frantically attempting to prevent the boats from being swamped by people. It was an ugly sight, pitiless, even murderous, as the people in the water were struck by oars or any kind of weapon to prevent them from grasping the sides of the rafts or boats. A few were taken on board, but not many, and for those left in the water there could be only one ending. Rapid hypothermia followed by unconsciousness and death. The intense cold quickly numbed the body. The hypothermia numbed the mind. After a while it was a quiet way to die.

*   *   *

The *Admiral Hipper* was drawn to the scene by the distress flares being fired from several of the lifeboats. The massive ship was itself a great danger to those struggling in the water and also in the boats and on the rafts. It would have been so tragically easy for the *Hipper* to begin sloughing through vast pools of people, crushing them with its bows and shredding them into a bloodied froth with its propellers. Captain Heningst was well aware of the dangers as the *Hipper* came up to the scene of the disaster, the first ship to arrive. He was also aware that the submarine that had attacked the *Wilhelm Gustloff* was probably still out there somewhere, submerged or on the surface, hidden by darkness and the thick curtains of snow. It was not uncommon for the Russians to sink one ship and wait around for rescue vessels to arrive so that they could also be attacked. Heningst knew this but in the darkness he could have no hope at all of rescuing the survivors unless the ship was stopped and the searchlights turned on. He had to make a terrible decision; to risk his ship, its entire crew and the 1700 refugees already on board, against the lives of the thousands of people now flailing about in the water. He hesitated for only a moment: 'Stop main engines,' he shouted. 'Man the searchlights.'

As the lights came on there was immediate panic by those still alive in the water. Many thought that a Russian ship had arrived and they were about to be machine-gunned, but Captain Heningst calmed them with a loudspeaker, telling them what ship it was and that they would soon be rescued. Among the survivors there was an almost immediate sense of intense relief. They were not to be killed. This was a rescue ship.

In reality few would be rescued by the *Hipper*. The ship was too large, too high in the water to be able to get survivors aboard easily, especially in such difficult weather conditions, and when the ship's sonar operator announced suddenly that he had detected a submarine closing quickly, the rescue attempt was immediately abandoned, the lights switched off and the *Hipper* was forced to make off in an attempt to hide from the danger that apparently lurked beneath the waves. What it must have been like for those still in the water to watch their rescue ship picking up speed and disappearing into the snow-blanketed night is almost impossible to imagine.

Off to starboard the destroyer TZ 36, which had been approaching the scene of the sinking, had also registered submarine contact close by. Lieutenant Commander Hering, who was one of the heroes of the entire *Wilhelm Gustloff* tragedy, standing on the destroyer's bridge, realised immediately what was happening when he saw the distant searchlights on board the *Hipper* wink off. A submarine was closing for the kill. The destroyer was rigged for anti-submarine work but there was little Hering could do. If he began to drop depth-charges into the water so close to the survivors it would be unlikely that any of them would survive. Like Captain Heningst aboard the *Hipper*, Hering now had to make an agonising decision, to flee and seek the anonymity of the night leaving thousands of people behind, or to risk his ship and stay in a courageous attempt to pick up as many survivors as possible. It took him only seconds to decide. 'Rig the nets', he ordered, 'and listen to every movement of that damned submarine.'

The asdic operators listened with owl-like intensity to the acoustics emanating from the Russian submarine, keeping Lieutenant Commander Hering fully informed of the enemy's movements so that he was able to calculate exactly when the submarine was manoeuvring into an attack position. Meanwhile the crew of TZ 36 went efficiently on with the business of rescuing hundreds of survivors. Seamen standing on the nets literally dragged men, women and children from the water and onto the nets and then passed them up to sailors above who, in turn, began passing the half-frozen and semiconscious survivors even higher on the nets until they could be dragged, more dead than alive, over the scuppers and onto the decks. It has to be said that Hering's superb organisational skills, coupled with the grim determination of the ship's seamen who were working under freezing and extremely hazardous circumstances, managed to save the lives of five or six hundred people that night.

Hering's actions were the only brief shining light in the entire miserable affair. He remained on the bridge throughout, directing operations, constantly harassing the asdic and radar operators for information about the submarine's movements. When it became obvious that the submarine was placing itself into the best position for an attack, Hering would counter its move intelligently, anticipating how the attack would be made and from what direction. It was like a deadly game of chess. All this manoeuvring was taking place while the rescue work was being carried out and Hering also had to consider not only the dangers facing those in the water, as the ship was moving among them, but also how best to ensure that as many people as possible were rescued. The work continued for what seemed like an agonisingly long time, the crew anticipating a torpedo attack at any moment.

Yet it could not last. The little ship was now stretching its luck beyond the boundaries of credibility. With the decks, cabins and every available space crammed with survivors, there seemed little room for more, and although Hering was determined to bring even greater numbers on board, he received an urgent message that another submarine had been detected on radar and that it too, semi-submerged, was in the process of manoeuvring for an attack. Hering, outnumbered and unable any longer to dance the ship around making it difficult for an attack to take place, reluctantly decided that the rescue mission would have to be truncated and ordered full-steam ahead. As he did so, two torpedo trails hissed past the ship on both sides. It was definitely time to get out of there.

*   *   *

Hundreds of people – many hundreds – were still alive in boats or in the water when TZ 36 was forced to leave the scene of the disaster. They had no way of knowing what was happening and when the ship turned suddenly and took off at high speed those left behind felt a terrible sense of abandonment. One ship had come and achieved almost nothing, disappearing into the night and snow like some grey wraith, and now the second ship was leaving too. True, it had managed to rescue many hundreds from the freezing sea and it was obvious that not everyone would be able to get aboard but where were the other rescue ships? Surely they should have been at the scene by now.

The agonising cries from those in the water had all but ceased by now. TZ 36 had made it a priority to rescue those in the water and those efforts had largely been successful. Many in the water were already dead, of course. In took only minutes to die in such temperatures and the corpses were floating silently away into the night, most of them never to be recovered. In the boats too, and also on the rafts, people were dying. Soaked through and frozen to the core, it did not take long to die, even when not in the water. There was little time or room for sentiment. As people died their bodies were placed into the sea to float away with the rest.

It was an intensive night of dying. Those struggling to survive could have no way of knowing that a massive rescue mission was already underway with small and large ships and boats racing to the scene from a variety of Baltic ports. Yet, despite these efforts the chances of survival for those awaiting rescue were becoming slimmer by the moment. Well below freezing to begin with, the temperature was now plummeting like a stone and soon it was hovering at around minus twenty degrees Celsius. The elderly, the weak, the children, were all dying like flies. A man, a woman and several children had managed to crawl onto an ice-floe in a desperate attempt to survive. When they were later found by one of the rescue vessels it was discovered that they had all died during the night and their bodies were already embedded in ice.

Captain Petersen miraculously managed to survive. In the end it transpired that most of those who would survive the sinking had already been picked up by TZ 36. Those remaining at the scene, or at least the majority of them, would die either before the rescue vessels arrived or soon afterwards, victims of hypothermia or of complications resulting from emergency surgery such as the amputation of frozen limbs.

Captain Alexander Marinesko was almost certainly the commander of one of the submarines that had stalked both the *Hipper* and TZ 36 as they had attempted to rescue the men, women and children in the water. He would have been attempting to get his submarine S-13 into position to launch an attack against one or both ships and it may well have been his torpedoes that narrowly missed TZ 36 at the moment Lieutenant Commander Hering had abruptly ended his rescue mission.

After the *Wilhelm Gustloff* had been torpedoed Marinesko had submerged to periscope depth to watch the results of his actions. What must have been going through his mind when he realised that he had been responsible for the deaths of so many people, mainly civilians and up to around five thousand children, has never been recorded. He was evidently sufficiently pleased with himself to take part in the attack on TZ 36 before that destroyer had taken off at speed, and Marinesko must have known that TZ 36 had taken on board hundreds of survivors from the *Wilhelm Gustloff* so one must assume that he felt nothing for these people nor did he have any remorse for killing them in such enormous numbers.

Marinesko did not attack any more vessels coming to the aid of the survivors, probably because they were so small and relatively insignificant that he believed them unworthy of his dwindling supply of torpedoes. S-13 was capable of carrying twelve torpedoes and Marinesko had used three on the *Wilhelm Gustloff* and possibly another two aimed at TZ 36. He was still on a war patrol and the Baltic was filled with ships carrying refugees to Kiel.

Marinesko's next target, and the last ship he would ever sink, was the German transport *Steuben*. It too would go down with an enormous loss of life, far more than twice the number lost in the *Titanic*, but mercifully only about half of those who had just been killed aboard the *Wilhelm Gustloff*.

The *Steuben* had been constructed by the company AG Vulcan of Stettin, Germany, and was owned by the Norddeutscher Lloyd Company. It had been launched in 1922 under the name of *München* and completed its maiden voyage in June/July the following year. Even now the *München* was making history. Following the armistice of the First World War, Germany was punished severely by the terms of the armistice, particularly with the need to make very costly reparations to the victorious nations. Constructing liners at such a time was both hideously expensive and extremely difficult. Yet the *München* was constructed and began its life successfully, although it was to have a chequered career. The *München* was the first liner to be built after the war and also the first such vessel to dock at New York Harbour after the war following a trans-Atlantic crossing. Sadly, its career as a trans-Atlantic liner was almost cut short after only seven years of operations. In February 1930 the ship arrived at New York and after its passengers and cargo had been landed a fire broke out in one of the ship's paint-lockers. These were particularly dangerous places, prone to fires, and being filled with paint and other highly flammable materials such fires were often difficult to control. This was certainly the case on 3 February that year when the paint-locker aboard the ship burst into flames. The fire quickly gained a hold on the ship and at least five fire appliances had to be brought in to fight the resulting conflagration. In the end the fire won the day and the *München* sank at its moorings. It took months and a vast amount of money to re-float the huge ship which was subsequently placed into a dry-dock and repaired. Following this disaster the owners decided to rename the ship and it became known as the *General von Steuben*, being named after Friedrich Wilhelm von Steuben, a famous German general of the American Revolutionary War era. In 1938 the ship's name was shortened simply to the *Steuben* and the following year it was pressed into service with the German *Kriegsmarine* as an armed transport ship and used to ferry troops to the eastern Baltic and to return with wounded for landing at Kiel.

Now, however, the *Steuben* was about to take part in its final and most terrifying voyage.

The *Steuben* was designed to carry around eight hundred passengers in modest comfort ranging from first to third class. Now, as a troopship, the vessel was rigged to accommodate far more in much less comfort. It had departed from Pillau on 9 February, 1945, reportedly carrying more than 5,000 people on board. These included about 2,800 wounded German soldiers, 800 civilian refugees and various numbers of servicemen, medical staff and crew.

Carrying on with his successful war patrol, Russian submarine commander, Captain Alexander Marinesko, was studiously studying the darkened sea on the night of 9 February when he recognised the outline of a large ship which was apparently on course for Kiel. This was just what Marinesko was looking for. His success in sinking the *Wilhelm Gustloff* would make him well known, he was sure, but to cap off that feat with another successful attack would raise him to almost legendary status among the close-knit Soviet submariners' fraternity. He quickly set up an attack plan and was soon launching two torpedoes at the completely unsuspecting liner.

Both torpedoes struck the ship on its starboard side, just forward of the bridge. Many of the crew were asleep in the mess-decks situated in that position and a large number of them were killed instantly. The ship began to list to starboard and sank within twenty minutes of having been attacked. Of more than 5,000 people on board, around 4,500 were killed during the disaster. The remainder, approximately 650 in number, were rescued by another German vessel, the torpedo boat T-196 which was able, in those few frantic minutes, to come alongside the stricken vessel and take the survivors straight from the decks of the sinking ship.

Following these murderous attacks on the two ships and their thousands of civilian passengers, Captain Alexander Marinesko was both right and also wrong in his estimate of his fame in the Soviet Union. He actually became the most successful Soviet submarine commander of the war, having sunk a total of 42,000 tons of shipping during his career. This might sound a lot on the face of it but compared to German U-boat commanders Alexander Marinesko's successes were minuscule. *Kapitänleutnant* Otto Kretschmer, for example, who was known as the 'Tonnage King' or 'Silent Otto', sank a total of forty-seven ships with a total tonnage of 274,333 tons, despite the fact that he was only operational until 1941 when his submarine, U-99, was attacked and sunk and Kretschmer was taken prisoner. He would remain a prisoner-of war in both the U.K. and Canada until December 1947.

Even so, Marinesko's successes were notable by Soviet standards and he had certainly killed more people than any other submarine commander in the war. With such a success he should have expected to have been awarded a coveted 'Hero of the Soviet Union' medal. However, his past life now caught up with him. At this time Marinesko was due to face a court-martial on charges associated with his alcoholism. This stain on his character meant that his superiors felt it impossible to make him a 'Hero of the Soviet Union' so Marinesko was instead given the lesser award of the 'Order of the Red Banner'. If this were not sufficient humiliation for the submarine captain then more was to follow. He was downgraded in rank to a mere lieutenant and subsequently dishonourably discharged from the navy. It should be pointed out that these punishments had nothing whatever to do with the fact that he had killed around 14,000 people in two attacks but merely because he was unable to handle his vodka and had been ignominiously caught visiting a brothel.

Marinesko later found work on a building site and was subsequently deported to Siberia. Yet he must have been a tough person because he managed somehow to survive the notorious gulags. His humiliation was not, however, to be permanent. In 1960 he was reinstated as a captain (third class) and given a full pension. He died of cancer in November 1963, aged just forty-six years, apparently never regretting for a second all those people he had put to death so terribly.

President Mikhail Gorbachev subsequently made Marinesko a posthumous 'Hero of the Soviet Union'.

*   *   *

Index

Miller
    Lieutenant Morrison R. 185, 191, 192
Milligan
    Professor Christopher 27, 42, 94, 97
Milne Bay 40, 69
Minas
    Captain Mavris 116
Mission to Seamen 77, 78
Mito
    Rear Admiral Hisashi 8
Mitsubishi Heavy Industries 180
Moate
    Ronald 'Ron'
        (chief pantryman) 14, 44, 45, 46, 54,
        58
Modified Air Warning Device
    (M.A.W.D.) 26
Mombasa 86
Montgomery
    Field Marshal Sir Bernard 'Monty' 172
Moreton Bay 81
Moreton Island 22, 26, 98
Morris
    Matthew 71
    Tom
        (radio officer) 14, 15, 43
Mossop
    John Coubro 142, 143, 144
Moston
    Sister Merle 36, 39, 40
Mount Taurus
    (vessel) 127
Mullins
    Marie (bombardier) 31
München
    (later the *Steuben*) 243
Murray
    George 4, 5, 7, 11, 45, 46, 55, 68, 70, 98,
        99
    Kenneth 60, 64
Musser
    William M. 190
MV *Anshun* 69
MV *Delane*
    (British vessel) 85
MV *Straat Soenda*
    (Dutch steamer) 92
MV *Sutlej*
    (sometimes reported as *Sutley*) 85, 86,
        88, 89, 95

Nagasaki 177, 202
Nakagawa
    Hajime ix, 1, 2, 3, 8, 9, 10, 11, 20, 21, 22,
        26, 29, 30, 49, 53, 59, 82, 83, 84, 85,
        86, 89, 90, 91, 92, 94, 95, 96, 97
Nakahara
    Jiro 208
Nambu
    Commander Nobukiyo 202, 205
National Socialist Party 216
Naval Officer in Command (Brisbane)
    (N.O.I.C.) 67
Naval War College (Japan) 180
Neuman
    Pierre 121
New Guinea 6, 67, 72, 79, 81
Newstead No. 3 [wharf] 71
Nilsson
    Captain David Martin 187, 188, 189,
        191, 196
Nishino
    Commander (..) 20
Norddeutscher Lloyd Company 243
Number 3 Interrogation Centre (UK) 144
Number 8 Fighter Sector (Brisbane) 27
Number 71 Squadron (R.A.A.F.) 61
Nuremberg 108, 173

Obori
    Lieutenant Hajime
        (submarine gunnery officer) 8, 9, 10,
        20, 21, 95
Ofuna prison camp 195
O'Gara
    Francis J. 191, 195, 196, 206
'O' Heavy Battery
    (also known as Rous Battery) 22, 23
Ohlsdorf cemetery, 173
Okinawa 201, 206, 208
Oliver J. Olson Company 187
Operation Crossroads 97
Operation Detachment 207
Operation Hailstone 201
Operation Hannibal 217
Oshima
    Baron
        (Japanese ambassador to Germany)
        94, 95
Outridge
    Lieutenant-Colonel Dr Leslie 56, 59, 74

About the Author

Tony Matthews is a Welsh-Australian author who has dedicated almost his entire adult life to writing and researching Australian and world history. He also writes extensively on military and espionage history with a specific emphasis on both world wars. He is the author of more than thirty books including several novels. He worked in the television industry for many years, writing, producing and directing, and during that time wrote a number of highly acclaimed historical documentaries which were broadcast on the Seven Network and ABC Television. He has also written and narrated more than five hundred historical programmes for ABC Radio. Tony Matthews' books and articles have been published in Australia, England, the United States and Europe and his television documentaries have been widely distributed to schools, universities, colleges and libraries across Australia.

Please visit the author's website for more details of his published and broadcast works: https://drtonymatthews.weebly.com

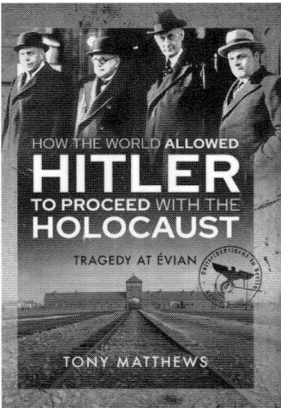

Also by Tony Matthews and published by
Pen & Sword
HOW THE WORLD
ALLOWED HITLER TO
PROCEED WITH THE
HOLOCAUST
TRAGEDY AT ÉVIAN
For more information see:
pen-and-sword.co.uk
&
penandswordbooks.com